Turning the Page

Turning the Page

Storytelling as Activism in Queer Film and Media

DAVID R. COON

Rutgers University Press
New Brunswick, Camden, and Newark, New Jersey, and London

Library of Congress Cataloging-in-Publication Data

Names: Coon, David R., 1974– author.
Title: Turning the page : storytelling as activism in queer film and media / David R. Coon.
Description: New Brunswick : Rutgers University Press, 2018. | Includes bibliographical references and index.
Identifiers: LCCN 2017055199 | ISBN 9780813593708 (cloth : alk. paper) | ISBN 9780813593692 (pbk. : alk. paper)
Subjects: LCSH: Sexual minorities in mass media. | Gay liberation movement—United States.
Classification: LCC P96.S58 C66 2018 | DDC 302.23086/64—dc23
LC record available at https://lccn.loc.gov/2017055199

A British Cataloging-in-Publication record for this book is available from the British Library.

∞ The paper used in this publication meets the requirements of the American National Standard for Information Sciences—Permanence of Paper for Printed Library Materials, ANSI Z39.48-1992.

www.rutgersuniversitypress.org

Manufactured in the United States of America

For all the storytellers and activists making the world a better place

Contents

Turning the Page

Introduction

Telling Stories for Social Change

On June 26, 2015, the United States Supreme Court ruled that same-sex marriage is a right protected by the Constitution. Although it represented just one portion of the larger fight for LGBTQ equality, this decision was a significant victory for gay rights advocates, and it marked the end of a long journey that had alternated between encouraging gains and discouraging losses. Building on previous court cases, legislative acts, and popular votes, this far-reaching decision was the ultimate result of the efforts of many activist organizations working for decades at the local, state, and national levels. One of the most prominent of these organizations, particularly at the national level, was Freedom to Marry. In early 2016, about six months after the Supreme Court decision, Freedom to Marry ceased its operations, noting that it had achieved its goals. To preserve the organization's legacy and offer support to other social activists, the leaders of Freedom to Marry decided to continue maintaining a website, providing a detailed story of how they organized their campaign, the lessons they learned, and advice for future campaigns. The website they created includes sections devoted to such processes as developing a vision and mission, working with news media, and fundraising.

Throughout the discussion of strategies and actions, the Freedom to Marry site emphasizes the importance of narrative and storytelling. The site includes an in-depth discussion of the value of storytelling in the organization's digital media initiatives and throughout the campaign. According to the site, "Freedom to Marry understood from messaging research and even just personal anecdotes that one of the key ways to change someone's mind on the freedom to marry is through conversation with a same-sex couple and being encouraged to get to know real people and authentic stories."[1] Campaign leaders collected the real stories of same-sex couples from all walks of life and all parts of the country, showcasing the range of people harmed by marriage discrimination. They disseminated these stories through social media, printed materials, paid campaign advertisements, and news coverage. Acknowledging their value in the overall campaign, the site notes that "the stories (real families, real journeys, real examples, both of love and commitment and of discrimination) were vital for demonstrating why the freedom to marry was so important,"[2] and they ultimately played a major role in the success of the campaign.

Freedom to Marry was an overtly political campaign organization dedicated to changing laws and policies related to the issue of same-sex marriage, and storytelling was just one of many tools they used in their efforts to bring about social change. On the other hand, there are many organizations for which storytelling is their primary purpose, as they create and share stories that are meant to entertain and inform audiences. The film and television industries in the United States, for example, are composed largely of companies dedicated to audiovisual storytelling. Just as social justice organizations like Freedom to Marry use stories along with other tools to further their cause, mainstream media organizations sometimes address social issues, including LGBTQ rights, as part of their overall mix of stories. However, very few organizations are dedicated to both media storytelling and social change, particularly with respect to the LGBTQ population. This book examines a handful of those organizations.

In the Life Media is a production company that documented important developments in the LGBTQ movements over the course of twenty-one seasons of a newsmagazine program that aired on public television. The Professional Organization of Women in Entertainment Reaching Up (POWER UP) is an educational organization and production company dedicated to training and supporting women and LGBTQ filmmakers in the early stages of their careers while producing films that expand and improve the representation of women and queer people on-screen. And Three Dollar Bill Cinema is a Seattle-based arts organization that produces queer and transgender film festivals and offers a filmmaking workshop for LGBTQ teens. All these organizations were created to use visual media to share the stories of LGBTQ people. While they may not engage explicitly in political campaigns in the way that Freedom to Marry did, their use of storytelling has just as much potential to influence social change, as the work of these organizations actively challenges myths and stereotypes about LGBTQ people that have been perpetuated by mainstream society.

Turning the Page explores these organizations and the work they have produced to demonstrate how the creation and dissemination of media content that is by and about queer people can be a valuable catalyst for social change and a vital component of the ongoing LGBTQ movements. My discussions in the following chapters show how organizations like In the Life Media, POWER UP, and Three Dollar Bill Cinema have made and continue to make contributions to the larger LGBTQ movements by giving a voice to a marginalized population that has long been silenced, educating future storytellers and audiences about media and LGBTQ experiences, broadening the range of available queer images and stories to come closer to representing the diversity of the population, and strengthening and expanding LGBTQ communities. In all these ways, LGBTQ-oriented media organizations help solidify a foundation that will enable queer people and their allies to protect the recent gains made by activists and continue the push for social and political equality.

My exploration of queer media storytelling takes a two-pronged approach, as I examine both the media organizations and the texts they create. My discussions of the history, mission, goals, and values of the organizations and the individuals working within them are based on personal interviews conducted with founders, executive directors, and other leaders involved with these organizations as well as observations of the events and workshops they have sponsored. These discussions are paired with and inform readings of the films, television programs, and festivals that the storytellers create. This approach builds on recent work in the area of critical media industry studies, which has highlighted, among other things, how social and cultural factors shape media industry practices, which in turn shape the resulting cultural products.[3] By examining queer media storytellers alongside the media they create and situating that examination within the context of ongoing LGBTQ rights movements, this book provides a more complete picture of the relationship between queer storytelling and LGBTQ social justice efforts.[4]

Voice and Authorship in Storytelling

In order to tell stories, an individual must find or develop and then be able to use their voice. Going beyond the mere physics of speaking (being able to generate audible sounds using the vocal cords), I use the word *voice* to refer here to the right and ability to tell one's own story or share one's opinion and to have that heard by one or more listeners. Discussing the political value of voice in a democratic society, Nick Couldry defines *voice* as an "expression of a distinctive perspective on the world that needs to be acknowledged."[5] Since each person has a unique experience, their perspective on the world will differ from the perspectives of others, particularly at the level of minute details. But as individuals affiliate with one another in the formation of groups, they find that their perspectives overlap in many ways. As such, groups and their members can develop a collective voice.[6] The inability of a collective voice to capture the unique perspective of every individual can lead to conflicts within a group, but a collective voice can also express shared concerns in a way that conveys strength in numbers. Both individual and collective voices are foundational to democratic societies, and denying voice to either an individual or a group is to prevent them from participating fully in society.

Whether individual or collective, voice and its use will change based on the scale of a particular situation. The smallest scale, for example, would involve direct, face-to-face interactions between individuals, while the largest scale would involve the international interactions of global organizations, including nations, corporations, and NGOs. Using one's voice to speak directly to another person is clearly different from harnessing the collective voice of a large group to speak to a national or global audience. As Couldry points out, there is a significant difference between the smaller scales, which allow for speaking and listening to be aligned and uninterrupted, and the larger scales, which necessitate "mechanisms of representation that defer and reorganize the matching of speaking and listening" that was sufficient for the smaller scales.[7] In other words, voice must be mediated in large-scale interactions so that ideas can be disseminated to larger audiences. This may happen by way of the written or printed word, visual images, audio recordings, or a mix of all three. However, individuals and many groups have limited or no access to the resources necessary to make their voices heard on a larger scale, as the tools of mass mediation and communication are concentrated in the hands of a relatively small number of organizations and individuals. It therefore becomes important for those who do have access to such channels of communication (including popular media) to make every effort to include a range of different voices in their work, as failure to do so effectively silences the voices of large portions of the population. Individuals and organizations like those discussed throughout this book contribute to the LGBTQ movements by marshalling the media resources necessary to reach large audiences and then sharing stories that give voice to individuals and groups who would otherwise be voiceless on larger scales.

Related to voice but perhaps even more complicated is the concept of authorship, which has long been a source of debate, in part because of the important functions that authorship serves in many cultures. From a social standpoint, people often want to be able to attribute a creative or intellectual work to a particular individual as a means of giving credit and celebrating achievement. The desire to celebrate authors as sources of creative ideas has been reinforced by academic practices, particularly within literary studies, which frequently examine creative texts with the goal of uncovering the author's intentions. And in a world driven by market exchanges, authorship takes on more than artistic, social, and intellectual value; it also has an economic value. John Hartley argues that modern societies have corporatized authorship as a way of monetizing creative ideas, noting that "the publishing industry required the *concept* of authors, as the originators of something that could be held as private property in order to be exploited."[8] This economic imperative necessitated copyright law to guide the assignment and management of authorship status and the financial implications of that status; the social, aesthetic, academic, economic, and legal significance of authorship continues to drive debates in such fields as literary studies, cultural studies, and film and media studies.

Within film and media studies, much of the discussion about authorship has revolved around the concept of the "auteur." This idea originated during the 1950s among critics working for the French film journal *Cahiers du Cinéma*, including François Truffaut, who would go on to be a leader in the French New Wave film movement. During the years following World War II, as large numbers of Hollywood films made their way to European audiences, these French critics took notice of the work of such directors as Alfred Hitchcock, Howard Hawks, and John Ford. Although these directors were working within the Hollywood system, which was known for the high-output, assembly-line environment favored by studio bosses, the critics argued that some directors were able to rise above the industrial efficiency to make films that exhibited a recognizable personal signature, typically evident in elements of visual style and thematic content. Directors earning the auteur label were those who expressed a creative personality across their body of work, despite the constraints placed on them by the industrial studio system, thereby differentiating themselves from other directors who were seen merely as cogs in the Hollywood machine.

The auteurist approach was further developed and introduced in American film circles by critic Andrew Sarris, who was particularly interested in using auteurism to evaluate directors and place them within a hierarchical system.[9] Sarris offered a set of criteria—including "technical competence," "distinguishable personality," and "interior meaning"—that could be used to measure directors' achievements.[10] Seeking to elevate some directors' work from commercial entertainment to respectable works of art, he wrote, "Ideally the strongest personality should be the director, and it is when the director dominates the film that the cinema comes closest to reflecting the personality of a single artist."[11] The auteur-oriented work of Sarris, *Cahiers du Cinéma*, and others following in this tradition generated an ongoing intellectual discussion primarily focused on aesthetics, essentially seeking to create a canon of the most accomplished filmmakers and establish guidelines for adding future directors to that canon.[12]

Over the years, the auteurist approach has been challenged and rejected by many scholars and critics who believe that identifying a single creative force is impossible in an expressive form that is built on collaborative efforts. Among those who have questioned auteur theory, Pauline Kael, a film critic for the *New Yorker* from 1967 to 1991, was perhaps the most prominent. She challenged the usefulness of Sarris's criteria and argued that writers, cinematographers, and others working on a film could be just as influential as a director in the creation of artistically accomplished films.[13]

While some have embraced the specifics of auteur theory and others have rejected them, the broader question of authorship has continued to be a significant component of the study of film and media.[14] Two of the most common strands within the discussion of media authorship have been those that explore the generally collaborative nature of media authorship and those that focus on the authorial contributions of specific artists other than the director. For example, in his analysis of the creation of *Strangers on a Train* (1951), Robert Carringer encourages collaboration analysis in film, which "entails the temporary suspension of single-author primacy . . . to appraise constituent claims to a text's authorship," suggesting that this approach provides a more accurate understanding of how creative ideas are shaped during a film's production.[15] Similarly, Colin Burnett offers the "intentional flux" model as a way of examining how the intentions of authors are in a constant state of flux as they respond to crises, changes, and the contributions of other creative minds throughout the course of production.[16] John Caldwell argues for the inclusion of authorial contributions from below-the-line workers in craft and technical positions, noting that their day-to-day work regularly involves "conceptualizing and generating textual and stylistic components" that may not have been anticipated by but help realize the ideas of writers, directors, and producers.[17] Building on the general belief that film and television are necessarily collaborative forms, some media scholars have emphasized the contributions of individuals including producers, composers, and production designers to argue that they also deserve to be recognized as authors of the media they help create.[18]

Around the time that Sarris and Kael were debating film auteur theory and inspiring other scholars and critics to forge new paths in the exploration of media authorship, the concept of authorship in general was being challenged by poststructuralist cultural critics like Roland Barthes and Michel Foucault, who argued that the author of a text was not as important as the meanings made by readers after the text was in circulation. Believing that attention to authorship imposed barriers on the dynamic interaction between readers and texts, Barthes argued that "to give a text an Author is to impose a limit on that text, to furnish it with a final signified, to close the writing."[19] Foucault argued that the concept of the author did serve important functions in terms of categorizing texts and making meaning from them but that this "author-function" should not be confused with the biological being assigned to the role of "author."[20] Many critics embraced this perspective and happily celebrated the "death of the author."

But not everyone was willing to accept that the author was dead. Many critics found it particularly unsettling that the concept of authorship was being dismissed just when many groups who had long been silenced—including women, racial minorities, and gays and lesbians—were joining together to make their voices heard and bring about positive social changes.[21] Recognizing the value of authorship to marginalized groups, Janet Staiger rejects the notion that authorship does not matter. She says, "It matters especially to those in non-dominant positions in which asserting even a partial agency may seem to be important for day-to-day survival or where locating moments of alternative practice takes away the naturalized privileges of normativity."[22] For those seeking to tell stories that do not simply reinforce the norms imposed by Hollywood and society as a whole, claiming authorship status can be the triumphant result of a difficult struggle. Referencing the work of filmmakers associated with the New Queer Cinema movement of the early 1990s, Amy Villarejo notes that "unlike their counterparts in mainstream cinema, they do not presuppose the prerogatives of authorial status; they fight for it, they earn it."[23] Rejecting the alleged death of the author, these and other critics examining the work of individuals from marginalized groups have shifted the discussion from one that focuses on the deceptively benign elements of aesthetics to one that explicitly reveals the political nature of authorship.

Scholars of queer film and media have taken a particular interest in questions of authorship precisely because of its political weight, and they have offered a variety of approaches for examining queer authorship. Some scholars, particularly those initially bringing queer readings to the study of film, have examined seemingly "straight" texts by filmmakers who were either fully or partially in the closet due to industry norms in various eras, seeking to reveal queer traces left by creators. Alexander Doty, for example, looks at the films of Dorothy Arzner and George Cukor and notes, "We might recognize a queer version of authorship in which queerly positioned readers examine mass culture texts—here Cukor and Arzner films—in order to indicate where and how the queer discourses of both producers and readers might be articulated within, alongside, or against the presumably straight ideological agendas of most texts."[24] As queer filmmakers and queer scholarship have become more common and open, many have shifted from uncovering hidden traces of queerness to examining the work of openly queer filmmakers. This often involves demonstrating how queer filmmakers have claimed the status of author and used it to critique the norms of heteronormative culture, either through the content of their films or by reimagining the cinematic language used to tell stories. For example, the lesbian independent film movement, which emerged in the 1970s, is notable for generating what Andrea Weiss describes as "films which in form and content declare their complete independence from and opposition to the dominant American film and television industries."[25] Similarly, Walter Metz demonstrates how John Waters refused to be assimilated into the norms of Hollywood, while Michael DeAngelis and Marcia Landy show how Todd Haynes has used his films to deconstruct and queer the language and structures of Hollywood films.[26]

Turning the Page continues the discussion of queer authorship in cinema by examining the collaborative work of organizations dedicated to telling and sharing stories by, for, and about LGBTQ people. As discussed previously, authorship functions simultaneously on multiple levels, including the creative and the political, and the latter is my primary concern here, as I consider how the authorial role of these organizations ties film- and media-making processes to broader LGBTQ social justice efforts.

The organizations examined in this book offer examples of authorship as stewardship—taking stories that originate in the lived experiences of the LGBTQ communities, shepherding them through the production process, and eventually delivering them to audiences who want and need to hear the stories. Unlike the auteurist approach, which confers authorship *status* on an individual who is identified as the creative force behind a media text, my discussion considers authorship as a *process* that involves many people along the way. The collaborative act of authoring a media text and stewarding a story through production, distribution, and exhibition goes well beyond the creative generation of original ideas. The stewardship model of authorship, though not unique to queer film, has significant political value for LGBTQ people or any other marginalized group. Authors find stories that matter—stories that need to be told—and then mold them into the form that will have the greatest impact in terms of advancing social movements. Queer authorship as stewardship thus becomes an important tool for supporting and advancing the broader activist efforts of the LGBTQ movements, making the process of authorship, or storytelling, a vital political act.

Storytelling, Counterstorytelling, and Social Movements

Storytelling is a valuable weapon in the fight against oppression, as narratives can be used to challenge dominant beliefs and replace misinformation with truth. Scholars working in the field of critical race theory (CRT) have long emphasized the value of individual and collective voice and the power of storytelling as a tool for combatting and overcoming discrimination against any marginalized group. Storytelling helps solidify bonds between groups of people, in part by representing a kind of cohesion and offering shared meanings and understandings of the world. Dominant groups circulate stories that naturalize the power and influence of their own group; marginalized groups and individuals can use stories to challenge that dominance, often by pointing out the flaws in the naturalized world views circulated by those in power. CRT scholar Richard Delgado argues that this "counterstorytelling" is one of the best tools to combat dominant viewpoints that people have accepted as natural.[27] As Delgado points out, "Stories, parables, chronicles, and narratives are powerful means for destroying mindset—the bundle of presuppositions, received wisdoms, and shared understandings against a background of which legal and political discourse takes place."[28] What Delgado refers to as a "mindset" can also be viewed as an ideology, and counterstorytelling becomes a tool with which emerging or marginalized ideologies may challenge the dominant or hegemonic ideologies of a society.

Individuals and organizations representing many different marginalized groups have used visual media as a tool for counterstorytelling in an attempt to resist hegemonic narratives. For example, African American filmmakers such as Oscar Micheaux, Richard Maurice, and William A. Foster worked during the silent and early sound film eras, making films that sought to challenge the racist imagery coming from Hollywood studios at the time.[29] Visual Communications, a grassroots Asian American filmmaking collective, was founded in Los Angeles in the early 1970s and aimed to improve the representation and participation of Asian Americans in film and television.[30] Appalshop, founded in 1969, is a media cooperative in Whitesburg, Kentucky, that works to constitute and preserve Appalachian identities in part by undermining the damaging representations of this population that have been perpetuated by mainstream media.[31] These and other media creators have used and continue to use counterstorytelling to challenge dominant ideologies, and the organizations examined in this book continue this tradition by emphasizing the experiences of LGBTQ people.

CRT scholars advocating for the importance of storytelling have argued that narrative has additional benefits beyond challenging dominant ideologies. Gloria Ladson-Billings notes, for example, that stories can help people overcome the internalized discrimination and condemnation that can result from long-term exposure to racist beliefs perpetuated by dominant groups. She says, "Historically, storytelling has been a kind of medicine to heal the wounds of pain caused by racial oppression. The story of one's condition leads to the realization of how one came to be oppressed and subjugated, thus allowing one to stop inflicting mental violence on oneself."[32] Similarly, Delgado and Jean Stefancic argue that "stories can name a type of discrimination; once named, it can be combatted."[33] Storytelling thus offers a clarification and demystification of existing situations, allowing marginalized groups and individuals to understand the sources of their oppression and identify clear targets and goals for social change efforts.

While storytelling can have benefits for individuals, its impact is greater when it is put to use in service of broader social movements, and organizations working for social change have used narrative in very strategic ways to support their causes. Storytelling is powerful because it can foster identification on the part of listeners by stimulating recognition and empathy[34] and by appealing not only to the intellect but also to emotions and imagination.[35] Stories can put a human face on otherwise abstract issues, causing people to see situations in a different light.

The narratives used in support of social movements are meant first and foremost to influence people's thoughts and actions. Individuals may align themselves with a social movement by connecting their own personal story with similar stories emerging from that movement. As Joseph Davis notes, "Culturally and institutionally embedded narratives with which we identify, then, shape the construction of our self-story."[36] In other words, individuals may redefine their own identities by situating themselves within preexisting social narratives. Individuals may also be motivated to join or support a movement as a result of a particular strategy used to structure movement narratives. As Robert Benford points out, "Whereas the temporal structure of most narratives includes a singular beginning, middle, and end, movement narratives suggest alternative middles and endings."[37] Typically, one middle and its corresponding ending represents the status quo and is portrayed as highly undesirable, while an alternative middle is shown to lead to a different, more desirable ending. Potential participants are encouraged to join the movement as a way of bringing about the more desirable ending to the story. In this way, storytelling serves as a vital tool in efforts to build support for and increase participation in social movements of all kinds. Like the narratives that come directly from activists, the counterstorytelling efforts of the media makers discussed in this book offer alternative middles and endings to many of the stories that have been circulated by heteronormative cultural institutions. In this way, they can also be considered "movement narratives," similar to those described by Benford, as they advance the cause of the LGBTQ movements by changing hearts and minds, ultimately contributing to an environment that enables the changing of laws and policies.

The LGBTQ rights movements have had a complex relationship to storytelling, given that narratives have been crucial both to maintaining the oppression of queer people and to pushing for their liberation. Historically, the stories of gay and lesbian identity and experiences—generated largely by religious, medical, and government institutions—have pathologized and criminalized individuals and groups rather than liberating them. As a result, stories about nonnormative sexualities have long been associated with embarrassment and shame and have often remained hidden. Christopher Pullen examines the potential for out queer cultural producers to shape discourses by offering a new set of narratives. He argues that the revealing and self-reflective practices of these storytellers reject "mythologies and histories of shame,"[38] which have long enabled the oppression of LGBTQ people. Pullen also notes that storytelling allows people to "challenge such subjugation through the production of discourse,"[39] thereby creating opportunities for community building and political visibility.

Coming out stories have been particularly significant within the LGBTQ rights movements. The act of coming out is difficult for a variety of reasons, not the least of which is because it means going against every heteronormative and cisnormative story that a person has heard throughout their life. An individual who wants to come out as queer—either privately or publicly—must challenge the dominant and naturalized narratives that have long silenced the LGBTQ population. For many individuals, a critical component of this coming out process is what Ken Plummer refers to as a "textual search," which involves scanning existing stories for evidence of one's own identity.[40] As more queer stories enter into circulation, individuals have more resources they can use to help understand and construct their own narrative identities. Such stories may be exchanged face-to-face between individuals who know each other, but many individuals in the process of coming out do not know any other queer people. Unable to connect with a face-to-face community, they may turn to what is essentially a discursive queer community, relying on mediated texts like books, films, or online videos to provide the traces of queer life that will help them understand their own.

In his book *Telling Sexual Stories: Power, Change and Social Worlds* (1995), Plummer considers the contemporary fascination with personal, intimate, sexually oriented storytelling, focusing particularly on the proliferation of rape survival stories, tales of sexual recovery and therapy, and coming out stories. In this discussion, Plummer identifies four levels over which such stories evolve, moving from the personal (when an individual is dealing with the motivations for telling their story) to the cultural/historical, which concerns "the moment at which a story enters public discourse—the moment of public reception."[41] It is during this fourth and final level that a story has the potential to influence public opinion and have a lasting impact. Plummer notes that timing is important when it comes to stories entering this level. He says, "Certain stories can only be told when key social worlds await the telling, when an audience is ripened up and ready to hear. Many stories are in silence—dormant, awaiting their historical moment."[42] For example, coming out stories emerge when cultures decriminalize and/or depathologize homosexuality. These stories continue to be important to the LGBTQ rights movements in the United States, particularly when they raise awareness of the presence of queer people in Hollywood, professional sports, politics, and the business world. But as a society, we are at a point where queer storytellers working in film and television have moved beyond coming out stories to tell more complex and nuanced tales about the lives people lead *after* coming out. The audience that is ready to hear these stories is growing, which allows the stories to have a wider impact.

The historical moment for these stories has arrived, and many cultural producers, including those discussed in this book, are capitalizing on this. Their work engages in counterstorytelling to challenge harmful stereotypes and ideologies circulating in mainstream culture, but challenging these views is no small task, since they have been reinforced for many years by society's most powerful institutions.

Queer Identities and Oppressive Narratives

People who do not fit the dominant norms of gender identity and sexual orientation have long experienced oppression from a normalizing mainstream society. This oppression has been created and reinforced by various sociocultural institutions that have generated and circulated stories about same-sex desire, gender nonconformity, and the individuals expressing these traits. These stories have sustained the hostile environment that the LGBTQ movements have always worked to change.

Long before queer people had opportunities to speak openly for themselves, psychiatrists and other medical professionals chose to speak on their behalf. Medical institutions presented queer people as sick and in need of treatment. Same-sex attraction was considered curable, and doctors offered a variety of treatments that they said could turn people straight. It wasn't until 1973 that the board of trustees of the American Psychiatric Association (APA) voted to remove homosexuality from its list of psychiatric disorders, a decision that was ratified by the full membership of the APA in 1974. Despite this formal shift on the part of the medical profession, the image of gays as diseased lingered in large portions of society; thus when the AIDS crisis erupted in the 1980s, it was easy for antigay leaders to revive the conflation of homosexuality with illness. And more than four decades after the APA's reversal, delegates to the 2016 Republican National Convention, still believing the stories of gay conversion through therapy, urged party leaders to include support for such treatment in the party's official platform.[43]

Through sermons, counseling, and printed materials, religious institutions have told equally damaging stories about LGBTQ people, often extending early medical diagnoses to present queer people not only as sick but as sinners in the eyes of the Lord. As the dominant religion in the United States, Christianity, in its various branches and denominations, has had the most significant impact on American society. Some denominations have embraced LGBTQ people in recent years, but most still have roots in antigay teachings. Conservative Christians have frequently drawn on a Bible passage from the book of Leviticus (18:22) to portray queer people as "abominations." Catholic doctrine has traditionally defined morally acceptable sexual activity as only that which is procreative, thereby categorizing all homosexual acts as sinful.[44] Other religious discussions have framed homosexual acts as "crimes against nature," leading to a definition of queer people as "unnatural."[45]

Educational institutions, which occupy positions of authority and respect when it comes to circulating accurate information, have not traditionally spread negative views of LGBTQ people. Instead, most schools (until relatively recently) tried to ignore homosexuality altogether, making queer people invisible in most areas of the curriculum. The majority of adults currently living in the United States grew up in an era when history books barely acknowledged homosexuality, if they did so at all. As just one example, the sixth edition of *The National Experience: A History of the United States*, from textbook publisher Harcourt Brace Jovanovich, was used by many high schools in the 1990s. The book is nearly a thousand pages long, and it only makes two (very general) references to homosexuals. In a discussion of cultural upheaval in the 1960s, the book says, "Students, blue-collar workers, convicts, and homosexuals began to reject the roles in which society had cast them."[46] Interestingly, LGBTQ people are placed after convicts in the list of unsatisfied groups. Later, the book offers a few sentences about the gay rights movement of the 1970s, sandwiched between comments about swingers and drugs in a section with the heading "Tribulations of the Permissive Society."[47] Until recently, the near absence of queer people in official accounts of history such as this one, as well as other areas of curriculum such as sex education,[48] allowed the harmful stories circulated by other institutions to become even more powerful.

Although there have been many improvements in recent years, historically, the U.S. government has also contributed to the harmful images and stories of LGBTQ people that have circulated in our society. The justice system, for example, ranging from local police officers up to the Supreme Court, has found many ways to cast queer people as criminals and then punish them accordingly. Sodomy laws, which were not completely eliminated until the Supreme Court's 2003 *Lawrence v. Texas* decision, made certain private sex acts between consenting adults illegal. This essentially made all homosexuals criminals by definition, which could then be used to prevent them from getting jobs, finding homes, or maintaining custody of children.[49] During the first half of the twentieth century, unevenly applied obscenity laws were often used to target queer people, making criminals of anyone who dared to possess or share materials about homosexuality, even if they were educational in nature. Until well into the 1970s, police regularly raided gay bars and clubs, generally on trumped-up charges of liquor code violations, and frequently cited patrons for vaguely defined "lewd conduct."[50] While courts and law enforcement turned queers into criminals, legislative acts and other government policies portrayed them as second-class citizens who were unfit to marry one another,[51] serve in the military,[52] or hold government jobs.[53]

Moving beyond the bounds of official government policies or religious teachings, many individuals, frequently merging politics and Christianity as part of the religious right, have told misleading stories about queer people in an attempt to gain support for various antigay initiatives. For example, in 1977, singer and former Miss America contestant Anita Bryant brought national attention to a Dade County, Florida, ballot issue that would make it legal to discriminate against people based on their sexual orientation. To generate support for her Save Our Children campaign, Bryant painted queer people as child predators, claiming she had proof that gays were trying to recruit children to homosexuality.[54] This argument was also used by California Senator John Briggs in 1978 when he pushed an initiative to remove gay teachers from public schools.[55] Reinforcing a myth circulated by many opponents of marriage equality, James Dobson, founder of the conservative advocacy group Focus on the Family, claimed in 2004 that LGBTQ activists were "working to implement a master plan that has as its centerpiece the utter destruction of the family."[56] Bryant, Briggs, Dobson, and many others speaking out against LGBTQ rights have circulated stories of monstrous, destructive queer people, relying on fear and ignorance to win support for their causes. And with the history of various social institutions presenting LGBTQ people as sick, unnatural, sinful criminals unfit to be treated as full citizens, it is no wonder that so many people have been willing to buy into the harmful myths.

Popular Film and Television

While plenty of damaging stories have come from medical, religious, educational, and government institutions, some of the most vivid and memorable images of LGBTQ people have been generated by institutions built on storytelling: the film and television industries. Representations of queerness on the big and small screens have evolved and improved over the years, but more often than not, they have done more harm than good.

In Hollywood's early decades, homosexuality was generally hinted at rather than shown explicitly. By the 1920s, both on-screen and off, male homosexuality had become equated with the stereotypical image of the pansy—an effeminate, mincing, and flamboyant man. Pansy characters generally appeared in bit roles and provided moments of comic relief, but they rarely contributed significantly to a film's plot.[57] The female counterpart to the pansy was the mannish woman, a character type that dressed in men's suits and hats and occasionally even smoked a cigar. As Laura Horak points out, a few films of this era upped the ante by showing brief glimpses of erotic physical contact between women or by making subtle references to real women who were known to be lesbians,[58] but most films relied on innuendo and stereotyping, allowing cross-dressing to suggest homosexuality.[59]

In the 1930s, in an attempt to avoid censorship from outside bodies, the film industry adopted the Hollywood Production Code, a listing of moral guidelines for film content. Among the many elements explicitly forbidden by the code were references to homosexuality. Despite this prohibition, many of the stereotypes and innuendoes of the precode years continued, though they had to be subtler to get by the code administrators. Effeminate men were officially heterosexual, as evidenced by references to wives or girlfriends, even if their behaviors and mannerisms suggested otherwise. As Vito Russo notes, these sissy characters hinted at homosexuality in part to serve as "yardsticks" for the heteronormative masculinity of the men around them.[60] The sexualized mannish women of the precode era were replaced by tomboys and spinster aunts who suggested stereotypes of lesbianism without explicitly enacting same-sex desire.

During the 1950s and '60s, as Hollywood filmmakers sought to incorporate more daring and racy material in their work, some began to include more overt references to homosexuality. Filmmakers pushed the limits of the Hollywood Production Code, and code administrators, recognizing nationwide shifts in social mores, loosened their restrictions. The presentation of homosexuality was no longer forbidden, but the code still did not allow for the sympathetic treatment of queerness. As a result, the films of this era generally present queer characters as either monstrous villains or tragic victims, and in both cases, they tend to be killed off before the final credits.[61] Films could engage with homosexuality, but they most certainly could not condone it.

After the elimination of the production code in 1968, filmmakers were able to explore homosexual issues and characters freely and openly. Despite this freedom, and aside from a few exceptions like *The Boys in the Band* (1970), *Cabaret* (1972), and *Dog Day Afternoon* (1975), Hollywood essentially avoided the topic for the next couple decades. In the 1980s, a few independent films, like *Desert Hearts* (1985) and *Parting Glances* (1986), dealt openly with queer characters, but aside from the box-office failure *Making Love* (1982), Hollywood generally continued to relegate queer characters to bit parts, often rooted in stereotypes and serving as villains, victims, or comic relief. In the 1990s, Hollywood began to feature more LGBTQ characters in both lead and supporting roles, but this increased visibility did not always translate to fully developed, nuanced, or accurate images of queerness. Films like *Philadelphia* (1993), *In & Out* (1997), and *My Best Friend's Wedding* (1997) focused on "respectable" queer characters that were white, homosexual, gender conforming, largely desexualized, and living in a predominantly heterosexual

FIGURE 1.1 Like many films of the 1960s, *The Children's Hour* (1961) presented queer identities as shameful and unbearable. Frame enlargement.

world, cut off from any visible queer community. The focus on safe, respectable queers was an improvement over the negative stereotypes of the past, but as Steven Seidman warns, including only these images can "establish a division between the good and the bad gay citizen,"[62] suggesting that those who do not fit the respectable image envisioned on-screen were still not accepted. Characters that were bisexual, transgender, or queer people of color were few and far between.[63] Hollywood was ready to embrace some queer people, but only if they were not too queer, a trend that has generally continued to the present.

Television began many decades after film, and by the time it reached a national audience, homosexuality had been forced into the closet by the Hollywood Production Code. Although television was not restricted by the code, as a medium that reached directly into people's homes, it was generally limited to more conservative content than film, especially in the early decades. As such, it is not surprising that homosexuality was essentially invisible on television during the 1940s, 1950s, and 1960s. Aside from the occasional homophobic joke in a sitcom, the most common site of homosexual representation during this era was news, talk, and public affairs programs, which typically offered a clinical approach to the topic. As Stephen Tropiano points out, these early representations brought a previously hidden topic into the public arena, but the designation of homosexuality as a social problem likely did "more to strengthen than to alleviate the public's growing fear" of gays and lesbians.[64] While the portrayals were not particularly flattering, they did offer participants in the homophile movement a chance to speak out publicly, which, as Edward Alwood notes, "countered the prevailing stereotype that painted gays as too timid and ashamed to make themselves known."[65] Such content, which almost always focused on men and ignored women, was limited to local programs in large cities until 1967, when CBS aired the special *CBS Reports: The Homosexuals*, a program that offered a nationwide audience a picture of sad, lonely homosexuals and a seedy underworld in which they existed.

During the 1970s, more gay and lesbian characters began appearing in fictional programming, but they were usually relegated to one-off guest appearances, and they frequently presented a problem or conflict for the regular characters to solve. This played out in two main ways: the queer guest character either came out as gay, with the regular cast then having to learn how to tolerate him or her, or filled the role of killer, child molester, or rapist.[66] Gay activist groups protested the more monstrous portrayals, and by the mid-1970s, all three major networks had promised to avoid negative stereotypes, and they began seeking advice from gay consultants during the production of their programs.[67]

The most offensively stereotyped representations decreased in the late 1970s and into the 1980s, but aside from a few recurring queer characters like Jodie Dallas on *SOAP* (1977–1981) or Steven Carrington on *Dynasty* (1981–1989), most LGBTQ characters on television appeared in guest roles on series or in stand-alone TV movies. As mentioned, regardless of whether they were in guest or recurring roles, LGBTQ characters tended to pose a problem—which in the 1980s was often AIDS—that the heterosexual characters around them had to deal with.[68] Queerness continued to provide conflict that was presented through a heteronormative lens and resolved by heterosexual characters.

As with film, television of the 1990s contributed to increasing visibility among LGBTQ people. Recurring and supporting queer characters became more common, and a few shows, like *Ellen* (1994–1998) and *Will & Grace* (1998–2006), featured queer characters in lead roles. But as with film, television primarily offered images of white, middle-class, gender-conforming gay men and lesbians presented as unthreatening to heterosexual audiences and perhaps, as Ron Becker argues, used strategically in an attempt to attract the "upscale, college-educated, and socially liberal adults" desired by advertisers.[69] Queers of color and bisexual and transgender characters were harder to find. Since the 1990s, the number of queer characters on television has fluctuated from season to season, and there have been improvements in many respects, but like Hollywood films, the mainstream television industry has been slow to provide a broad range of representations that accurately reflect the diversity of the LGBTQ population.

Queer Media Storytelling as Activism

To tell a story that challenges the dominant narratives and images circulated by heteronormative institutions is to alter the frameworks that have oppressed LGBTQ people for generations. Because it engages in this way, the work of queer storytellers should be considered a kind of advocacy and activism. The terms *advocacy* and *activism* are closely related and often used interchangeably, but the work they represent differs in important ways. Advocacy is generally understood as the act of supporting a cause by arguing publicly in favor of it. It is often seen as a more diplomatic way of talking through issues and winning support. Activism, on the other hand, involves more assertive actions such as protests, strikes, and other disruptive demonstrations as ways of supporting or opposing a particular cause.[70] The aggressiveness often associated with activism is sometimes seen as generating rather than solving conflict, and it can lead some individuals and groups to shy away from identifying themselves or their efforts as activist in nature. Nonprofit organizations may be particularly sensitive to this, because identifying their work as activism may raise concerns about violating the laws governing such organizations.

Carrie Rentschler defines two different types of activities that would fall into the category of media advocacy. On one hand, media advocacy can be "the strategic use of the mass media . . . in support of community organizing to push public policy initiatives"; on the other hand, it can involve efforts "directed at the mass media in order to create a more democratic media system."[71] In other words, media advocacy can use media as a tool to address other social issues, or it can address media as the problem that needs to be fixed. The organizations examined in this book certainly engage in both of these activities. They use media in support of broader efforts to achieve social justice for LGBTQ people, and they call attention to the inequities and lack of diversity that have come to define the workforces and output of the mainstream media industries.

But their work goes well beyond advocacy. They are not just speaking out and encouraging social change; they are actively making change. The mass media landscape is a significant part of everyone's lives. Through our engagement with media, we learn about ourselves and each other. We see dominant ideologies reinforced and challenged, and we see new world views introduced. The treatment of LGBTQ people in the media shapes their treatment and acceptance in the rest of society. Recognizing that popular media images are a major part of the problem and not just a reflection of it, the organizations examined in this book create alternative images and stories, actively changing the media landscape that has long supported the erasure and marginalization of LGBTQ people. They are using storytelling as a creative form of activism.

The production, distribution, and exhibition of queer media can also contribute to the creation and maintenance of LGBTQ communities, which supports further activism. At the local level, film festivals and other screening events can bring large numbers of viewers into contact with one another to help embody a lived community occupying a shared time and space.[72] Additionally, the stories told by LGBTQ filmmakers and television producers can make the larger imagined community more real, helping individuals feel connected to others like them.

As Jeffrey Weeks argues, "A web of narrative, a proliferation of stories, has developed in a particular set of historical circumstances, which gives meaning to the idea of a sexual community for many people."[73] As stories circulate and attach meanings to the idea of an LGBTQ community, that community comes into being as a lived reality. Even for those who might not have direct interactions with other queer people, stories circulating by way of popular media let them know that they are not alone. As Kath Weston suggests, feeling connected to LGBTQ communities "need not entail meeting other [queer] people, but rather becoming convinced of their existence."[74] Learning about and sharing the experiences of other queer people by way of mediated storytelling can be an important way for individuals to feel connected to something bigger than themselves. The following chapters explore the work of organizations that demonstrate how film and television can be valuable tools for making these crucial connections.

Chapter 1 builds on the concepts established in this introduction by providing a broader context for the book. Following the earlier discussion of the harmful myths created and perpetuated by powerful social institutions, I examine some of the ways that LGBTQ groups and individuals have pushed back against those myths in an attempt to secure equal citizen status in the United States. I offer a brief historical overview of the evolving LGBTQ movements, emphasizing the ongoing tension between radical liberationist strategies and more pragmatic assimilationist approaches—a tension that can also be seen in the work of the organizations explored throughout the book. As part of this discussion, I consider some of the queer storytellers who have used film and other media to challenge repressive heteronormativity over the years, including avant-garde and documentary filmmakers in the 1970s, those involved in the New Queer Cinema movement of the early 1990s, and the creators of more recent hits like *Milk* (2008), *The Normal Heart* (2014), and *Carol* (2015). These examples help situate the organizations studied throughout the book within the broader landscape of LGBTQ media, showing how these storytellers both build on the work of others and make their own unique contributions.

Chapter 2 focuses on a nonprofit educational organization and production company called In the Life Media. While many filmmakers have created dramatic and comedic films inspired by the lived experiences of LGBTQ people, In the Life Media aimed to document the actual experiences of real LGBTQ people and share those stories on television. The organization was founded in 1992 to increase visibility of LGBTQ people on television and expose social injustice by chronicling the experiences of the LGBTQ population in American society. In the Life Media is best known for producing twenty-one seasons of *In the Life* (1992–2012), a newsmagazine-style program documenting the LGBTQ movements. *In the Life* originally aired on public television and is now available online through the UCLA Film and Television Archive. This chapter considers the goals and philosophies of the organization while exploring the program's use of documentary storytelling to encourage social change. I also examine the challenges and benefits of In the Life Media's relationship with PBS and the significance of archiving this particular program in a public venue. I argue that *In the Life* successfully documented the most important aspects of the LGBTQ movements for two decades, encouraging positive social change when the show aired and preserving a record of twenty years' worth of progress toward LGBTQ equality.

Chapter 3 examines a nonprofit production company dedicated to nurturing filmmakers who can turn queer stories into fully realized short and feature films. POWER UP is an educational organization and production company that provides training and mentorship for aspiring women and LGBTQ filmmakers. This chapter focuses on the educational aspects of queer media storytelling, using the programs and films of POWER UP as case studies. The discussion incorporates concepts from the field of critical pedagogy, which is primarily concerned with identifying and challenging the social hierarchies that limit educational opportunities for marginalized groups. I argue that POWER UP's programs exemplify many of the ideals of critical pedagogy and serve as a model of antioppressive education. This chapter examines POWER UP's training programs along with some of the media content produced through those programs, including a handful of lesbian-oriented short films, the award-winning lesbian feminist feature film *Itty Bitty Titty Committee* (2007), and a series of public service announcements (PSAs) in support of marriage equality. Focusing on the pedagogical aspects of this film and video output, my analysis of these texts demonstrates how the antioppressive education of POWER UP's work goes beyond training aspiring filmmakers to educating media audiences as well.

Chapters 4 and 5 investigate a range of programs offered by the Seattle-based nonprofit arts organization Three Dollar Bill Cinema. Chapter 4 considers the exhibition of queer film and media through a discussion of TWIST: Seattle Queer Film Festival and Translations: Seattle Transgender Film Festival. I suggest that while organizations like those discussed in previous chapters produce media content and then work to find an audience for that content, Three Dollar Bill Cinema creates and nurtures an audience and then provides media content for them. By assembling groups of people for media viewing experiences, the organization helps make abstract, imagined LGBTQ communities into something more concrete and real, which in turn supports additional organizing and solidarity for LGBTQ movements. This chapter considers diversity in festival programming, the spatial and temporal characteristics of film festivals, and the cultural work that such festivals perform, arguing that in addition to pulling together communities, these festivals also inspire improved queer storytelling and help educate audience members—all of which support ongoing efforts for positive social change.

Chapter 5 pulls together many threads from earlier discussions to examine another program sponsored by Three Dollar Bill Cinema. Reel Queer Youth is a week-long summer filmmaking workshop for LGBTQ teens and their allies. This chapter examines the Reel Queer Youth program to consider how it prepares the next generation of LGBTQ storytellers and activists. Placing Reel Queer Youth within the contexts of media literacy programs and the representation of queer youth in mainstream media, this chapter examines issues of youth storytelling and community formation to show how Reel Queer Youth prepares participants to be actively engaged citizens who can make positive changes to the world around them. I argue that Reel Queer Youth demonstrates how critical media literacy training with a focus on production can help give voice to LGBTQ youth and connect them to a supportive community, thereby empowering them to speak out against oppression and push for positive social change.

In many ways, this book is an extension of the work being done by the storytellers that I study. These media producers collect and draw inspiration from the lived experiences of LGBTQ people and shape those experiences into stories that are delivered to audiences through film and video. In doing this, the storytellers document and make visible the lives and experiences of a group of people that has long been erased from and hidden by mainstream society. This documentation and visibility is, therefore, an important political act that contributes to the increasing acceptance of difference in our society. I too am collecting and telling stories, but my stories focus on a narrower group of people, as I work to document and interpret the experiences and output of some of those who create and disseminate LGBTQ media. I want to acknowledge the importance of these creators and their work by sharing their stories with other scholars, students, and activists interested in media, culture, gender, and sexuality. With this book, I offer a handful of stories that will hopefully contribute to the ever-growing body of narratives that document and advance the push for LGBTQ social justice. Groups like Freedom to Marry have made significant progress, but the 2016 election of Donald Trump and the ensuing appointments of anti-LGBTQ individuals to powerful cabinet posts served as reminders that the fight is not over. The work of the LGBTQ movements will have to continue as long as there are people who want to reverse the advances those movements have made. The following discussions highlight some of what queer storytellers have accomplished so far and will hopefully provide inspiration for those continuing the fight.

1

Challenging Oppressive Myths

LGBTQ Activism and Storytelling

Lesbian, gay, bisexual, transgender, and queer people have been working for more than a century to combat the oppression caused by harmful, inaccurate, and incomplete stories circulated by powerful social institutions and to secure equality and acceptance within larger society. The social justice work of queer people has taken a variety of forms over the years, from peaceful demonstrations and vigils, to aggressive and occasionally violent street protests, to creative acts of artistic expression. Some of this work has been aimed directly at government policy makers, while other work has targeted institutions like churches, schools, corporations, and the media. Still other efforts have sought to reach individuals on a more personal level, with the hopes of building support for the cause one person at a time. Some of the messages generated by advocates for queer social justice have circulated within the LGBTQ population with the goals of generating a sense of unity and inspiring action. Others have been designed to reach out to the rest of society in order to build broader support and encourage the participation of allies.

A central component of my argument in this book is the belief that storytelling is a vital form of activism and a crucial part of the fight for LGBTQ equality. Whether it is the messaging of lobbying groups seeking to change policies or the personal stories of artists hoping to change hearts and minds, storytelling has always been integral to queer social justice efforts. This chapter reviews some efforts of the LGBTQ movements more obviously recognized as activism as well as storytelling practices that perhaps have not been seen as activist in order to help situate the discussions that follow within the context of queer social justice efforts and demonstrate how storytelling has always supported other forms of LGBTQ activism.

Pushing Back: A Brief History of the LGBTQ Movements

The fight for LGBTQ equality has been defined by stops and starts, achievements and setbacks, and disagreements about strategies and goals. As such, it would be a mistake to try to identify a single LGBTQ movement, as that would suggest a coherence and unity that has not existed. It is more accurate to consider a series of sometimes intersecting and other times diverging LGBTQ movements—all working toward similar goals but using different strategies and methods in response to differing sociohistorical contexts.

There have been many changes in the evolving LGBTQ movements over the years, but a defining feature of the entire history of LGBTQ organizing is an ongoing tension between two broad strategies: assimilation and liberation. These are, of course, not the only strategic options, and many individuals and organizations blend elements of the two to fall somewhere in between, but a consideration of these approaches is helpful to understanding the dynamics of the LGBTQ movements. Assimilationists tend to favor a rights-based approach, working within the existing democratic system and arguing for inclusion in that system. Those favoring this approach generally accept that change will be incremental and progress will be slow, as this is the nature of the U.S. government and society. Liberationists, on the other hand, push for more radical change that is "transformational in nature and often arises outside the formal structures of the U.S. political system."[1] In general, assimilationists see the United States as a fundamentally good society, and they push for queer people to be included as citizens in that society. Meanwhile, liberationists see the country as a broken society in need of significant repairs. For them, the rights-based agenda favored by assimilationists "amounts to a wish to be integrated into a flawed, repressive society," leading liberationists to believe that real progress requires more revolutionary changes.[2] Both approaches have been present throughout the development of the LGBTQ movements, demonstrating a diversity of opinions within the population and constantly pushing the movements forward.

Although there were earlier efforts to organize in Europe, including the 1897 founding of the Scientific Humanitarian Committee in Germany and the 1914 founding of the British Society for the Study of Sex Psychology,[3] similar efforts in the United States did not begin until the years following

World War II. As John D'Emilio argues, social changes and upheavals brought on by the war created situations that allowed many homosexuals to discover and develop new sexual identities. Mobilization for the war uprooted many young men and women, separated them from their families and communities of origin, and often placed them in sex-segregated environments, all of which opened the door for increased experimentation and exploration of sexual identity.[4] When the war ended, many men and women who had discovered a homosexual identity in themselves settled in large urban centers rather than returning to their families, and this planted the seeds for the development of communities of homosexuals in cities such as New York and San Francisco. The 1948 publication of Alfred Kinsey's *Sexual Behavior in the Human Male* revealed, among other things, that a significant proportion of men had at least some homosexual experiences in their lifetimes, even if they did not identify as exclusively homosexual. Although some critics challenged or dismissed Kinsey's findings, his report brought all kinds of sexual activities into the spotlight and made society recognize that homosexuality was more prevalent than previously thought. This increased awareness of homosexuality, combined with postwar anti-Communist fears—which led to the policing of all kinds of difference, sexual or otherwise—put gays and lesbians on the defensive and ultimately sparked efforts to organize as a movement.

The first group organized as part of what would become known as the homophile movement was the Mattachine Society, founded in 1950 by Harry Hay and a handful of other gay men with ties to the Communist party. Drawing on principles learned through their work with the Communist party, the founders of the Mattachine Society originally envisioned it as a radical group aiming to "develop among the gay population an awareness of its status as an oppressed minority"[5] so that gay people could come together to resist heterosexual hegemony. As the organization grew and the fear of Communists in the United States became more pronounced, Mattachine Society members decided to distance themselves from their radical origins and connections to Communism, leading to Harry Hay's expulsion from the group in 1953.[6] Under new leadership, the group adopted a less radical agenda, encouraging gays and lesbians to see themselves not as a distinct cultural group but as people who should try to be integrated into mainstream society. As such, their efforts focused on getting scientists, doctors, and politicians to view them as "normal," and they encouraged members to present themselves as respectable, productive citizens so as to win support for their cause.

ONE Inc. was a Mattachine spin-off that was founded in 1953 to publish *ONE* magazine[7] and eventually led to the ONE Institute of Homophile Studies, which offered seminars and produced reports to educate people about the movement. The politically moderate, assimilationist approach favored by the revamped Mattachine Society and ONE Inc. was also adopted by

Del Martin and Phyllis Lyon, the key founders of the women's group Daughters of Bilitis. Originally founded in San Francisco in 1955 as a safe, private social club for lesbians, the group (with some protest from concerned members) soon added social action and outreach to their mission and began coordinating some of their efforts with other groups.[8] Daughters of Bilitis joined the Mattachine Society and ONE Inc. to form the core of the homophile movement during the 1950s and 1960s. Although there was some dissent within the movement—particularly from activists like Barbara Gittings and Franklin Kameny, who pushed for more radical forms of protest—the accommodating, assimilationist approach prevailed within the broader movement until the end of the 1960s.[9] The homophile movement of this era never attracted large numbers of supporters to its cause, even though it had chapters in cities across the country, and it failed to make substantial changes to laws and policies governing homosexuals in the United States. But as D'Emilio argues, this "first generation of gay activists did open a debate on the topic . . . and through its persistence managed to rupture the consensus that shaped social attitudes toward homosexuality and society's treatment of gay people."[10] The homophile movement thus laid the groundwork for the more radical gay liberation movement that followed.

In the late 1960s, as social attitudes about sexuality became more liberal, the concept of a radical challenge to gay and lesbian oppression became more viable. Inspired by the aggressive tactics of other political activists such as antiwar protestors and the Black Power movement, gay and lesbian activists were willing to move beyond the generally polite efforts of the homophile organizations. The growing sense of unrest, coupled with a willingness to fight back, provided the backdrop for the events that took place at New York's Stonewall Inn in late June 1969. When police raided the bar late one night, as they had done many times before, some of the bar's patrons—including cisgender and transgender men and women of various racial and ethnic backgrounds—fought back, hurling physical objects and verbal epithets at the police. The disturbances continued in the neighborhood for several nights following the initial protest, demonstrating the local LGBTQ community's unwillingness to tolerate continued abuse.

The Stonewall Uprising was not the first protest of its kind, as it was preceded by the 1966 Compton's Cafeteria riot in San Francisco and others that did not receive widespread news coverage.[11] Nor was Stonewall the beginning of the gay rights movement. But as Martin Duberman points out, the violent protest at Stonewall "became a symbolic event of international importance,"[12] marking a dramatic shift in the tactics of the LGBTQ movements. Rejecting the assimilationist approach of the homophile organizations, new groups pushed for more radical changes in the name of gay liberation. Within weeks of Stonewall, a group of young men and women formed the Gay Liberation

Front (GLF), which quickly organized regular meetings, action groups, and demonstrations. Inspired by other liberation movements of the era, the GLF refused to see antigay bias as disconnected from other forms of oppression and sought (unsuccessfully) to build coalitions with other groups that were similarly oppressed. Dissatisfied with the group's broad scope, some members left the GLF to form the Gay Activists Alliance (GAA), which adopted a single-issue focus, aiming to achieve civil rights for gays and lesbians rather than challenging all interconnected forms of social oppression.[13] Both groups sought to achieve sexual freedom and liberation rather than an integration of sexual minorities into mainstream society.

As a centrally organized movement, gay liberation was relatively short-lived. The belief in a complete cultural revolution became harder to sustain, and many began to raise concerns about the abilities of a centralized movement to incorporate the differing concerns of women and people of color. The GLF dissolved in 1972, and the GAA weakened in the mid-1970s before coming to an end in 1980. A separate lesbian feminist movement emerged, led by women who felt excluded from both the women's and gay liberation movements.[14] Less radical, more rights-focused groups also developed, some of which became well-funded, permanent institutions. Former members of the GAA, for example, founded the National Gay Task Force (NGTF) in 1973, an organization that has changed its name (first to the National Gay and Lesbian Task Force and eventually to the National LGBTQ Task Force) but continues to fight for equality four decades later. Despite some growing pains and internal divisions, the LGBTQ movements of the 1970s made significant strides in terms of raising awareness about the oppression of LGBTQ people. As a significant component of their work during this era, the GLF, GAA, and NGTF, as well as the Los Angeles–based Gay Media Task Force, all took actions to fight against harmful stereotypes of gay people in media representations. They staged protests and boycotts and eventually served as consultants for some television programs to help minimize negative portrayals and maximize positive visibility.[15] But increased awareness and visibility eventually led to backlash, as conservative forces began to organize in opposition to the growing acceptance of queer identities.

The citizens of Dade County, Florida, as discussed in the previous chapter, voted in 1977 to repeal an ordinance that made it illegal to discriminate against people based on their sexual orientation. Spokesperson Anita Bryant and other leaders of the campaign framed the repeal as necessary for the protection of children. Cities and counties around the country soon followed Dade County's example, and laws protecting gays and lesbians were repealed in cities like St. Paul, Minnesota, and Wichita, Kansas. The conservative right gained strength as Ronald Reagan was elected President in 1980, ushering in a new conservatism that was not hospitable to advancing gay rights. Worsening the hostile political environment was the emergence of the AIDS epidemic in the early 1980s. Because the earliest diagnoses of the illness were in gay men, AIDS was quickly, though incorrectly, labeled as a "gay disease" by many conservative politicians and religious leaders who used the disease as an excuse to target homosexuals, arguing that AIDS was punishment for a deviant lifestyle.

The fear and confusion that dominated the early years of the AIDS epidemic forced LGBTQ leaders to put equality campaigns on the back burner, as they were essentially in crisis mode dealing with an illness that nobody yet understood. Not surprisingly, AIDS was a setback for the LGBTQ movements, but it eventually brought activists together with a renewed sense of purpose. Leaders organized groups like the Gay Men's Health Crisis (New York), Boston's AIDS Action Committee, and the San Francisco AIDS Foundation to provide counseling, education, and health care when the services of established medical providers were inadequate. As the initial fear of AIDS turned into anger over the unsatisfactory responses of the government and pharmaceutical companies, Larry Kramer and a group of fellow activists in New York formed the AIDS Coalition to Unleash Power (ACT UP). ACT UP, which quickly developed chapters in large cities across the country, staged public rallies, marches, "die-ins," and other acts of civil disobedience. These demonstrations were directed at public and private agencies that activists felt were dragging their feet with regards to dealing with the epidemic, and they were performed in front of news cameras whenever possible.[16] As men and women worked together to address the AIDS crisis, the LGBTQ movement gained new strength, and this was translated into additional efforts during the 1990s.

Queer Nation was founded in 1990, drawing on the activist spirit of ACT UP but pushing beyond AIDS to address other issues facing LGBTQ people. Using the term *queer* not as a pejorative but as a claiming of identities that, in various ways, exist outside normative, binary definitions of gender and sexuality, Queer Nation aimed to challenge mainstream society rather than seeking a place within it. Queer Nation existed for less than two years as a stable organization, but the queer sensibilities that the group encouraged survived in other activist organizations, popular culture, and academia.[17]

Aside from the radical activities of Queer Nation and a few organizations inspired by their efforts, the LGBTQ movements of the 1990s and beyond have been defined by a focus on civil rights issues such as military service and marriage equality. Led by well-organized and well-funded groups like the Human Rights Campaign and the National Gay and Lesbian Task Force, the movements generally embraced an assimilationist approach, arguing that LGBTQ people should be granted equal rights because they contribute to the nation as productive and valuable citizens. During the 1990s, this push for civil rights was part of a general increase in LGBTQ visibility that went beyond political discussions to include media, popular culture, and the marketplace. As news outlets covered gay rights struggles with greater frequency and depth, Hollywood began incorporating more LGBTQ characters (often sidekicks, best friends, or siblings instead of primary protagonists) into mainstream film and television productions. While some saw this increasing visibility as a cause for celebration, critics encouraged a more cautious approach, warning that being visible is not the same as being understood or accepted.[18] And as Suzanna Walters points out, "At times, cultural visibility can simply be synonymous with commercial exploitation or with the 'degaying' of gayness for heterosexual consumption."[19] Indeed, the producers of mainstream popular culture and media work in a profit-driven environment and are more concerned with the bottom line than with equality and civil rights. And as part of a trend toward increased market segmentation, marketers in the 1990s increasingly embraced the LGBTQ population as a valuable target audience. In a 1995 book aimed at business leaders, Grant Lukenbill proclaimed that there was "a dynamic infusion of economic opportunity for American business," which he identified as "the power of the gay and lesbian consumer dollar and all that it represents."[20] Many businesses, including the mainstream media industries, were eager to embrace this market segment, further increasing their visibility.

Unfortunately, the increased visibility of the 1990s did not translate to major victories in the realm of civil rights. In fact, two of the issues that LGBTQ leaders pushed most aggressively during this period—open inclusion in the military and marriage equality—were defeated, as the government, led by supposedly LGBTQ friendly President Bill Clinton, enacted the "Don't Ask, Don't Tell" policy in the military and passed the Defense of Marriage Act to formally codify a narrow, heteronormative definition of marriage. In the 2000s, the institutions of the mainstream LGBTQ movement continued to push for civil rights, honing their political, legal, and cultural strategies and working through all three branches of government to eventually achieve victories in the battles over marriage equality and military service. But even with these victories, the LGBTQ movements have continued to face resistance and backlash from religious and political conservatives threatening to reverse some of the advances made by queer people and working to prevent any further progress.

In addition to resistance from opponents, the heavily funded, rights-focused organizations, which have been the most visible LGBTQ groups in recent decades, have faced resistance from within the LGBTQ population, as critical queer and trans activists have argued that the continued focus on inclusion in institutions like marriage and the military has led to further marginalization of queer people who do not want or are unable to assimilate to dominant society.[21] As it has from the beginning of the LGBTQ movements, the push for a radical politics of transformation continues to offer an alternative to the liberal politics of inclusion, pushing for ever greater change and progress for all members of the LGBTQ population.

Building Queer Communities

Participants in the LGBTQ movements have not always agreed on the best strategies to advance their causes, but central to all movements has been the recognition that in order to achieve any success, individuals must work together and make themselves known and heard as a group. As such, a central component of the movements has been an effort to build and support strong LGBTQ communities as a way of achieving success.

The LGBTQ population in the United States has organized itself in various ways and on different scales over the years. As John D'Emilio discusses, the gay liberation movement of the 1970s was characterized by a strong impulse to "create organizations and to build community—to build, really, something of a 'queer nation.'"[22] At the local level, this manifested in the creation of gay-friendly religious groups, sports teams, community centers, newspapers, bookstores, and professional organizations.[23] LGBTQ individuals who lived in or moved to cities where such organizations appeared could easily find other people to connect with, allowing them to tap into a local LGBTQ community. And while very few LGBTQ organizations existed at a nationwide level, there was a sense that many of the same types of groups were developing across the country, expressing shared concerns, hopes, and desires. The common ground uniting various local communities formed the foundation for what D'Emilio refers to as the "queer nation."

The concept of a queer nation, held together by shared beliefs rather than any defined organization or personal relationships, has much in common with Benedict Anderson's ideas about "imagined communities." In his discussion of national identity, Anderson argues that the development of such an identity is generally predicated on the notion of community, but he notes that a nation is necessarily composed of such a large number of people that it would be impossible for everyone to know each other on a personal level. Their sense of connection with one another is therefore imagined—they believe that they share commonalities that bind them together, and in living out this belief, the bonds become a social reality.[24]

As concrete, geographically defined LGBTQ communities developed in various cities and towns, so too did the imagined LGBTQ community, composed of lesbian, gay, bisexual, transgender, and queer people across the nation. Identifying this community as an imagined one is not to diminish its significance, as imagined communities can have very real effects. Dorothy Noyes argues that even when communities are imagined, we can see their ideas "living in concrete realizations: texts, performances, and objects, all transmissible and open to recontextualization."[25] In other words, an imagined community produces concrete artifacts that then circulate in our culture and solidify the community's existence, providing a source of strength and connection for the individuals who identify with it.

The LGBTQ population is a very diverse group, and referring to this group as a community has the potential to obscure the significant differences that exist among its various segments. In fact, the concept of a unified community with shared concerns and goals, popularized by the 1970s liberation movement, lost credibility by the start of the next decade. Women and people of color objected to the fact that the concerns of gay white men were dominating the liberation movement, and the differences that these objections revealed made the image of a single community harder to sustain.[26] Further complicating attempts to define a unified community is the intersectional nature of most individuals' identities, which can pull people in multiple directions; identifying with multiple communities can make it harder to connect with any one of them. Kath Weston has noted that in the face of such potentially damaging divisions, "some political activists have endeavored to fabricate a solidarity capable of spanning 'the community' without denying differences that divide its members."[27] United by resistance to a shared oppression but divided by concerns and perspectives unique to individual subgroups, the LGBTQ population is perhaps most accurately described as a collection or coalition of communities rather than as a single monolithic community.

Whether singular or plural, local and concrete or nationwide and imagined, LGBTQ communities can provide personal emotional benefits for the individuals who connect with them. At a very basic level, a sense of belonging is considered one of the most important human needs, following only physiological needs and safety.[28] LGBTQ individuals often find themselves cast out of family groups, religious institutions, and other organizations, and connecting with a queer community can help reestablish a lost sense of belonging, making it a key element in an individual's well-being and even survival.[29]

In addition to the emotional benefits offered to individuals, communities can generate political benefits that help the entire group and often society as a whole. Jeffrey Weeks, for example, argues that groups who feel threatened, as is often the case for queer people, "construct out of this a community of identity which provides a strong sense of resistance and empowerment,"[30] which can then be mobilized for activist purposes. Similarly, Patricia Hill Collins argues that community identification is important to grassroots political movements: if groups see themselves as communities, they are more likely to believe that when the group is harmed collectively by some outside force or social policy, the group is "best helped through collective response."[31] In other words, if individuals see themselves as part of a community, they are more likely to share the pain and frustration caused by injustices aimed at that community, and in turn, they are more likely to take action to contribute to finding solutions. There is social and political strength in numbers, and creating a sense of community is an important step toward mobilizing those numbers. Storytelling has the potential to help in the formation of communities, and as the following chapters demonstrate, organizations dedicated to producing and disseminating LGBTQ stories make those communities visible and give individuals opportunities to connect with them.

Telling Their Own Stories

In order to support the development of queer communities and their efforts to achieve social justice, the organizations examined in this book tell stories that challenge those that have come from the mainstream—including those that have been overtly negative and harmful as well as those that may have been well intentioned but were ultimately incomplete or inaccurate. But these organizations are not the first to do this. They build on a history of queer activists who have challenged repressive heteronormativity and strengthened LGBTQ communities simply by sharing their own stories.

As a marginalized minority group with limited access to resources, the LGBTQ population has not always had an easy time communicating with one another, let alone sharing their stories with a wide audience. Long before the development of nationally distributed queer magazines, films, or television programs, LGBTQ people had to find creative, inexpensive, and often covert ways of connecting with one another. Martin Meeker argues that for many decades, publishers, doctors, ministers, police officers, judges, and parents essentially acted as censors, aiming to prevent the flow of communication among LGBTQ people. But despite this censorship, Meeker notes, "Those who wished to communicate about homosexuality or with homosexuals found holes in the nets of censorship, and they developed strategies for communicating in ways that avoided the attention of censors or even subverted their actions to enable new modes of communication."[32] For example, some relied on heavily coded ads in classified sections of periodicals like the *Hobby Directory*, which offered a forum for individuals to connect and correspond about their hobbies. Hobbies such as flower arranging, interior decorating, and collecting photos of athletic models often signaled homosexuality and prompted readers to exchange contact information.[33] Bar guides such as *Damron's* provided lists of LGBTQ-oriented bars and clubs across the country, letting queer people know where it was safe to meet others like them.[34] While these resources did not offer stories per se, they did help establish and maintain the existence of a queer population, however dispersed, that was eager to connect with one another and would eventually form the core audience for the queer storytelling that was to emerge.

In 1947, a woman using the name Lisa Ben wrote a magazine called *Vice Versa*, which she printed herself using carbon paper before hand-distributing it in a few Los Angeles bars.[35] As a solo effort, *Vice Versa* did not reach a very large audience, but other magazines soon followed. As part of their efforts to win supporters to their cause, the homophile organizations of the 1950s all published magazines. These were small-scale, somewhat amateur magazines, but they were distributed, albeit in limited numbers, in cities across the country. *ONE* started in 1953, while the *Mattachine Review* and the *Ladder* (from the Daughters of Bilitis) were both launched in 1955. In 1960, Virginia Prince started *Transvestia* magazine, the country's first long-running transgender-oriented periodical.[36] As with *Vice Versa* before them, these magazines included editorials, fiction, entertainment reviews, and letters from readers. Through various forms of narrative, the magazines helped queer readers see that there were many others like them and recognize some of the sources of their oppression while encouraging them to join the fledgling social movements.

Toward the end of the 1960s and into the 1970s, as the gay liberation movement gained strength, publishers saw the potential for commercial publications aimed at LGBTQ readers. The *Los Angeles Advocate*, an activist newsletter transformed into a commercial newspaper about LGBTQ issues, was launched in 1967. Soon renamed the *Advocate*, it would become the first national gay newsmagazine, focusing on coverage of all aspects of the growing LGBTQ movements.[37]

As some were making connections and sharing stories via print media, others took it upon themselves to produce their own films and videos to document and dramatize queer experiences. Experimental, avant-garde, and underground filmmakers worked well outside the bounds of Hollywood to create works that explored and expanded the bounds of film as a medium while challenging a variety of social norms, including those centered on gender and sexuality. The work of Kenneth Anger, for example, draws on ideas from pagan spirituality along with iconography from gay erotica—including images of sailors, bikers, and muscle men—to represent and play with notions of sexual pleasure and gay desire.[38] His film *Fireworks* (1947) depicts a young man wandering through a mysterious dreamscape filled with erotic and occasionally violent encounters with masculine sailors. Anger's *Scorpio Rising* (1963) features a soundtrack of 1960s pop music and images of cultural icons like Marlon Brando and James Dean as it explores the relationships between homosocial bonding and homosexual desire.[39] Many gay underground films of the 1960s, including Jack Smith's *Flaming Creatures* (1963), use a camp aesthetic to explore queer subcultures and comment on mainstream Hollywood storytelling and imagery. Famous for much more than just filmmaking, Andy

Warhol also contributed to the gay underground movement, producing films with a minimalist aesthetic that challenged the norms of Hollywood through the use of long takes, little to no editing, and nonprofessional actors. These films generally appealed to a small art-house film audience, but the screenings of these films made an important contribution to the developing LGBTQ movements. As Janet Staiger points out, the gathering spaces associated with underground queer cinema in the 1960s "endorsed and even rewarded resistance" and aided in "building a community that would later erupt into a revolution."[40]

As the gay liberation movement of the 1970s gained strength, many filmmakers gravitated toward documentary films, hoping to fuel the liberation movement by capturing and sharing the true experiences and stories of a wide range of LGBTQ people. Ken Robinson's *Some of Your Best Friends* (1971) broke ground by presenting openly gay citizens discussing details of their personal and professional lives. As a student film with minimal distribution, its impact was minor, but it set the stage for a much bigger breakthrough later in the decade.[41] *Word Is Out: Stories of Some of Our Lives* (1977) was shot, directed, and edited by a team of six filmmakers—three gay men and three lesbian women—known as the Mariposa Film Group. The film features gay and lesbian men and women from varying races, ethnicities, regions, and walks of life telling their own stories in their own words. Interview segments are woven together to paint a broad portrait of the difficulties encountered by gays and lesbians over the years. Arthur Bressan's *Gay U.S.A.* (1978) moved away from people's everyday lives to interview participants in large-scale pride parades and festivals in cities like New York and San Francisco. Using these celebrations as a backdrop, the film emphasizes the public celebration of sexual diversity, explicitly politicizing the personal nature of individuals' stories. Documentaries like these featured individuals from all walks of life to show that queer people were everywhere, thereby offering "cinematic extensions of the coming-out strategy" that was so important to the gay liberation movement[42] and inspiring countless films that document and preserve queer experiences, including *The Times of Harvey Milk* (Rob Epstein, 1984), *The Brandon Teena Story* (Susan Muska and Greta Olafsdottir, 1998), and *How to Survive a Plague* (David France, 2012).

In the late 1970s, a movement of lesbian-feminist filmmakers including Barbara Hammer, Jan Oxenberg, and Anne Severson adopted a different strategy for telling queer stories. Based on the belief that conventional filmmaking was rooted in and reflected sexist and patriarchal values, these women challenged the very language of cinema, creating, as Andrea Weiss describes them, "films which in form and content declare their complete independence from and opposition to the dominant American film and television industries."[43] The most prolific of these filmmakers, Barbara Hammer, often included

FIGURE 1.2 The documentary *Word Is Out: Stories of Some of Our Lives* (1977) features gay men and lesbians from many different backgrounds telling their own stories in their own words. Frame enlargement.

herself in the films she directed, positioning herself as an active sexual subject to challenge the more common voyeuristic view of lesbian lovemaking. Her film *Women I Love* (1976) offers a series of portraits of women in Hammer's life interspersed with images of vegetables, flowers, and other organic materials shot in ways that suggest vaginal imagery. Hammer appears in multiple intimate sequences, which, as Richard Dyer observes, connect the filmmaker to her subjects and "dissolve the strict boundary between who films and who is filmed."[44] While films like this embody the political spirit of feminism, others engage with politics in a more direct and explicit manner. For example, Lizzie Borden's *Born in Flames* (1983) is set ten years after a peaceful socialist revolution transformed much of the government of the United States but preserved the basic framework of patriarchy. In response, a group known as the Women's Army organizes a resistance and, with increasingly militant tactics, pushes back against the government. The film includes a fragmented narrative that blends the aesthetics of documentary and scripted drama and is punctuated by energetic musical interludes. The main characters are women of color, many of whom express their dissatisfaction with the exclusionary approaches of liberal white feminism, and the film serves as a call to arms, urging all women to fight back against misogyny, racism, homophobia, and the surveillance of women by social institutions largely run by men. Like the experimental and underground films before them, the lesbian-feminist films of the 1970s and 1980s generally appealed to a small audience of like-minded viewers, but they provided that audience with alternatives to the oppressive images of mainstream media and encouraged them to continue pushing for social change.

Also pushing for social change in the 1980s was a smaller movement known as queercore, the name of which refers to its queer approach to hardcore punk. Started by queer media artists G. B. Jones and Bruce LaBruce, queercore was a transmedia movement that incorporated film, music, zines, and performance art. Queercore rejected not only mainstream ideals but also the values of two oppositional groups: the gay and lesbian rights movement and the punk scene. As Curran Nault describes, queercore emerged "in pointed distinction to the homophobia of hardcore punk and the lifeless sexual politics of the gay and lesbian majority."[45] Pushing for a fully inclusive punk scene that rejected heteronormative phallocentrism and celebrated all forms of sexual and gender variance, queercore espoused a politics of transformation through its varying forms of storytelling.

Another important movement in the history of queer media storytelling emerged during the late 1980s, when LGBTQ people were searching for ways to combat the growing AIDS epidemic. To coincide with street protests and other demonstrations organized by groups like ACT UP, many activists decided to use video as an additional tool to advance the movement. Recognizing that mainstream media outlets were not responding effectively to the epidemic, activists in New York and other cities formed loosely organized AIDS activist video collectives, relying on inexpensive video equipment, minimal training, and guerrilla filmmaking tactics to produce their content.[46] The videos produced by these groups were meant to document the efforts of activists, provide countersurveillance and protection from overly aggressive law enforcement, and educate and inform people in the hopes that those who saw the videos might join the activist efforts. Without access to mainstream distribution channels, the activist collectives found other ways to get their videos in front of audiences: they were shown on public-access cable channels, in bars and clubs, at activist meetings, in galleries, at fundraisers, and as a part of gay and lesbian film festivals.[47]

These video collectives were often short-lived, as they formed around a particular project and then dissolved as members moved on to other projects and created new collectives. One of the better known and most prolific groups was DIVA TV (Damned Interfering Video Activist Television), which focused on the members of ACT UP as both its primary subject and target audience.[48] Embracing a low-tech, amateur aesthetic, DIVA TV and the other video collectives focused on the political value of their content. As Alexandra Juhasz notes, AIDS video collectives allowed activists to use video "to form a local response to AIDS, to articulate a rebuttal to or a revision of the mainstream media's definitions and representations of AIDS, and to form community around a new identity forced into existence by the fact of AIDS."[49] The stories told by these video activists were not intended to amuse or entertain, as is generally the goal of Hollywood productions; rather, they demonstrate how the tools of video storytelling can be used in specific ways to advance the work of AIDS activists as well as the larger LGBTQ movements.

While AIDS activist videos were fairly narrow in scope, a much broader range of topics and styles can be found in the wave of queer films that came to be known as the New Queer Cinema. Coined in an essay by B. Ruby Rich, the term *New Queer Cinema* refers to a group of films that won the acclaim of critics and audiences when they hit the festival circuit in the early 1990s. Films such as *Paris Is Burning* (1990) and *Poison* (1991), which earned top awards at the Sundance Film Festival, along with *Edward II* (1991), *My Own Private Idaho* (1991), *Swoon* (1992), and *The Living End* (1992) were surprise hits that dealt openly and honestly with a variety of queer issues and demonstrated that queer films "could be both radical and popular, stylish and economically viable."[50] New Queer Cinema was not a formal movement, and there was no organization among those who contributed to it, nor was there a shared visual aesthetic or subject matter. But as Rich notes in the essay that first identified the trend, New Queer Cinema films all exhibit "traces of appropriation, pastiche, and irony, as well as a reworking of history with social constructionism very much in mind." Rich goes on to describe them as "irreverent, energetic, alternately minimalist and excessive."[51]

Perhaps most importantly, the films of the New Queer Cinema are united by an attitude that Michele Aaron identifies as "defiance."[52] They defy the conventions of mainstream cinema, both in their focus on marginalized queer people and in their reimagining of form and genre. By presenting flawed (and sometimes criminal) queer characters without apology, they defy the logic that pushes for "positive" queer representations as the best way to advance the LGBTQ movements. They defy accepted homophobic accounts of history by revisiting the past and reinserting queerness where it has previously been erased. And as Aaron points out, "The films in many ways defy death,"[53] particularly when they challenge dominant views on AIDS by refusing to treat the illness as a tragic death sentence.

The defiant attitude of New Queer Cinema reflected the mood of the late 1980s AIDS activists, who angrily confronted government agencies and corporations over their slow response to the health crisis. Not surprisingly, some of the New Queer Cinema filmmakers were involved with this activism before turning to feature filmmaking. Tom Kalin, for example, was a founding member of Gran Fury, the AIDS activist artist collective that used techniques from graphic design and installation art to publicize the work and message of ACT UP. Todd Haynes was also involved with ACT UP and Gran Fury before turning to film. Kalin's first feature, *Swoon*, is based on the true story of Leopold and Loeb, two men who killed a young boy for sport. Previous films had been made about these killers, but Kalin's was the first to openly address their queer sexuality. While some criticized Kalin for reinforcing stereotypes about deviant queer killers, many others felt that the film actually challenged the construction of such stereotypes by confronting them. Haynes's film *Poison* was also controversial. The film tells three separate stories, each shot in a different visual style and cut together so as to encourage the audience to see links between the stories and their themes. While some applauded the film's self-reflexive play with style and genre, others labeled the film as pornographic and objected to the support it received from the National Endowment for the Arts. As two of the breakthrough films of New Queer Cinema, *Swoon* and *Poison* helped establish the trend of films that were not afraid to alienate some viewers in their efforts to challenge cinematic norms.

Along with her initial observations celebrating the arrival of New Queer Cinema, B. Ruby Rich also offered a critique of the trend, noting that most of the initial wave of films came from white men. There were, however, a few exceptions. Marlon Riggs's *Tongues Untied* (1989), for example, appeared just ahead of the first big wave of New Queer Cinema films. An experimental documentary that includes elements of poetry, autobiography, and social critique, the film explores the challenges and complications of being black and gay in the United States. A few years after the first New Queer Cinema wave, lesbian filmmakers made a big splash with *Go Fish* (1994). Written by Rose Troche and Guinevere Turner—directed by Troche and starring Turner—the film is essentially a romantic comedy, but it challenges cinematic norms not only by focusing on lesbian romance but also by breaking up the straightforward narrative with avant-garde sequences that offer political commentary about gender and sexuality. Cheryl Dunye's *The Watermelon Woman* (1996), a rare example of a film made by and about African American lesbians, is a self-reflexive pseudodocumentary that critiques the marginalization of black women, lesbians, and particularly black lesbians in cinema as well as society as a whole. Dunye stars as a version of herself, an aspiring filmmaker who sets out to uncover the true identity of a black character actress from early Hollywood credited only as "the watermelon woman" in the films in which she appears, eventually learning that the actress was romantically involved with a female director, even though family members and historians repeatedly deny this information. *Tongues Untied*, *Go Fish*, and *The Watermelon Woman* exhibit many of the hallmarks of New Queer Cinema, including self-reflexivity, formal experimentation, and a defiant attitude while broadening the range of voices telling queer stories.

New Queer Cinema was a relatively brief wave of films. In an article written about eight years after she first gave a name to the trend, Rich herself noted that it was more of "a moment than a movement."[54] By the second half of the 1990s, queer characters began appearing more frequently in mainstream and independent media as marketers and producers saw the incorporation of queer content as a mark of hipness and a way to reach a lucrative market segment. The defiant activist drive was replaced somewhat by a commercial imperative, and many filmmakers began to produce content that aimed to reach queer viewers as just one piece of a broader audience.

While the wave of films widely recognized as the New Queer Cinema eventually subsided, some of the filmmakers associated with those films have gone on to achieve much in the industry. One of the most successful is producer Christine Vachon. Vachon studied film and semiotics at Brown University and was involved with ACT UP and other activist organizations, all of which helped her realize the social power of film and the importance of engaging in meaningful work. She notes the impact of feminist film theory on her changing perception of the industry, saying, "Suddenly there was a lot more at play when you went to the movies than just sticking popcorn in your mouth. . . . After you start thinking this way, there's no way you can go and simply tell a story."[55] Seeking to tell stories that could make a difference, she partnered with her friend Todd Haynes to produce his first feature film, *Poison*. She then moved on to produce *Swoon*, directed by Tom Kalin, who she had met through their shared work in AIDS activism. Upon learning of Vachon's association with these films, Rose Troche and Guinevere Turner, who had run out of funding partway through the production of what would become *Go Fish*, reached out to Vachon for help. She joined them as a producer, helped raise the funds to complete the project, and soon had another successful queer film playing at Sundance. With these accomplishments, she quickly gained a reputation as a queer producer—a title that she hates. She says, "I'd never make a film solely because it's edgy or provocative or features a gay subject, and I'd never refuse to make a film solely because it doesn't."[56] Instead of focusing specifically on queer stories, she aims to produce unique and original ideas from writers and directors who are deeply passionate about their projects. She says, "When you stop retreading the conventional fairy tales—when you quit with the fairy tales entirely—you make better art. You also make people a little nervous."[57] In 1995, Vachon joined with Pam Koffler to found Killer Films, a company driven by Vachon's willingness to take risks and go after stories that have not been told.

Given Vachon's approach to moviemaking, it is not surprising that many of Killer Films's projects have been queer in form and/or content, including major successes like *Boys Don't Cry* (1999), *Far from Heaven* (2002), and *Carol* (2015). In many ways, these films continue the spirit of the New Queer

Cinema movement, but they also take some steps toward making queer content more appealing to mainstream audiences. *Boys Don't Cry*, for example, is based on the true story of Brandon Teena, a trans man who was beaten, raped, and murdered by two friends after they discovered that he was not biologically male. The film carries on the legacy of New Queer Cinema by pushing the boundaries of media storytelling—telling a story that many were not ready to hear and not giving them a way to ignore the brutality of what happened. The film's transgressive status was highlighted by the fact that the MPAA originally assigned the film an NC-17 rating, objecting not only to the brutal rape scene but also to a tender love scene between Brandon and his girlfriend, Lana.[58] Vachon and director Kimberly Peirce agreed to cut a few frames to get the film an R rating, and it eventually went on to earn multiple Oscar nominations, including a win for Hilary Swank, who played Brandon. Although Brandon passed some bad checks, the film basically establishes him as the hero, giving audiences a trans person they can root for and weep for, even if it pushes them slightly out of their comfort zone.

Far from Heaven adopts the style of 1950s melodramas by such directors as Douglas Sirk and Max Ophuls, telling the story of a middle-class suburban housewife named Cathy Whitaker (Julianne Moore), whose perfect world begins to fall apart when she discovers that her husband is gay and then develops romantic feelings for her black gardener. The film pushes boundaries by raising issues of sexism, racism, and homophobia, but by using a 1950s setting and a highly stylized aesthetic, it puts distance between the story and the audience, making it easier for some viewers to see these behaviors a part of our society's past rather than our present. And partially in keeping with the norms of the era being presented, the film avoids any graphic depictions of sexuality. Although the original script featured Cathy catching her husband performing oral sex on another man,[59] this was eventually downgraded to a kiss, and the film overall remains very chaste in its presentation of sexuality.

Carol, another film directed by Todd Haynes, is also set in the 1950s. It tells the story of a young photographer (Rooney Mara) who begins an affair with an older woman (Cate Blanchett) going through a difficult divorce. Given the rarity of wide-release films that focus on lesbian romance, *Carol* certainly marks a step forward for queer cinema. But unlike New Queer Cinema standouts *Go Fish* and *The Watermelon Woman*, there is a stylistic polish that situates the film closer to the mainstream in terms of its narrative and visual aesthetic. As with most of Killer Films's projects, *Carol* tells the kind of story that studios and most independent producers overlook, helping bring queer lives and experiences to a wider audience. But the presentation of these stories adopts a stance that is politically more liberal than radical. While the films of the New Queer Cinema rejected heteronormativity as well as polite gay and lesbian society to embrace an outsider status, the later work of Killer Films aligns more with the broader LGBTQ political movements from the late 1990s onward, which have tended to favor integration over transformative liberation. This stance is further emphasized by the company's diverse slate of films. As previously noted, Vachon has argued that she is not just a queer filmmaker. Films such as *One Hour Photo* (2002), *The Company* (2003), and *Still Alice* (2014) broaden Killer Films's portfolio. By highlighting queer stories without focusing on them exclusively, Killer Films has been able to create content with a broad appeal for viewers, critics, and investors,[60] an approach that mirrors the integrationist political strategy adopted by the LGBTQ movements' most visible contemporary activists.

While the diversified approach has proven successful for Killer Films, some companies have chosen to focus solely on queer storytelling. An example of this approach is a company called Mythgarden, which was founded in 2003 by three openly gay men—Christopher Racster, Chad Allen, and Robert Gant. Racster had previously made a name for himself on the business side of the entertainment industry, working in marketing and public relations before producing a handful of short and feature films that played at festivals around the world. Allen had been working as an actor since childhood, starring or recurring in television shows like *St. Elsewhere* (1983–1988) and *Our House* (1986–1988) before his long-running stint on *Dr. Quinn, Medicine Woman* (1993–1998). Gant had earned a law degree from Georgetown University but left the legal field to pursue acting, eventually landing a costarring role on the second through fifth seasons of *Queer as Folk* (2000–2005). The three men knew each other socially and had crossed paths in the industry but had never worked together. Then Allen came across an unproduced film script about two men who find love at a Christian ex-gay ministry center. The three decided not only to adapt and produce the script into a film but also to found a company dedicated to LGBTQ storytelling. Believing that there was a market for well-made LGBTQ films with a message, they formed Mythgarden as an investor-supported, for-profit company.

The mission of Mythgarden, according to its founders, was to raise the quality of LGBTQ filmmaking and tell important stories that would help advance the queer community. In both internal and public conversations about the company, the founders characterized the work of Mythgarden as "turning the page" on LGBTQ filmmaking in regard to both quality and message. This meant focusing on technical and aesthetic excellence while expanding beyond the coming out stories and AIDS dramas that had come to dominate serious queer filmmaking. Racster says that the founders of Mythgarden were passionate about "telling the stories that no one else was telling . . . turning the page on what was considered LGBT content."[61] Allen concurs, saying that his interest in Mythgarden was "born out of a desire to find good stories and find a way to tell them," adding that the company was primarily trying to "provide an outlet and a voice for LGBT storytellers."[62]

The mission and goals of Mythgarden were rooted in the social justice work of the company's founders. As Racster notes, "We had all been incredibly politically active. All three of us had done different things for different charities and different political groups within the community, and we really recognized the ability for good queer content to make a difference, big or small, whether it was just in the community making people feel good about themselves or outside the community helping to shape opinions." The men had worked with LGBTQ charitable organizations like Point Foundation, the Matthew Shepard Foundation, the Human Rights Campaign, Lambda Legal, and GLEH (Gay and Lesbian Elder Housing). Drawing parallels between his philanthropic work and the work of Mythgarden, Gant says, "I appreciate the opportunity to be of service and to be a part of the solution."[63] Similarly, Allen points to the importance of blending social justice work and filmmaking. He says, "I continue to be dedicated to my role as an activist—as a person who's involved in the civil rights struggle for gay and lesbian Americans—as much as I am dedicated to being an actor and a storyteller." Racster, Allen, and Gant recognized that their experiences and connections gave them a public voice and access to an industry that would allow them to maximize that voice on behalf of others. Mythgarden provided an opportunity for its founders to continue their philanthropic and activist work within the context of film.

With the company's framework established, the producers moved ahead with the script they had acquired, which they eventually turned into the film *Save Me* (2007). While the original script was a comedy, the producers hired Robert Desiderio to rewrite the screenplay and turn it into something that would take a serious look at ex-gay ministries and the larger relationship between Christianity and homosexuality. Rather than fueling division between gays and Christians, the completed film recognizes that many people are both gay and Christian and that people who see themselves as being on one side or the other can actually find common ground through dialogue. *Save Me* had its premiere at the Sundance Film Festival, followed by a tour of film festivals around the world, a limited theatrical release, a Gay and Lesbian Alliance Against Defamation (GLAAD) media award nomination, and a DVD release. It was not a blockbuster of Hollywood proportions, but by independent film standards, it was a big achievement for the new company.

The success of *Save Me* generated much attention, and soon Mythgarden was flooded with scripts and story ideas from LGBTQ writers looking for someone to produce their work. The partners began developing some of the projects, but before any of those came to fruition, the company closed its doors. The primary catalyst for this was the desire of one partner

FIGURE 1.3 *Save Me* (2007), the debut film from independent production company Mythgarden, examines the relationship between homosexuality and Christianity. Frame enlargement.

to leave Mythgarden, which triggered a contractually stipulated dissolution of the company. But even before this, the partners had begun to worry about the financial viability of a for-profit production company dedicated entirely to LGBTQ storytelling. The recession of 2008 made fundraising harder for all filmmakers, and Mythgarden's narrow focus only increased the challenge. Allen notes that the increase in queer stories and representation in mainstream film and television might have actually led to a shrinking of smaller, independent markets. He says, "It shrunk so severely that it became obvious that there wasn't a market for profitable storytelling in that arena. It became such that we couldn't in good faith take people's money and expect that we could give it back to them."

Before disbanding, the partners briefly considered the possibility of shifting their business model to emphasize queer-friendly content over strictly queer-focused content, an approach similar to that embraced by Killer Films. The fact that Logo, originally launched as the first national cable channel built around LGBTQ programming, also made a shift to broader content in 2012 suggests that others in the industry had similar concerns about the profitability of a business built solely on LGBTQ content. This may also explain, at least in part, the nonprofit route chosen by the organizations examined later in this book.

While companies dedicated entirely to LGBTQ content may struggle in the marketplace, queer storytellers are increasingly finding success within the commercial enterprises of Hollywood, particularly in television. Openly gay writer/director/producer Ryan Murphy, for example, has brought prominent queer characters, storylines, and performers to mainstream television by way of such hits as *Nip/Tuck* (2003–2010), *Glee* (2009–2015), and *American Horror*

Story (2011–), all of which use multiple storylines and ensemble casts to incorporate queerness as just one piece of a larger narrative structure. Similarly, Alan Ball, the openly gay writer/producer behind *American Beauty* (1999), *Six Feet Under* (2001–2005), and *True Blood* (2008–2014), regularly incorporates queer characters and themes into stories that are not, on their surface, primarily LGBTQ-focused. Writer/producer Dustin Lance Black placed queer issues front and center in the ABC miniseries *When We Rise* (2017), which chronicles the major developments of the LGBTQ rights movements in the United States. While the success of these storytellers indicates a degree of progress, queer women and people of color continue to be woefully underrepresented as storytellers in mainstream media. Additionally, while mainstream media outlets seem willing to accept images in line with liberal assimilationist strategies, radical messages about social transformation for queer people are far less likely to appear.

For those who do not have access to the resources associated with Hollywood, or even those of small-scale independent film, the world of online storytelling has become a popular option. The growth of online storytelling has been fueled by the rapid development of social media, online video distribution portals like YouTube, and easy access to cameras via smartphones and laptops. Essentially anyone with a smartphone, a computer, and internet access (still not everyone, but by now, the vast majority of people in the United States) can share their stories online using words, images, sound, and video. One of the most common forms of online queer storytelling is the coming out story. Sometimes individuals speak directly to the camera and, by extension, their online audience, while others come out to a friend or family member in front of the camera. Other videos involve individuals telling stories on topics ranging from oppression, fear, and suicidal thoughts to accomplishments, loving families, and hopes for the future. Some even go so far as to create short dramatic or comedic films, some with relatively high production values. But as Jonathan Alexander and Elizabeth Losh point out, the majority of individual online videos "are rarely viewed and infrequently commented upon. Thus such videos may have more affective and political power in aggregate."[64] The impact of online storytelling, in other words, can be enhanced by pulling many stories together in one place and putting some promotional effort behind them.

One attempt to harness the power of aggregating online videos is the It Gets Better Project, which was started in 2010 by sex advice columnist Dan Savage and his husband, Terry Miller. Savage was inspired by a series of high-profile suicides committed by teens who were bullied because they were queer or at least perceived to be queer. He notes that as a well-known gay writer, he was often asked to speak on college campuses but was never invited to speak to middle school and high school students, even though these younger students are often far more vulnerable and in need of support. Realizing that social media was a way to reach out to younger queer people, Savage and Miller posted a YouTube video discussing the happiness they had found as adults, hoping to provide comfort and inspiration for queer youth facing discrimination, bullying, and harassment.[65] The idea caught on quickly, and the project received thousands of user-created videos from celebrities, athletes, politicians, and everyday people sharing stories and messages about overcoming struggles and finding happiness in life. The project quickly reached its limit on YouTube and had to move to its own website, eventually spawning a book, MTV specials, an online docuseries, and a line of merchandise. Not every online story becomes part of such a phenomenon, but the It Gets Better Project demonstrates the potential for using the wide reach and low barriers to entry associated with the internet to find new ways to support queer storytelling in various forms.

The LGBTQ movements have come a long way since their formal emergence in the 1950s. The act of storytelling, embraced by radical liberationists as well as liberal assimilationists, has always been one of the most valuable tools for bringing about social change and progress. In the early days, LGBTQ activists had to fight just to make themselves visible so that society could not ignore their existence. They had to push back against the harmful stories generated by religious groups, government institutions, and mainstream media producers, attempting to erase the stereotypes and myths that support homophobia and transphobia. Those stereotypes and myths are so firmly embedded in our culture that LGBTQ activists and storytellers are still working to eliminate them, but a significant sign of progress is the fact that straight storytellers and media producers are not only avoiding the reinforcement of harmful myths but producing high-profile projects that encourage support for and understanding of a range of gender and sexual identities. As examples, popular and critically acclaimed films like *Brokeback Mountain* (2005), *The Danish Girl* (2015), and *Moonlight* (2016) were directed by straight men and starred straight performers, indicating support among allies willing to work to advance the cause of the LGBTQ movements.

The increase in queer stories coming from mainstream media outlets and straight storytellers is encouraging, but the LGBTQ movements cannot and should not settle for that. Queer people need to tell queer stories to make sure their voices are heard. In addition to being the subjects of stories, queer people need to be the tellers of stories to ensure a range of perspectives on the experiences of LGBTQ people. Some queer storytellers can work effectively through mainstream, profit-driven channels, incorporating queerness into stories in a way that will appeal to mainstream audiences. But it remains important for some storytellers to pursue other routes so they do not have to worry about pleasing a large enough audience to turn a profit. They need to be able to tell honest stories that might not always draw a huge audience but will reflect and validate the experiences of other queer people who may feel marginalized and silenced by the expectations of society. The rest of this book focuses on nonprofit organizations dedicated to helping queer storytellers share stories from the LGBTQ experience. These organizations have used and are continuing to use storytelling to express and work through the struggles that queer people face, to make the broad range of LGBTQ people visible to one another and to mainstream society, to strengthen LGBTQ communities, and to support continued progress for all people, regardless of their sexuality or gender identity.

2

Documenting and Preserving Stories from the LGBTQ Movements

In the Life Media

In the penultimate episode of *In the Life* (1992–2012), titled "Foster Care's Invisible Youth," a young man named Anwar Bible discusses his experience as a gay teen in the foster care system. Describing his life with foster parents who did not accept his sexual orientation, Anwar says, "Living with them made me kind of miserable. Coming out to them was a problem. Eventually I just stopped caring, 'cause they kept assuming that I was wanting to be with their son, and I was like, 'No, I don't want—I just need a brother.'" He goes on to say, "Feeling so unaccepted like that, at the age I was at, you contemplate suicide." Later in the episode, a young woman named Shaquana Green talks about how her mother called her "a child from hell" and "Satan's child" after finding out that Shaquana was gay. She also describes being beaten regularly by the boyfriend of her foster mom while she was in foster care, saying, "I never had somebody come and check to see if the home was OK."

Anwar and Shaquana are just two of the hundreds of individuals featured on *In the Life* over the course of the show's two decades on public television. They provide emotional, firsthand accounts of their lives, allowing viewers to see details of the LGBTQ experience from the perspective of those who live it every day. They also epitomize the storytelling approach favored by the organization that produced the show, In the Life Media, which was founded

FIGURE 2.1 Shaquana Green shares her story on *In the Life*. Courtesy of Outfest UCLA Legacy Project / UCLA Film and Television Archive.

to document and preserve real-life stories that challenged the invisibility and stereotypes that have long defined media representations of LGBTQ people.

This chapter examines In the Life Media and its television program, *In the Life*. Drawing on interviews with key staff members working at In the Life Media during its final seasons of production, I examine the goals, challenges, and accomplishments of the organization as well as the content of *In the Life*—from its beginnings as a variety show through its transition into an issue-oriented newsmagazine, to the show's expansion into web content and its eventual preservation in a publicly accessible online archive. During its two decades of existence, while mainstream media outlets frequently ignored or misrepresented LGBTQ people, In the Life Media engaged in vital acts of counterstorytelling, providing a queer perspective on important events taking place in the world. It created a record of twenty years of the LGBTQ movements, capturing not only the events that took place and the issues at stake for LGBTQ people but the personal, emotional responses of queer individuals experiencing those events and issues. Refusing to allow the lives of LGBTQ people to be ignored or erased, In the Life Media documented those stories in a way that highlighted the urgent need for social change when episodes originally aired and that will preserve those valuable stories for years to come.

In the Life Media

In the Life Media was, as former executive director Michelle Kristel describes it, "a not-for-profit educational organization that produce[d] media."[1] The stated mission of the organization was to bring about change "through innovative media that exposes social injustice by chronicling lesbian, gay, bisexual, and transgender life."[2] Founded in 1992 on the premise that "visibility in media is vital to achieving equality and social justice for LGBT people,"[3] the organization stirred controversy immediately. Even before the first episode of *In the Life* aired (on six public television stations), the program was condemned by political conservatives, including then Senate minority leader Bob Dole, who cited *In the Life* and its positive portrayals of gays and lesbians as evidence that PBS was misusing taxpayer money.[4] Dole's argument was off base, given that *In the Life* did not, in fact, receive financial support from PBS, but his comments highlighted the need for the program, as Dole expressed a desire to silence the voices of LGBTQ people. The controversy is not surprising, given how infrequently queer people were featured on television in the early 1990s. The few LGBTQ people who did appear in this era were generally presented as problems (often dying of AIDS or struggling to come out) that straight characters had to deal with. While televisual representations of queer people increased and expanded throughout the decade, In the Life Media's plan to present a wide array of real LGBTQ people and stories in a nonfiction television program was somewhat revolutionary at the time of its premiere.[5]

In the Life Media was a small organization with a few full-time staff members supported by a network of freelance producers, interns, and volunteers. Over the course of the organization's history, all the original staff members moved on to other projects or retired, and the staff members running the organization in its final years all came to In the Life Media after it was firmly established. These people came from a variety of backgrounds but all had similar motivations for joining the organization. Michelle Kristel had worked for many years in the finance industry but left Wall Street in part because she found it to be an inhospitable environment for out lesbians and women in general and in part because she wanted to find a more personally fulfilling job. Realizing that she "wanted to contribute in some way to the LGBT movement for equality," she was drawn to the mission of In the Life Media. Because she did not have a background in television or nonprofit work, she started as a volunteer and "learned about the business of production hands on, from the ground up" and eventually worked her way up to being the executive director. Series producer Jacqueline Gares did have a background in television production, including some time working on the documentary series *P.O.V.* (1988–present). Just prior to joining In the Life Media, she had been working in commercial television, producing awards shows and specials for various cable channels. While she enjoyed this, she says that she "wanted to change [her] personal mission and make work that was meaningful," and as a lesbian, she was particularly drawn to the content of *In the Life*.[6] Director of new media Erik Satre also had a diverse background in the media industries, working in film production before moving into video editing and eventually online coding. He says he was drawn to In the Life Media by the nature of the work and particularly appreciated the opportunity to "move from the commercial environment into something more focused on civil rights."[7]

Marketing director Chuy Sanchez had worked as a senior media strategist with the Gay and Lesbian Alliance Against Defamation (GLAAD) and had also worked as a film and television producer for an independent Latino production company. While these professional experiences working with marginalized communities and media prepared him to work at In the Life Media, he was drawn to the organization by much more personal motivations. He recalls discovering *In the Life* while channel surfing as a teenager in Chicago. He says he was "astounded" because he had previously "not been exposed to positive LGBT representation in media," and the "powerful impact" of the program stayed with him and eventually led him to work for the organization.[8] Communications coordinator Eleanor Moonier came to In the Life Media right out of college, starting as an intern and then doing some freelance work before joining the staff full time. She says that she was drawn to the world of noncommercial media because she was dissatisfied with the stories covered by commercial outlets. Although she identifies as straight, she appreciated the specific content of *In the Life* because she has many gay family members and therefore "grew up as a part of the LGBT community" and knew "the language of LGBT issues."[9] Although the staff members followed different paths to get to In the Life Media, they shared a belief in the power of media and its ability to have a positive impact on the LGBTQ movements. In other words, they were all motivated, at least in part, by visual storytelling's potential as a tool for social change.

When asked about the goals of In the Life Media, staff members offered a range of interpretations of the organization's mission and the strategies used to work toward that mission, but their comments highlight three main goals: (1) representing diversity, (2) informing and educating audiences, and (3) moving people to action. One of the original goals of *In the Life* was simply to present positive and accurate representations of LGBTQ people, which was an important step given that the series premiered at a time when the few images of queer people on television were generally rooted in stereotypes, and most of those characters either were the butt of jokes or faced tragic endings. By the end of the series's run, the number of representations of LGBTQ people on television had increased significantly, but *In the Life* continued to focus on providing a depth, breadth, and accuracy of representation that was rarely visible on commercial television. As Moonier points out, while the numbers of representations increased over the years, they still tended to favor "upper-middle-class white gay men" rather than presenting the full diversity of the LGBTQ population. In response to this problem, Gares says that one of the key goals for the show was "to represent diversity within the [LGBTQ] community . . . diversity as a source of strength and not as a weakness or an impediment—to show how our differences make this movement as strong as it is now."

Going a step beyond accurate and diverse representations, Kristel says that another important goal was "to inform a national television audience and a larger online audience about LGBT people and issues." Similarly, Gares points to the importance of covering issues in such a way that "people can educate themselves as to what LGBT people go through while struggling for civil rights." With an eye toward preserving stories for future generations, Kristel highlights the significance of "documenting the history of the LGBT movement by creating this record, at least in the last twenty years, of the LGBT experience in America," and Gares similarly identifies the need to "chronicle the movement and the experiences of the community."

The stated goals that involve providing diverse and therefore accurate representations along with efforts to "inform," "educate," "document," and "chronicle" fall within the realm of objective journalism, which is, in part, how In the Life Media always presented its work. But these goals also support activities oriented more toward activism and social justice. These ideas come through in some of the other goals identified by staff members, including efforts to reach particular audiences and ultimately bring about positive social change.

Kristel points to the importance of connecting with a broad audience, saying that the program was always intended to reach "beyond the LGBT community. If the LGBT movement is going to realize full equality, we must have allies in this fight." She goes on to say that *In the Life* provided a "great opportunity to reach those allies and potential allies." Referring to these potential allies, Sanchez highlights the importance of reaching the "moveable middle—the mainstream community that is undecided about issues around the LGBT: issues of acceptance, issues of separation of church and state, issues of adoption, marriage equality, et cetera." He explains that an important goal of In the Life Media was "to influence that moveable middle to understand our issues from our eyes, from our voices, from our faces."

Convincing undecided individuals to sympathize with the LGBTQ movements is a step in the right direction, but in order to bring about change, those new allies have to take some sort of action. Kristel sees In the Life Media as contributing to this, noting that in addition to making issues visible, the organization also provided "tools for people to learn more and to take action on the issues presented." Emphasizing viewers' ability to shape government actions, Satre suggests that a key component of In the Life Media's mission in its later years was to "motivate people around issues and legislation." Expressing hopes that the content of *In the Life* might convince viewers to take action by voting in particular ways and influencing legislation, these comments highlight the activist intentions embedded in the work of In the Life Media. While their nonprofit status prevented the organization from formally lobbying or openly advocating for legislative change, the comments from In the Life Media staff clearly express an understanding of the potential for storytelling to change hearts and minds, which is the first step toward improving the legal and political status of the LGBTQ population.

In the Life Media's goals of highlighting LGBTQ diversity, informing and educating viewers, and moving people to action made the organization and its program unique within the American media landscape, and its status as a nonprofit organization was often helpful in achieving those goals. Discussing the value of the organization's nonprofit status, Kristel says, "We're not beholden to corporate or commercial interests . . . so our content is not driven by commercial interests." While the producers of commercial programs may be pressured by advertisers to put viewers in a "buying mood"[10] and are expected to generate ratings high enough to justify continued production, the producers of *In the Life* were freed from such constraints. As a result, they could focus on storytelling efforts that were, as Moonier describes, "dictated by what's really relevant rather than what brings the largest viewership and sells the most expensive advertising." This freedom from corporate/commercial control was especially important in the early days of the program, given how few advertisers were willing to be associated with LGBTQ content at that time, but it continued to be crucial in the later years, as it allowed the show to incorporate a greater diversity of perspectives and tackle tougher issues than mainstream commercial broadcasters were willing to include.

The organization's nonprofit status may have helped the producers of *In the Life* maintain editorial control, but it also brought significant challenges. The majority of the organization's annual budget was provided by charitable foundations, with additional funding coming from private donations and memberships. While foundations like the Ford Foundation, the Rockefeller Foundation, and the Nathan Cummings Foundation regularly support public television projects, Kristel notes that In the Life Media did not have any success getting regular funding from what she refers to as the "mainline public television foundations." Since the responses to rejected grant applications rarely offer explanations beyond having a large pool of applicants, there is no way to know if the queer content of the program influenced funding decisions, but In the Life Media did have much greater success at getting funding from foundations that frequently supported LGBTQ causes.

Key funders of *In the Life* included the H. van Ameringen Foundation, the Arcus Foundation, and the estate of Richard Wyland, all of whom supported a wide range of LGBTQ organizations and projects. While these and other funders provided money year after year, they only covered part of the annual budget, meaning that fundraising was an ongoing process, and it was always a challenge—largely because many potential funders do not consider media production to be the most worthwhile use of charitable money. As Kristel points out, "When you look at a media production company versus a food bank or a homeless shelter, a lot of people are going to go with what they consider essential services." As a result, the organization worked very hard to try to convince potential supporters of the value and power of media as a tool for social justice. A fundraising letter sent to potential donors by the In the Life Media in 2010 argues that "the right-wing, anti-gay media machine . . . poisons young minds, political discourse and popular opinion every hour of every day." The letter goes on to note that "it takes media to fight media—persuasive, innovative and high-impact media that tells the truth about LGBT lives and issues, and motivates our supporters to act in greater numbers than ever before."[11] While the staff of In the Life Media may have struggled to raise the funds necessary to keep the show in production, they generally agreed that facing these challenges was worth it if it gave them the freedom to tell the stories they felt were the most important to tell.

Story ideas for episodes of *In the Life* were drawn from a wide variety of sources through what Gares refers to as "an open process." While some ideas originated with staff members, others came from outside producers or suggestions from viewers. Regardless of the origins of ideas for segments and episodes, Gares says that in the end, producers did their best to allow the subjects of the segments to tell their own stories. She says that the organization's top priority was to "treat our subjects and their stories with respect and really have it be their story . . . we try to really represent the personal story through the person's own words." The producers' stated goal of letting subjects speak for themselves should not be mistaken for complete objectivity, which is, of course, an unrealistic expectation. As Bill Nichols notes, nonfiction media "draws on and refers to historical reality while representing it from a distinct perspective."[12] As noted previously, staff members of In the Life Media were guided by various personal and organizational goals, and their efforts to achieve those goals are evident in their shaping of the program. This does not mean that they falsified or fictionalized stories, but they, like all media producers, presented one perspective on reality—in this case, to fit their goals of challenging harmful stereotypes by offering positive images of LGBTQ people.

Whether the ideas for segments of *In the Life* were generated by the staff of In the Life Media, freelance producers, or viewers of the show, all stories had their roots in the lived experiences of LGBTQ individuals and communities. Those experiences were shaped into compelling narratives by the professional storytellers of In the Life Media, providing an example of what I described in the introduction as authorship as stewardship. In this case, rather than offering a fictionalized narrative that captures the essence of many people's lived experiences, as some authors do, the storytellers aimed to document and present real experiences in a way that would reflect and resonate with those of other LGBTQ people. When *In the Life* began, the mere act of putting real LGBTQ people on television was fairly radical, and as the show developed, producers remained focused on sharing stories that represented the lives of LGBTQ people as accurately as possible.

In the Life

The form and content of *In the Life* evolved significantly from the pilot episode to its final season, partially in response to changes in the political climate with regard to the LGBTQ movements. As noted earlier, hostility and fear often dominated political discussions of queer people in the early 1990s, and positive LGBTQ images on television were few and far between. In the film world, filmmakers whose work would be labeled as part of the New Queer Cinema movement were offering edgy and somewhat radical films that aggressively challenged the status quo both politically and aesthetically. As a program planned for public television and designed to reach out to potential allies, *In the Life* took a far less radical stance. In an episode celebrating the show's fifth anniversary, host Katherine Linton explains that the program was originally conceived as a variety show that would provide "quality entertainment and celebrity performances for gay men and lesbians." The pilot episode, which aired in June 1992, opens with a performance by the New York City Gay Men's Chorus, followed by a monologue by comedian and host Kate Clinton, who acknowledges the groundbreaking nature of the show by sarcastically remarking that the audience was probably thinking, "Gosh, not another show on gays and lesbians on television!" The episode also features musical performances by Casselberry-DuPreé, John Kelly, and the Lavender Light Gospel Choir; performances by dancers Amy Pivar and Scot Willingham and the theatrical troupe Five Lesbian Brothers; a mock commercial for a collectible line of Stonewall-inspired dolls and a real PSA for the AIDS Coalition to Unleash Power (ACT UP); and a panel discussion about LGBTQ images in film, featuring filmmakers Su Friedrich, Hilton Als, Martha Gever, and Todd Haynes (offering a nod to New Queer Cinema without adopting its more controversial tone). The range of performers and content offers a snapshot of the diversity that defines the LGBTQ population and the cultural expressions they produce.

Equally significant in the pilot episode is the audience. The program was recorded in front of a large studio audience, and members of that audience frequently appear on-screen. They are generally shown applauding, laughing, or otherwise reacting to the performers on stage but do not participate directly in the show's proceedings. There is no roll call during which audience members announce their sexual orientation, but it is safe to assume that the audience is composed primarily, if not entirely, of LGBTQ people, potentially with some allies mixed in. Simply by being present and visible, this audience expands the range of images of gays and lesbians offered by the show, creating a mini queer community in the studio and serving as an on-screen stand-in for the larger queer audience around the country. In this sense, the pilot episode simultaneously visualizes queer performers and queer audiences, placing them both on national television in a way that had not previously been attempted.

For the remainder of the first season and the first two episodes of the second season, the producers of *In the Life* explored various formats for the program, blending live performances and discussions in the studio with prerecorded clips from field reporters covering issues relevant to the LGBTQ population. The first season finale abandons the studio (and variety format) entirely, focusing on a 1993 gay rights march and demonstration in Washington, DC, with hosts Karen Williams and Garrett Glaser covering the event with interviews and commentary. This turn to more overtly political content covered by field correspondents eventually became the norm, and beginning with the third episode of the second season, producers formally adopted a newsmagazine format to replace the variety format that had launched the series.

While early episodes presented nonthreatening artistic performances as a way of making real LGBTQ people visible on television, later seasons placed

FIGURE 2.2 *In the Life* correspondents Garrett Glaser and Karen Williams cover gay rights demonstrations in Washington, DC. In the Life Records (Collection 2178). UCLA Library Special Collections, Charles E. Young Research Library, UCLA.

a greater emphasis on providing information that might motivate viewers to take action with respect to current political issues. Coverage of the arts remained part of the program throughout its run, but rather than offering up performance pieces as entertainment, the show examined cultural products in order to reveal their relationship to and impact on the larger issues that came to define the program's focus. As *In the Life* settled into a newsmagazine format, some episodes would be built entirely around specific topics, such as LGBTQ youth in the foster care system, while others would pull together a more eclectic mix of stories connected only by their relevance to LGBTQ lives.

The changes in format and content are mirrored by a shift in the storytelling practices of the program, but from beginning to end, it emphasized the importance of queer storytelling as a tool for positive social change. As a variety show, *In the Life* offered queer artists a chance to perform in front of a queer studio audience, and the artists offered numerous stories expressing hopes, fears, and desires. Some performances offered glimpses of larger stories, as in the case of the pilot episode segment featuring the New York City Gay Men's Chorus. They sing the lyrics, "Just think about how far we've come / Think of all we have shared / It's a wonder we survived / But here we are, and we're alive / Can we hold on, hold on? / Take a moment to celebrate."[13] While the song does not present a detailed narrative from beginning to end, it clearly references the struggles and achievements of the gay community as a whole, inviting the listener to reflect on their own stories. Also in the pilot episode, Amy Pivar and Scot Willingham use dance and dialogue to tell a story about a developing relationship between a straight man and a lesbian, and the members of the Five Lesbian Brothers theater troupe perform an excerpt from a story about young lesbian girls in an orphanage.

These and other acts from the early episodes use a variety of performance techniques to offer expressive interpretations of the real-life experiences of countless gays and lesbians. When these shows aired, queer storytelling of any kind was hard to find on American television, so even these stories were fairly radical in their context, and they served the program's early purpose of increasing visibility of lesbians and gays on television. But because these stories are presented by singers, dancers, and actors—all individuals marked explicitly as performers—interpreting and expressing the ideas and feelings of writers, the stories are presented in a less immediate and more indirect way. This is not to say that fictional stories and trained performers cannot express emotions and ideas in ways that can change the hearts and minds of audiences. But as the form and content of *In the Life* evolved, the program moved away from using performers and artists to tell stories, highlighting instead the actual experiences of real people and using the words of those individuals to tell their own stories whenever possible.

As a general rule, the stories presented in episodes of *In the Life* address issues of concern to everyone involved in the LGBTQ movements, but they focus on the experiences of individuals to humanize those issues and make them real to viewers. Describing the strategy behind this approach, Gares says, "Any time you can put a human face on an issue, that's when you can create some kind of change." Moonier notes that this is one characteristic that sets *In the Life* apart from other coverage of the LGBTQ movements. She says, "While mainstream television is talking about the fight back and forth about gay marriage, we're telling the story of a couple—just one couple—and we let the audience get to know that couple and their struggles and how they met. So that couple illuminates the issue in a way that is much more personal . . . these are the people that you're voting against if you vote against gay marriage." As a rhetorical strategy, this personal approach aims to influence its audience via ethos and pathos, as the subjects establish credibility by sharing their own lived experiences and then appeal to the audience's emotions by displaying the pain, heartache, joy, and love that accompanies those experiences.[14]

A particularly powerful example of the firsthand storytelling approach is a segment titled "A Call to Duty," which aired in the premiere episode of season fifteen. In the introduction to the episode, guest host Cherry Jones emphasizes this approach when she says, "This season, *In the Life* renews its commitment to tell real-life stories from the LGBT communities." The segment focuses on former army specialist Jeff Howe, who shares some of his experiences as a soldier serving in Iraq, including being kicked out of the army for being gay. The segment opens with Howe explaining that the events of 9/11 convinced him to leave his life as an openly gay man working in Silicon Valley behind so that he could serve his country—a decision that required him to go back into the closet, given the military's ban on homosexuals. He describes the camaraderie and teamwork of his military unit but also talks about having to put up with homophobic jokes that referenced beating and torturing gay men. He discusses the friendship he formed with his captain and the difficulty of having to lie to him. He ultimately reveals that he was kicked out of the army when someone discovered an old profile that he had posted on a gay and lesbian community website, describing how he was hurriedly evacuated from his camp by helicopter without being able to say good-bye to his fellow soldiers.

The segment runs approximately fourteen minutes, and Howe's is the only voice included. Much of the segment is presented in interview format, with Howe speaking directly to an off-screen interviewer and indirectly to the audience. This is supplemented by Howe's voice playing over images of him and his unit in Iraq as well as excerpts from a blog that Howe wrote during his tour of duty, with text appearing on-screen as Howe reads the words. The blog posts offer examples of Howe's thoughts and state of mind while he was serving in Iraq, and these are combined with his reflections from the present day of the interview, bringing two time periods together to provide a multilayered picture of Howe's experience—all from his point of view. This foregrounds his personal reality and emotions, putting a human face on the problems created by the military's antigay policy. The only portion of the segment that moves away from Howe's personal story is some on-screen text at the very end, which announces that "11,000 gay service members have been discharged under 'Don't Ask, Don't Tell.'" A second screen adds, "Discharging and replacing these soldiers has cost the Pentagon nearly $369 million." The statistics provided by these screens help place Howe's story in context, building on the emotions conveyed by his personal experience to show that his is not an isolated case and that the damages caused by the policy go well beyond an individual soldier. While most segments from *In the Life* incorporate multiple voices, including narrators or other interview subjects to flesh out a story, this segment relies on just one voice to capture what Michelle Kristel identifies as a hallmark of *In the Life*'s later seasons: "Using personal stories as a vehicle to talk about larger issues."

As the show's storytelling approach moved from having artists and entertainers present stories indirectly through their staged performances to having individuals share their own stories firsthand, the role of on-screen professionals evolved as well. During the variety show era, each episode featured a host who would serve as a master of ceremonies, introducing each act for the studio audience and often providing a comedic monologue. When *In the Life* shifted to a newsmagazine format, the program initially adopted the model used by most local newscasts, featuring anchors who sat at a news desk in the studio, setting up segments and introducing field correspondents who then relayed coverage of individuals and events back to the anchors. The anchor-correspondent relationship gave way to a single host doing the work of both anchor and correspondent, introducing stories either from a studio or from the field. For many seasons, this role was handled by a permanent host, Katherine Linton, and then the program moved to a rotating roster of celebrity guest hosts, including Alan Cumming, Janeane Garofalo, and Rosie O'Donnell. Season sixteen returned to having a permanent host, Michael Billy, and seasons seventeen to twenty-one eliminated the role of the on-screen host, relying instead on a voice-over announcer to welcome the audience and introduce segments. This evolution of hosts, anchors, correspondents, and narrators reflects the changes in storytelling style. While the initial hosts interacted directly with the performers and the live audience, thereby serving a prominent role in the storytelling process, the anchors and hosts of the newsmagazine era did little more than welcome the audience and provide basic context, while the narrators at the end of the series were even less prominent. The role of professionals in the series became less visible, placing an increased emphasis on the individual subjects featured in the segments, highlighting their stories and eliminating the need for a visible intermediary to authorize the stories of everyday people.

Documenting and Performing LGBTQ Experiences

While the program format and storytelling style evolved significantly over *In the Life*'s twenty-one seasons, the emphasis on presenting stories and images in the service of positive social change was part of the series from beginning to end. Of the many ways in which the show sought to bring about positive change, three stand out as particularly significant. First, the content of *In the Life* counters lies, myths, and stereotypes about queer people by emphasizing the diversity that defines LGBTQ communities. Second, *In the Life* highlights the status of LGBTQ people as citizens who make valuable contributions to society and deserve equal treatment. Finally, the content of *In the Life* pushes for social change by exposing oppressive power structures that harm LGBTQ people. All this is done within a framework of nonfiction television, drawing heavily on the traditions of documentary film to capture and share the lived experiences of LGBTQ people.

As discussed previously, producers of the early seasons of *In the Life* experimented with various formats before settling into the newsmagazine approach that would define the bulk of the program's run. While the series occasionally provided brief updates or commentary about current events, thereby drawing on elements of journalism, most of the individual stories included in any given episode embody the styles and approaches associated with documentary media. Episodes generally play out as collections of documentary shorts that are grouped together by a particular theme. Viewed in this way, the stories presented on *In the Life* might be seen by some as more valid or more persuasive than fictional ones because they are grounded in reality. While the producers of the program did aim to counter the myths and lies told about LGBTQ people, *In the Life* should not be read as purely factual or completely accurate just because it is nonfiction. As is the case with all documentaries, *In the Life* offers a particular interpretation of reality. As Nichols argues, "The story a documentary tells stems from the historical world, but it is still told from the filmmaker's perspective and in the filmmaker's voice."[15] This does not diminish the value of *In the Life* or any other documentary, but it does shape how we interpret the finished product.

Stella Bruzzi argues that rather than debating the objectivity or reality of documentaries, we should embrace them as "performative acts" that offer a "truth that emerges through the encounter between filmmakers, subjects and spectators."[16] Thomas Waugh similarly emphasizes the role of performance, which he defines as "the self-expression of documentary subjects for the camera in collaboration with [the] filmmaker/director."[17] As Bruzzi and Waugh suggest, the performance that defines documentaries is an endeavor shared by those in front of and behind the camera and ultimately offered to the viewer for interpretation. Bruzzi adds that the interaction between performance and reality is what gives a documentary meaning, noting that "a documentary only comes into being as it is performed."[18] As a variety show offering dance, theater, music, and comedy, the early episodes of *In the Life* foreground widely recognized types of performance, but as the previous comments suggest, the documentary format embraced by the show as it evolved can also be read as a kind of performance, and considering the program in this way illuminates the continuity of strategies guiding the show across its changing formats. With these ideas in mind, I want to consider how the producers and subjects of *In the Life* perform particular expressions or interpretations of reality in support of their efforts to educate and inform the audience about LGBTQ experiences and the need for social change.

From its pilot episode, *In the Life* worked to counter the myths—based largely on ignorance—about LGBTQ people that circulated in society. In the absence of accurate and positive images, it is much easier for homophobic groups and individuals to paint queer people as harmful, destructive deviants. *In the Life* aimed to combat these dangerous myths by offering strategic performances of diversity, presenting a wide range of LGBTQ people on stage, in the audience, and in prerecorded packages. In many cases, episodes of *In the Life* demonstrate the diversity of the LGBTQ population by focusing on the unique experiences of people who are both queer and part of some other subset of the larger population, be it race, age, geography, or some other defining feature. For example, the season three episode "Different Drummers" features a segment on LGBTQ Native Americans, discussing how the oppressive ways of European colonizers hindered the acceptance of Two-Spirit individuals in many tribes. Other segments focus on the unique experiences of queer people who are also African American, Latino/a, Asian American, Muslim, elderly, homeless, or mentally ill, to name just a few. By performing these intersectional identities, the subjects challenge any beliefs about all gays and lesbians being the same, and they make it clear that being queer is not the only defining feature of a person's identity. Segments emphasizing the lives and experiences of LGBTQ people in rural areas, small towns, and cities, states, and regions around the country challenge stereotypes that suggest all queer people live in large cities on the coasts.

In addition to calling out diverse identity categories and geographic locations with segments devoted specifically to them, *In the Life* features a range of individuals incorporated into all of its episodes. By featuring interview subjects, experts, politicians, artists, and entertainers that represent a variety of races, ethnicities, gender identities, ages, and occupations, *In the Life* offers a view of the LGBTQ population that is defined by diversity, which not only helps break down stereotypes but also helps show potential allies that they have at least something in common with many LGBTQ people.

The images of people presented by *In the Life* are certainly diverse, but that is not to say that everyone is presented equally or that nobody is left out. For example, while drag queens appeared regularly as entertainment in early seasons of the series, transgender individuals were rarely included. As the transgender movement gained recognition and as gay and lesbian activists began to incorporate transgender issues more fully into the larger LGBTQ movement, *In the Life* also increased its attention to transgender people. More segments focusing on transgender individuals appeared, and in the show's final seasons, transgender people are featured with regularity.

While the attention to transgender people and their stories increased over the years, something that remained relatively absent during the series run is depictions of radical sexuality. Even depictions of not-so-radical sexuality are minimal. The show's focus on nonheterosexual people and their stories does automatically introduce sexuality at a certain level, but *In the Life* rarely examines that sexuality in any depth. Instead, the program acknowledges sexuality and then focuses on other things. Sometimes, the focus of an episode is on the ultimate impact of sexual orientation—how it restricts rights and opportunities or how it alters relationships with family members and coworkers. In other cases, sexuality is introduced and then immediately pushed to the background so that a segment can explore how an individual has overcome the limitations imposed on them based on their sexuality and has succeeded as an entertainer, politician, or businessperson. In many ways, this makes sense. It is, after all, the sexual acts of queer people that are most often condemned by those who oppose equal rights. As discussed in chapter 1, shifting emphasis away from sex and onto other aspects of queer people's lives is a key element of assimilationist strategies. Given the already difficult nature of getting *In the Life* aired on public television, this strategy becomes even more logical. But as liberationists argue, minimizing or ignoring sexual activity erases what is an important component of many people's lives. Just as leaders of the early homophile movement sought to downplay their sexuality so as to create a more respectable, rights-oriented movement,[19] the producers of *In the Life* may have minimized references to sexuality in order to keep their program on television. Rather than trying to reproduce the full range of the LGBTQ experience, producers and subjects of *In the Life* strategically performed a particular version of LGBTQ diversity. They offered a wide range of ethnic, racial, economic, and geographical identities but avoided more radical performances of difference that might inhibit assimilationist efforts by making it harder to reach the "moveable middle" that producers were after.

In addition to highlighting (most of) the diversity that exists across the LGBTQ population, the producers and subjects of *In the Life* worked together to create a performance of citizenship, emphasizing the status of LGBTQ people as contributing citizens who deserve the same rights and recognitions as everyone else in the nation. As Christopher Pullen argues, documentary film and other nonfiction forms (like reality TV) have frequently offered LGBTQ people opportunities to make a claim to citizen status. Pullen points to films associated with the 1970s gay liberation movement as marking a significant shift in the representation of queer people, moving away from treating them as specimens to be studied and pitied or vilified and giving them the chance to act as "agents representing themselves."[20] He identifies *Word Is Out: Stories of Some of Our Lives* (1977) as a film that "foregrounds the emergence of the independent gay citizen who as a social actor becomes a highly influential agent working toward change through storytelling."[21] After setbacks brought on by the conservative backlash against gay liberation, which was fueled by homophobic fears surrounding the AIDS epidemic, groups like ACT UP and Queer Nation aimed to reignite the LGBTQ rights movements. If the 1970s liberation movement marked the emergence of the independent gay citizen, the early 1990s might be seen as a reemergence of the independent gay citizen, and similar to *Word Is Out* in 1977, the appearance of *In the Life* in 1992 gave queer people opportunities to represent themselves and perform queer citizenship as a way of working toward social change.

Many episodes and segments highlight the citizen status of LGBTQ people, often doing so in subtle ways, but a pair of episodes from seasons five and six titled "As American as Apple Pie" and "American as Apple Pie II" take citizenship as their explicit focus. The first of these episodes demonstrates how LGBTQ people are woven into the fabric of the nation's workforce as a way to establish that queer people contribute significantly to the economic well-being of the United States. Segments in the episode focus on Ron Woods, a Chrysler factory worker who spoke out about homophobic harassment in his workplace and was eventually elected as a delegate to the United Auto Workers bargaining convention; Sabrina Soujourner, the first out black lesbian elected to Congress; farmers in rural Wisconsin; circus workers and sideshow entertainers; and executives and other employees of the Walt Disney Corporation. Showing these individuals working hard in a variety of sectors, from agriculture and auto manufacturing to government service and family-oriented entertainment, the episode showcases the contributions they make to the economy and the nation as a whole. The producers and subjects of the stories work together to present a performance of good citizenship. The logical follow-up

FIGURE 2.3 Philadelphia's Independence Hall provides a patriotic backdrop for an *In the Life* episode about the citizen status of LGBTQ Americans. Courtesy of Outfest UCLA Legacy Project / UCLA Film and Television Archive.

is to argue that since LGBTQ people contribute to the nation's success, they should benefit from it as well by being granted equal rights and privileges. This argument becomes the explicit focus of the second episode of the pair.

"American as Apple Pie II" opens with an introduction from host Katherine Linton, who is standing in front of Independence Hall in Philadelphia, a national landmark that evokes thoughts of liberty, democracy, and citizenship—supporting Linton's performance of "Americanness" even before she speaks. Linton notes that LGBTQ people "share the same hopes, aspirations, and values as other Americans and are working for their share of the proverbial pie." She says, "While gay men and lesbians may be American citizens, they have not been granted the full rights of citizenship" and goes on to explain that the opening segment examines how gay people are demanding access to "America's traditional institutions, from the military to the family . . . even the Boy Scouts." The piece that follows surveys a list of rights that LGBTQ Americans have regularly been denied over the years, including the right to privacy, the right to equal protection under the law, the right to serve (in the military), and the right to form families. While some of these are not considered official rights as laid out by the Constitution or any other formal documents, they are generally perceived as activities and values that are important to our society. To emphasize this, each right is introduced with a title screen that includes text superimposed over a waving American flag, visually linking the named rights with American citizenship. Laying out all the ways that LGBTQ people have been denied various rights makes it clear that despite their contributions to the nation's well-being (detailed in the previous episode), they are not being treated equally by the laws and policies governing the country.

A third episode that highlights the performance of LGBTQ people as loyal citizens takes a very different approach, aiming to link a few individuals to an emotional event that in many ways brought the nation together—the attacks of September 11, 2001. The tenth-season episode "Comfort in Crisis" opens with a segment called "Victims of 9/11." Correspondent Jonathan Capehart introduces the piece by saying, "Next, we meet some Americans who are not only having to cope with the loss of their life partners but also with the burden of having to prove that their relationships were valid." Introducing these individuals as "Americans" is a significant choice here. Given that the vast majority of people featured on *In the Life* are from the United States, a subject's status as American is generally the default and not worth calling out. In this case, however, it serves a narrative strategy by explicitly linking LGBTQ individuals to the nation as a whole. As the segment develops, the three interview subjects share their recollections of the morning of 9/11 and express the pain and heartbreak they felt after losing loved ones in the attack, often breaking down or wiping away tears during their interviews. The stories reveal that one of the lost loved ones worked in security at the Twin Towers and helped 3,700 employees evacuate, while another was a government worker at the Pentagon.

The first part of the segment clearly embeds the three couples within an event that united the nation in a period of shock, anger, and mourning. In the second part, the interview subjects describe being deprived of many of the benefits that were granted to the families of other 9/11 victims—largely because in the eyes of government agencies, these same-sex couples were considered legal strangers. The overall segment paints a picture of three loving couples who experienced the loss and trauma of 9/11 alongside their fellow Americans but were then denied access to the national healing process because of their sexual orientation.

As with the episodes described previously and many others throughout the run of the series, this segment paints the LGBTQ community as a loyal, contributing segment of the population that earns, but is frequently denied, equal status as full citizens. This episode of *In the Life* does not just present facts and hope that the audience will be moved; instead, producers and subjects collaborate to offer a performance of citizenship wrongfully denied, suggesting that such a practice is not just unethical but un-American. The performance is carefully calibrated to present an image of earnest, hardworking queers who are politely asking to be treated as equals. Generally missing from *In the Life* are loud, visible expressions of rage accompanied by demands for immediate and radical change. Such elements were common to the protests and street theater of groups like ACT UP and Queer Nation, but the producers of *In the Life* embraced the pragmatic strategies associated with assimilationist politics—likely the best option for an already controversial show being beamed into people's living rooms via public television.

In addition to performing diversity and citizenship as a way of showing how LGBTQ people are woven into the fabric of the nation, *In the Life* engages in activist counterstorytelling by exposing the power structures that generate and reinforce the unequal treatment of queer people. As such, the program moves beyond generating sympathy for the oppressed and works to reveal the oppressors and their tactics. In this way, *In the Life* is aligned with what Rahat Imran refers to as the "cinema of accountability." As Imran describes it, "This category is positioned to investigate, expose, take to task, and press for accountability from the state, judiciary, policy makers, and society regarding the historical and ongoing violation of human rights."[22] The power structures examined through segments and episodes of *In the Life* fall into two broad categories. First, the show looks at formal laws and policies that have been enacted by government entities at various levels. Second, the program examines less-obvious forms of oppression and power—those that are not codified by any government policies but still marginalize and oppress queer people. In all cases, the program aims to hold institutions and occasionally individuals accountable for the ongoing marginalization of queer people.

The most visible sources of oppression, and those that most directly prevent LGBTQ people from feeling like equal citizens, are written laws and policies used by government bodies at federal, state, and local levels. Many such policies have been repealed or altered since *In the Life* premiered, and each episode provides a kind of time capsule that reflects the relationship between queer people and the government at the time the episodes aired. The twenty-one seasons of *In the Life* feature many episodes and segments that tackle these kinds of policies head on or point to them as causes of other issues being examined. For example, the season twenty episode "Married but Not Equal" looks at the burdens placed on same-sex couples whose marriages are recognized in their home states but who lack federal marriage recognition as a result of the Defense of Marriage Act (DOMA). The "Victims of 9/11" segment discussed earlier also references unequal marriage laws by explaining that such laws are the reason same-sex partners of 9/11 victims were denied certain benefits. A segment called "The Golden Years" from episode 1209 focuses on the unique challenges facing elderly LGBTQ individuals, noting that in addition to discrimination in health care and assisted living facilities, elderly queer people often have unequal access to partners' social security benefits, 401(k)s, pensions, and inheritance—all generally the result of being denied marriage rights.

In addition to marriage laws, episodes of *In the Life* examine a variety of other government policies, including the military's "Don't Ask, Don't Tell" policy, adoption laws, and the lack of employment protection for queer people. Building on one of the show's common strategies, these kinds of segments expose the harmful effects of antigay laws and policies by focusing on the personal experiences of one or two individuals and then directly connecting their pain and struggle to the regulations causing the problems.

Government policies are not, of course, the only medium through which queer individuals and groups are harmed. The oppression that queer people face comes from a wide variety of sources that may not be as visible and obvious as codified government rules but are just as powerful and often build on or support the official actions of the government. Many episodes of *In the Life* investigate these other sources, including antigay rhetoric from religious figures and conservative politicians, antigay bias in mainstream news media, and homophobia in professional sports. Segments like these draw attention to the multitude of ways that LGBTQ oppression is reinforced in our society, educating people about social injustice and potentially inspiring them to work for change.

While the emphasis of any given segment may be on either codified rules or the more informal means of exerting oppressive power, *In the Life* frequently hints at the relationships between these two and occasionally highlights those connections explicitly. The episode "Beyond the Rhetoric," from the twenty-first season, is an example of this approach. The episode begins with a segment about the frequent use of antigay rhetoric by conservative politicians, citing a study by the Human Rights Campaign that surveyed ten thousand LGBTQ youth and revealed that more than 90 percent of youth say they regularly hear negative messages about being gay, and more than 60 percent hear such messages from their elected officials. A later segment focuses on the Anoka-Hennepin school district in suburban Minneapolis, which made headlines after nine students committed suicide in the span of about two years. A study by the Southern Poverty Law Center revealed that about half of the suicide victims were either LGBTQ or perceived as LGBTQ and suggested that the homophobic environment of the school likely contributed to their deaths. Art teacher Jefferson Fietek says in an interview that the homophobic environment of the school was reinforced by a school board policy prohibiting teachers from talking about homosexuality. While the policy was presented as a neutrality policy, meaning that faculty and staff would avoid all discussions of sexual orientation and leave those conversations in the hands of parents, the end result was that teachers could not openly provide support or advice for queer or questioning youth who might be the targets of bullying or harassment.

Drawing connections between antigay political speech, school policies, and teen suicide and then weaving those together with personal stories and testimonials, the episode demonstrates how the complex web of heteronormative power and oppression can have devastating effects on LGBTQ people.

Throughout the series's twenty-one seasons, creators of *In the Life*, including those in front of and behind the camera, offered carefully crafted performances of a diverse LGBTQ population seeking equal-citizen status and calling out the powerful institutions standing in the way of that status. *In the Life*'s content was driven largely by the organization's stated goals of documenting the diversity of the LGBTQ movements and educating and informing viewers. At the same time, the program was also shaped by the desire to reach (and not offend) potential allies, the placement of the program on public television, and In the Life Media's status as a nonprofit educational organization. These latter elements prevented the inclusion of aggressively radical content, which likely disappointed those embracing liberationist political strategies. In this case, however, adopting an approach in line with integrationist strategies allowed the producers of *In the Life* to work within their constraints to argue persuasively for social justice for LGBTQ people and to take that argument directly into people's homes.

Distribution via Public Television

LGBTQ media content is frequently distributed through channels aimed specifically at queer audiences. The distribution of *In the Life* was unique, given that its original and primary outlet for distribution was public television, which is, by definition, intended to reach a very broad audience. This situation presented a number of opportunities as well as some challenges as the show's producers worked toward achieving their stated goals—particularly with respect to informing and educating audiences.

Airing *In the Life* on public television offered opportunities for both the producers of the show and the stations airing it. In the Life Media was able to draw on the positive aspects of the reputation associated with public broadcasting in this country while gaining access to an audience that producers saw as desirable. In return, *In the Life* provided content that addressed many of the concerns raised by critics who have argued that public broadcasting in this country has not lived up to its potential as a service that could reflect and nourish the diversity of the nation while supporting its democratic ideals.

With the Public Broadcasting Act of 1967, Congress created the Corporation for Public Broadcasting (CPB) and eventually the Public Broadcasting Service (PBS), which gave the United States a nationwide public television system supported in part by government funding. The creation of this system was driven largely by desires for reform and the belief that commercial television was not serving the public's best interests. Critics were concerned that commercial television, driven by ratings and advertiser dollars, favored crowd-pleasing and escapist entertainment at the expense of more challenging and enriching programming. A 1961 speech by FCC chair Newton Minow, in which he famously referred to the commercial television landscape as a "vast wasteland," captured many people's feelings about the medium and encouraged political and educational leaders to look more seriously into possible alternatives.

As Laurie Ouellette points out, support for public television was initially guided by two broad arguments. The first supported a public alternative to commercial television "on the grounds that it would bypass the tastes and expectations of the indiscriminate mass audience and operate at a higher level."[23] In this way, public television was seen as having the potential to provide content for a highly educated and discriminating audience that felt underserved by commercial television. The second argument suggested that the benefits of public television could be extended to a mass audience, "effectively serving the people by improving them."[24] Thus public broadcasting was seen by some as a tool for cultural uplift of the American masses.

As supporters celebrated public television's potential to provide "quality" programming for everyone, critics accused both PBS and the larger public television system of being elitist, claiming that the programming and policies served only a small portion of the population and cast the rest of the population as somehow inferior. William Hoynes, for example, argues that such programming is largely defined by its appeal to "corporate funders, well-off members of the public, and prestigious critics," noting that these "quality" programs "clearly differentiate public television from commercial television—largely along class lines."[25] Although television reformers and supporters of public broadcasting presented quality as something easily identifiable based on commonsense criteria, any notion of quality in something as subjective as television content is bound to be tied to particular experiences, perspectives, and tastes, meaning that only those with the "right" cultural capital will find their own tastes aligned with the predetermined notions of quality that a particular group presents.

Despite the critiques aimed at the narrow parameters used to define quality in public television programming, many audience members and content creators still respond in a positive way to the reputation that the system has built. Barry Dornfeld, a documentary producer and anthropologist, notes that even in the face of criticism, "public television in the United States is infused with a kind of authority, legitimacy, and importance not given to other channels and formats of broadcast media."[26] The staff of In the Life Media embraced this image, referencing it as a benefit of associating their program with public television and identifying it as a motivating factor behind their decision to work at In the Life Media.

As Michelle Kristel points out, *In the Life*'s presence on public television, combined with the nonprofit status of the organization producing it, went "a long way in solidifying [their] credibility as a journalistic endeavor." She says, "Commercial and corporate interests have really corrupted media in many ways" because so many news organizations "have their eye on the bottom line." She goes on to note that freedom from corporate interests allowed them to avoid the "race to the lowest common denominator that we see in so much of commercial television." Eleanor Moonier concurs, saying, "I wanted to work in media that I thought was smart and that I thought was relevant . . . that's what drew me to public television."

The comments from In the Life Media staffers suggest that although critics find fault with public television's approach to "quality programming," content creators still see the ideal of quality as a motivating factor in their work. In embracing the notion of high-quality programming while producing a show about LGBTQ issues, the creators of *In the Life* reinforced certain aspects of the accepted version of quality while challenging others. After its early years incorporating variety and entertainment with discussion of social issues, the program eventually settled into a recognizable public affairs documentary/journalism format, adopting a serious tone to address contemporary issues. Aesthetically, this fit the style of newsmagazine shows associated with PBS's version of quality programming. But while critics have argued that "high-quality programming" typically caters to a particular portion of the population, *In the Life* clearly strayed from this norm by offering a program that reached beyond the heteronormative mainstream to embrace a marginalized LGBTQ population and issues of concern to them, thereby broadening the scope of what could count as "quality programming."

In addition to believing that television could and should provide quality programming rather than responding solely to ratings, supporters of nationwide public broadcasting argued that such a system had the potential to be an agent of democracy. Proponents have suggested that it can support democracy by exposing viewers to the differences that define our population, disseminating information about important social issues, and encouraging the discussion and debate of those issues.

To do this, public television can serve the broadest possible audience, one that reflects the makeup of the nation's population. As Ouellette points out, public television officially "promises 'universal service' to everyone in the United States,"[27] but many critics believe that it has failed to deliver images of and content for the diverse population that it supposedly serves. As James Ledbetter argues, "Almost any group of Americans that can claim to be underserved by commercial television—women, the elderly, the disabled, rural populations—can make the same claim about public television."[28] Despite a few important exceptions, like *Sesame Street* (1969–) or *P.O.V.* (1988–), the programming of public television in the United States has historically served white, wealthy, educated, heteronormative audiences rather than reaching the broad population it claims to serve.

In the Life helped public television get closer to realizing the goal of providing universal service by programming content that spoke to the underserved LGBTQ population. The program offered stories that were directly relevant to the lives of queer viewers and gave them an opportunity to see their struggles and triumphs presented on-screen, addressing them as full and equal citizens even when local, state, and national governments refused to recognize them as such. Furthermore, it helped make the LGBTQ population visible to itself and the broader population of public television viewers who may not have had personal experiences with queer people.

In addition to the potential to serve and reflect a diverse national population, proponents of public television claim that it can support democracy by providing a kind of mediated public sphere that allows for rational discussion and the democratic exchange of ideas, encouraging civic engagement and possibly bringing about positive social change. Patricia Aufderheide, for example, suggests that "mass media can foster the communication essential to formation of a public sphere," arguing that while commercial media outlets fail in this regard because they are beholden to corporate interests and profits, "public media could be different."[29] Similarly, Glenda Balas argues that the push for public broadcasting in the United States was rooted in the principles associated with a thriving public sphere. She says that the agenda of the reform movement that ultimately led to the creation of a nationwide public broadcasting system "included problem-solving public discourse, democratic process, and broad access to media outlets that granted underserved audiences a voice and adequate representation. These possibilities were public sphere possibilities."[30]

Despite the possibilities that Aufderheide and Balas identify, public television has rarely lived up to its potential as a facilitator of public-sphere processes, in part because the desire for broad participation was overshadowed by the positioning of public broadcasting as an alternative to commercial television. Blaming the failures of commercial television on the lowbrow tastes of the mass audience, the elected and appointed officials leading the development of public television created a system that was, as Ouellette describes it, "*for* the people, not *by* the people" and ultimately governed by "top-down, bureaucratic control," which reinforced hegemonic perspectives rather than opening up to all voices.[31]

In the Life was a rare exception that took a step toward improving television's public-sphere potential by giving marginalized voices a platform on which they could share their counterhegemonic views and experiences so as to assimilate particular perspectives into broader cultural discussions. Queer voices were incorporated on two levels, as LGBTQ individuals appeared on-screen as subjects of featured stories and behind the camera as producers of the program. When it comes to the production of documentaries, the producer's voice and perspective are often just as significant as that of the on-camera subject, given the producer's ability to shape the development of the story into what eventually appears on-screen. Bucking the trend identified by Ouellette, in which public television has been produced *for* the people by a select group with a narrow perspective, *In the Life* came closer to the ideal of being produced *by* the people, thereby contributing an alternative perspective to public discussions.

Despite *In the Life*'s ability to help public television serve a diverse audience with high-quality programming that could inform public discussions in support of democratic processes, thereby responding to many of the criticisms aimed at public television over the years, the show was rejected by PBS and the CPB. During its life on the air, *In the Life* never received financial support from PBS or CPB, and PBS declined to include *In the Life* in the lineup of programming that it distributed to member stations across the country. While PBS and CPB do not publicly explain their reasons for refusing to fund or distribute particular programs, John Scagliotti, the original executive producer of *In the Life*, said in an interview not long after the show's launch that he believed a fear of right-wing backlash was to blame. Referring to his disappointment with PBS, he said, "Frankly, it's pretty outrageous how they've been treating us."[32] In addition to its general avoidance of controversial programming, PBS may have been especially skittish about airing any LGBTQ-oriented programming as a result of some events that preceded the launch of *In the Life*.

In 1991, the PBS documentary series *P.O.V.* (1988–) aired Marlon Riggs's *Tongues Untied* (1989), a prominent New Queer Cinema film that examines the lives of black gay men and the silencing and repression that this segment of the population has endured over the years. The film had played to critical acclaim at festivals around the world, and the producers of *P.O.V.* decided that it was perfectly in line with their program's mission, which executive producer Marc Weiss identified as "to provide a platform for voices which are unheard elsewhere on public television."[33] Despite this, nearly two-thirds of the stations that usually carried *P.O.V.* refused to air *Tongues Untied*, and many conservative politicians, spurred by right-wing groups like the American Family Association, publicly condemned the film and attacked both PBS and the National Endowment for the Arts for supporting the program. A month later, PBS canceled the broadcast of a scheduled documentary called *Stop the Church* (1991), which documented a demonstration by ACT UP at New York's St. Patrick's Cathedral. Arriving on the heels of these programs, *In the Life* was likely viewed as a threat—a program that would invite enough trouble that PBS wanted to keep a safe distance from it.[34]

Throughout the series's twenty-one season run, PBS never changed its mind about *In the Life*, which meant that the creators of the program had to rely on other funding sources and a different distribution outlet. As discussed earlier, some financial support for the program came from memberships and individual donors, but the bulk of the funding was from foundation grants. As for distribution, In the Life Media turned to American Public Television (APT). If the program had been distributed by PBS, it would have been sent out to all affiliate stations as part of the nationally agreed-upon package of programs. APT, however, functions more like an à la carte syndication system. Public television stations pay an annual fee to subscribe to APT, which gives them access to any of the content that is included in APT's Exchange program. This package includes a variety of programs—including cooking, travel, and lifestyle shows—that are usually generated by local public television stations or independent producers.[35] APT does not pay producers a licensing fee and will only distribute programs that are fully funded by outside sources. Before they can submit a program to be considered for APT distribution, producers are required to have a presenting organization, frequently a local station, "to oversee the submission and offer process, provide technical support, and assist with promotion."[36] In the case of *In the Life*, the presenting organizations were public television stations WNYC and WNET.[37] While APT provides some promotional services, they do the same for all the programs in their catalog, meaning that in order to make their own content stand out, producers and presenting organizations have to actively promote their shows to stations that might air them.

As individual stations work to fill up their programming schedules, they choose from the various programs offered by APT, which then compete with locally produced content and content from other stations and distributors and are ultimately scheduled in the slots not already taken by programs coming directly from PBS. When they were launching the program, the staff at In the Life Media had to reach out to station programmers across the country to urge them to schedule *In the Life* on their stations. And over the years, they constantly had to nurture relationships with individual station programmers, making sure that stations airing the program continued to do so and trying to convince new stations to add the program to their lineups. Communications coordinator Eleanor Moonier explains that building such relationships is particularly challenging because every station is different, and there is very little uniformity in terms of their beliefs and practices. She notes that there are still many stations that are "afraid to air LGBT content . . . and get a lot of pushback when they do." To get around this, In the Life Media staff members worked to remind programmers that "LGBT people don't just live in New York City and in San Francisco." LGBT people are a part of every community, and part of the mandate for public television stations is that they carry programming that reflects their communities.

Chuy Sanchez adds that for many station managers, an argument coming from someone in New York City is not as persuasive as one that comes from their own local constituency. As a result, the staff of In the Life Media worked with various regional and local organizations to try to persuade station managers to air the show. For example, when the courts in Iowa mandated marriage equality, *In the Life* produced a segment about this decision and the backlash that many of the judges faced. At the time, Iowa Public Television (IPT) was not airing *In the Life*, so staff members worked with organizers from One Iowa (an LGBTQ activist group), who recruited local volunteers to send emails and make phone calls to remind IPT of their mission to serve all of the community, including LGBTQ people. IPT eventually agreed to air the program and followed it with a locally produced discussion segment. A couple years later, *In the Life* was once again absent from IPT's schedule, serving as a reminder of the ongoing nature of this process. Even in markets that regularly aired *In the Life*, viewers sometimes had trouble finding it because it would be shown at odd hours, like Tuesdays at 1:00 a.m. Thus the staff at In the Life Media also tried to convince programmers to air the series at times when more people would be likely to watch it. This is something that had to be done individually with each of the more than 250 stations that aired the show, so just keeping the show on the air in decent time slots was an extremely laborious task.

From its premiere to its final episode, *In the Life* was marginalized. While the controversy that greeted the beginning of the series eventually died off and the program ran for two decades, *In the Life* was never fully embraced by the most powerful organizations in public television—PBS and the CPB. Despite the program's ability to address many of the weaknesses pointed out by critics of American public broadcasting, the lack of support from PBS meant that the producers of *In the Life* had to find alternative ways to keep their show on the air in pursuit of their goal to inform and educate audiences. But as with the LGBTQ movements that their program profiled, In the Life Media successfully worked around the system to put their stories and ideas in front of an audience in an effort to open minds and encourage action.

Beyond Public Television: On the Web and in the Archive

By documenting the realities of life for gay and lesbian people—past and present—*In the Life* aimed to provide a foundation based on truth and fact so as to counteract the myths and lies that have long circulated about LGBTQ communities. This base allowed the content produced by In the Life Media to serve as an educational tool for a variety of audiences. Educating the general public by way of television was one part of this, but perhaps the more significant educational use was when individual segments and episodes were presented directly to policy makers. While the nonprofit status of In the Life Media prevented staff members from directly lobbying elected officials and policy makers, content created for *In the Life* was picked up by other advocacy groups and used to inform and educate members of Congress and other government organizations, potentially influencing some of the decisions they made. For example, the episode titled "The Cost of Stigma" (December 2010) tells the stories of individuals who have been persecuted because of their HIV status. When legislation related to HIV criminalization was introduced in Congress, the Center for HIV Law and Policy gave presentations to inform legislators about the problems related to existing HIV laws, and they used video content from this episode as a primary component of their presentation. Marketing director Chuy Sanchez points to this example as a case where content from *In the Life* had "a very direct role in the legislative process in terms of educating people who [were] going to be making decisions about this new piece of legislation."

Another example involves an *In the Life* segment called "Bullycides" (March 2010), which focuses on the rise of bullying-related suicides among gay teens. When a high number of such suicides in a short period of time made national headlines and became a topic of nationwide discussion, the Department of Education picked up the *In the Life* segments and used them as part of a campaign to teach students, teachers, and school administrators about the harmful effects of bullying. The "In the States: Ohio" segment (March 2010) documents the lack of protections in the areas of housing, employment, and public accommodations and highlights the resulting discrimination faced by LGBTQ Ohioans. This piece was used by the civil rights group Equality Ohio as a tool for fundraising, recruiting, and lobbying when the state legislature was considering a nondiscrimination bill. In all these examples, segments from *In the Life* were adopted by activist groups outside In the Life Media and used to try to influence policies that would bring about positive social change for various members of the LGBTQ communities.

Another way that the content created for *In the Life* moved beyond the bounds of public television was through its online presence. In the last few years of the program, production staff made efforts to take advantage of the distribution opportunities offered by the internet. While the World Wide Web is not the panacea or virtual utopia that some optimists had hoped for, it does have great potential as a tool for social activism, and it offered In the Life Media the chance to take the content of its program beyond the boundaries of public broadcasting.

The internet has the potential for forming horizontal linkages, allowing individual users to connect with one another in a way that television never has. Additionally, the interactive nature of the web allows users / viewers / audience members to do more than passively consume. Jens Jensen reminds us that there are a number of modes of interactivity when it comes to the web, including transmissional, registrational, and consultational interactivity, all of which involve only minimal engagement between the creators and the users of web content.[38] Graham Meikle argues that a fourth type of interactivity—conversational—is what holds the most potential for activism. Conversational interactivity is present when users have the ability to influence and contribute to the content of media exchange;[39] it is a multidirectional form of communication that allows users to also be creators. Tim Berners-Lee, widely considered to be the creator of the World Wide Web, believes that this creative collaboration is a crucial characteristic of the web. He uses the term *intercreativity*, which he defines as "the process of making things or solving problems together."[40] The horizontal, conversational, and intercreative potential of the internet has been harnessed by some activist groups, and in its final years, In the Life Media explored this distribution channel as a way of widening their reach and strengthening their impact, especially in regard to their stated goal of moving people to action.

Although there were some challenges in the process of building an online presence, the basic form of *In the Life* was its advantage. While episodes of the television series are thirty or sixty minutes in length, and each episode has a theme holding it together, the episodes are typically composed of shorter segments on related but separate topics. Given the nature of internet video consumption, which tends to favor shorter segments that can be completed in a few minutes in between other tasks, this segmentation was beneficial for *In the Life*. In the Life Media's director of new media Erik Satre notes that individual segments are "very focused and targeted, meaning smaller, concise pieces of online content or components can be targeted much more to a specific direction or a specific topic." The early versions of In the Life Media's website did not take full advantage of this potential, as clips from the program were organized by season and by episode, thus relying on a television model to guide viewers through the content that was being made available online. Then in fall 2011, In the Life Media introduced an updated website design that was more suited to the behavior of web users. While complete, intact episodes were still available, individual segments were also accessible as stand-alone clips arranged by topic rather than airdate. Browsing the website by topic led to categories such as "Allies," "HIV/AIDS," "History," and "International Issues." Satre notes that the goal of the new website layout was to be "searchable in a very, very intuitive way," because people "want information fast." Meikle argues that successful activist users of the web must understand its differences from television, particularly the "archival nature of the web and its status as a medium which we *consult*—rather than have on all the time in the corner."[41] The redesign of the site was an important step in the process of changing *In the Life* from an informative television program to a resource that could fuel further discussion and action. Rather than stumbling upon the program late at night or being surprised by the content of an episode that was otherwise planned viewing, web users could approach the site with specific ideas about what they wanted to learn and narrow the content to better suit their needs. Beyond the content created for *In the Life*, the website also had links to resources related to the featured stories, giving viewers immediate access to additional information and opportunities to get involved, ultimately expanding the activist potential of *In the Life*'s storytelling by creating opportunities to turn stories into action.

The portability of content on the website also helped enhance its effectiveness, as users were able to forward links to and share materials with others. Erik Satre describes a particular segment that dealt with the injustices faced by individuals who identify as transgender, saying that "it was a huge success because . . . it reached a community. They [the trans community] are a heavy online community, and they . . . participated in a big way in just watching it and sharing it and posting it and moving it around." As this example demonstrates, the segmented, online version of *In the Life* had the potential to reach audience members in ways that the television version probably never could. But that's not to say that the television program became insignificant in a world of online video consumption. After all, the show's twenty-year history on public television generated a measure of credibility that other online videos do not have. While any video that strikes the right cultural nerve can go viral and reach a massive audience, not all such videos come with ties to a well-regarded, nonprofit, journalistic program like *In the Life*. This connection became incredibly important when content was used as a resource to inform policy decisions.

While the earlier examples related to HIV criminalization and bullying involved formal presentations to government officials, groups and individuals were also able to forward relevant clips and links to their own representatives at the local, state, and federal levels. The content created by In the Life Media thus become a powerful tool for grassroots activists and organizers, allowing them to connect local concerns to national issues by way of a professionally produced piece of visual media, accessed and circulated via the web. While viewers did not have a significant say in the creation of content for the website, the ability to use the site's content as raw material for further activism can be seen as a form of the "intercreativity" that Berners-Lee identified as part of the web's important potential.

When In the Life Media ceased production of its public television series in 2012, the staff also stopped producing and maintaining content for the organization's website. But this was not the end of *In the Life*'s online presence. The board of directors and leading funders of In the Life Media wanted to find a way to preserve and share all the work that the organization produced throughout its multidecade run. They contacted the UCLA Film and Television Archive, which had previously partnered with Outfest to create the Outfest UCLA Legacy Project for LGBT Moving Image Preservation, the largest publicly accessible collection of LGBT films in the world.[42] In 2013, UCLA announced that it would be adding the entire run of *In the Life* to its collection

FIGURE 2.4 All episodes of *In the Life* are available through an online research portal hosted by the UCLA Film and Television Archive. Courtesy of Outfest UCLA Legacy Project / UCLA Film and Television Archive.

and that with financial support from some of the foundations that had funded the television series, the collection would be digitized and made publicly accessible through an online portal. In 2015, the UCLA archive launched its digital research portal, including every episode of *In the Life* arranged chronologically by season. A press release announcing the launch included a quote from In the Life Media board member and donor Henry van Ameringen, who said, "We're committed to preserving this invaluable resource and maximizing access to it with an online presence that will continue to advance equality in new and innovative ways."[43] This comment highlights the funders' belief that *In the Life* had played and would continue to play a valuable role in the movement for LGBTQ social justice.

The shift from public television to an archival collection housed at a major research institution was more than just a change in content delivery format. Preserving and archiving elements of queer history is a complex issue with significant political weight, as it involves collecting stories that have long been suppressed and hidden and making them visible. *In the Life* is, in many ways, an unusual archival collection, and it serves as a valuable example of the significance of archiving queer materials.

An individual's identity and their understanding of their place in society are heavily influenced by knowledge of their own history and the history of any groups with which they are associated. One of the more important ways that we learn about our individual and collective histories is "through the examination of material records of the past."[44] Archives are an important way of preserving evidence of collective histories. The value of such materials is highlighted in the "Universal Declaration on Archives" issued by the International Council on Archives and endorsed by the United Nations Educational, Scientific, and Cultural Organization (UNESCO) in 2011: "Archives record decisions, actions, and memories. . . . They play an essential role in the development of societies by safeguarding and contributing to individual and community memory. Open access to archives enriches our knowledge of human society, promotes democracy, protects citizens' rights and enhances the quality of life."[45] Archives are a valuable way to preserve the history of all segments of society, but given the efforts to silence and deny the experiences and stories of LGBTQ individuals over the years, the work of archives to collect, preserve, and share documentation of queer history is absolutely crucial.

In the Life is, in some ways, a natural fit for an archive of LGBTQ materials. One of the primary goals of the show was to document and preserve important developments in the push for LGBTQ equality in the United States. This goal feeds directly into similar concerns about documentation and preservation that drive the creation and maintenance of any archive, meaning that *In the Life* arrived with much of the archivist's work already done. In most cases, archives rely on a significant amount of luck and chance, as they are frequently assembled based on whatever artifacts and documents happened to survive. With the exception of government agencies and perhaps some corporate entities, individuals and organizations rarely save and organize materials with the idea that they will someday be archived for public use. Rather, collections tend to be composed of whatever donated materials did not get thrown away or destroyed. As a result, archival collections often require users to fill in gaps and provide context in order to weave individual artifacts into any kind of coherent narrative. *In the Life* is a very different case. While the original producers may not have specifically imagined their work ending up in an archive, they did create each episode with the idea that it would capture a moment in history so that it would be presented to an audience in an engaging and enlightening way. As such, individual episodes and segments, as well as the series as a whole, present organized, contextualized narratives that give the impression of completeness. It is important to remember, however, that while the collection of *In the Life* episodes might not have the obvious missing pieces that are common in other archival collections, the polish of the television production obscures some of the production decisions about what did or did not make it into the program in the first place. Additional materials housed in the archive (which will likely be made available online as well)—including production paperwork, press releases, B-roll footage, and interview outtakes—fill in some but not all gaps. While the collection may provide a complete picture of the series as it aired, it should not be read as a complete picture of the LGBTQ movement during that time period. This collection may feel complete, but as with any archival collection, it is still just a portion of the bigger picture.

All archival collections are defined by a noticeable tension between what is included and what is excluded. As Jack Halberstam notes, archives can be seen as "places that hold and exclude, collect and reject, represent and obliterate, legitimize and disqualify."[46] There are a number of factors that determine what does or does not get included in an archive. Individuals make choices every day about what to keep and what to throw away. People who donate to archives may choose to send some items and not others. Archivists with limited storage space and large volumes of donations may decide that not everything can be saved or that certain materials do not fit with their larger collection. In a heteronormative and often homophobic society, closeted individuals or ashamed family members may actively erase traces of a queer existence, eliminating even the possibility of their appearance in an archive. As a result, the act of seeking knowledge from queer archives necessarily involves "an appraisal of presences and absences"[47] in the construction of a coherent narrative.

The presences and absences of queer archive material vary significantly from one collection to the next, sometimes based on the type of archive. For example, scholars attempting to uncover evidence of early gay and lesbian history have generally had to resort to materials that were not specifically intended to record queer experiences. With alternative sexualities being hidden and shunned, archivists, museum curators, and librarians were generally not collecting materials related to queer life. But government records still provide many traces of homosexuality, particularly related to the criminalization of certain behaviors. As Sara Edenheim points out, "Bureaucracy does not much care about ordinary people; it cares more about the wrongdoers, the illicit, the banned, those who do or may instigate a threat to the social order."[48] While arrest reports and housing records may give some indication of the numbers and locations of gays and lesbians, they do little to provide insight into their way of life or daily experiences. In recent years, mainstream archives (not specifically LGBTQ oriented) have become more open to collecting materials that document queer life, but in many cases, they emphasize "famous gays" who are deemed historically significant, either for their work in social movements or for something entirely unrelated to sexuality, such as success in the arts or business.[49] By focusing on exceptional individuals, these collections leave out the more typical experiences of most LGBTQ people.

The nature of *In the Life* minimizes some of the absences that plague other collections. For example, a significant absence in many archives (LGBTQ or otherwise) is authorship. Frequently, materials make it into an archive without any trace of who created them. This is especially true of queer archives, given that many creators feared the potential repercussions of being connected to explicitly queer artifacts. As David Frantz and Mia Locks point out in their discussion of the art collection held by the ONE National Gay and Lesbian Archives, "there are a handful of works by anonymous makers, others that are signed only with initials, and others that are signed with pseudonyms."[50] Given that *In the Life* was produced with the explicit goal of publicly documenting the LGBTQ movement and within the context of a media industry that has standardized practices related to attribution and credit, it is not surprising that the creators and participants are easily identifiable. And since the program aimed to document a range of LGBTQ lives, from government leaders and celebrities to everyday people, the collection is not limited to the stories of "famous gays." That is not to say, however, that there are no absences or exclusions in the collection.

While the producers of *In the Life* set out to provide a range of images of LGBTQ people and document the history of the LGBTQ movements during the time of the program's production, the archival collection is limited by the decisions that determined the content of the original show. Given that story segments were selected by an editorial board—based on ideas submitted by producers and viewers—and sometimes timed to coincide with specific events or anniversaries, the content of *In the Life* was defined by a process of filtering, compromise, and committee decision-making. As a result, the show is not a record of all aspects of the LGBTQ movements from 1992 to 2012 but rather a record of what was important to the producers at the time. These decisions about story selection, along with production decisions made during shooting and editing, shaped the content of each episode to fit with the larger goals of the series, generally aiming to present LGBTQ communities in a positive light that would help advance equal rights and social justice.

The emphasis on these kinds of stories may have led to the erasure, or at least the marginalization, of queer lives and expressions that could be perceived as being more radical. Given the political hostility toward the LGBTQ rights movements when the series began production in the early 1990s, coupled with the need to persuade individual public television station managers to air the program, it is not surprising that producers would choose representations of LGBTQ people that would be the least likely to generate controversy. This happened, in part, by toning down references to any erotic or physical aspects of sexuality in favor of highlighting political efforts, rights violations, and the desire for equal treatment under the law. While hostility toward the program declined over the years as the LGBTQ movements advanced, *In the Life* continued to emphasize public political struggles while minimizing any erotic content. As Marc Stein points out, LGBTQ archives have frequently struggled with questions of what to do with sexually explicit materials, and such materials are often left out so as to avoid offending users/viewers of the collections.[51] Stein goes on to demonstrate how historical accounts of the homophile movement in the 1950s and 1960s have focused on politically oriented publications like *Mattachine Review* and *Ladder* and have ignored the more sexually explicit and transgressive magazine *Drum*, despite the fact that it had a larger circulation than the other magazines. Other scholars have treated these historical studies as definitive accounts of the era, leading to what Stein calls the "canonization of homophile respectability."[52] While the producers of *In the Life* may have had valid reasons for including some aspects of the LGBTQ movement while excluding others, future users must remember that like any archival collection, *In the Life* is defined by what it includes as well as what it excludes, and the history documented by the program must be balanced with other accounts to reveal a more complete picture of the era.

However, the *In the Life* collection successfully includes content that many other archives leave out by contributing to what Ann Cvetkovich refers to as an "archive of feelings." Traditional archives are often filled with documents that provide evidence of LGBTQ people's existence along with traces of their words and actions, but such materials are less effective when it comes to capturing emotional experiences, which are a crucial part of what makes the queer experience unique. As Cvetkovich points out, "Lesbian and gay history demands a radical archive of emotion in order to document intimacy, sexuality, love, and activism—all areas of experience that are difficult to chronicle through the materials of a traditional archive."[53] As a film/video documentary,

In the Life was able to go beyond the evidence that might be available in a printed document to capture moving images and sounds that reflect many of the emotions involved in living the LGBTQ experience. Cvetkovich notes that documentary filmmaking can be an effective form of archiving, given the ability of documentaries to find "an unexpected range of materials that archive emotion and feeling."[54] Whether it is anger in the voice of a man discharged from the army for being gay, heartbreak in the face of a mother whose child committed suicide after being bullied, or hope and excitement in the laughter of a child adopted by two fathers, *In the Life* demonstrates the power of audiovisual storytelling to convey and preserve emotions. As an organized collection of images, sounds, and stories, *In the Life* helps archive feelings about alongside evidence of political actions, organizations, and historical events.

While the mere existence of queer materials protected in an archive is valuable in the sense that it acknowledges and respects the experiences of LGBTQ people, a queer archive is far more valuable if it is used in some way. In other words, the value of archival queer materials increases if those materials can have some kind of impact beyond the confines of the archive. In order for this to happen, an archive must first be accessible. As previously noted, the "Universal Declaration on Archives" states that it is "open access to archives" that makes them so valuable, and most archives consider public access to be a significant part of their mission. The level of access can vary significantly from one collection to the next. Smaller collections that are managed by volunteers or part-time staff will have limited hours of availability, and even collections housed in large institutions are likely to close at some point. In many cases, the only way to access desired materials is to physically enter a reading room, request an item, and wait for a staff member to deliver it. Anyone not living near the archive may find travel prohibitive, and in some cases, users must document their affiliation with an institution or research project to gain access. Some archival collections have been digitized and made available online, but even these can be restricted by membership status, as users may have to access materials through a university or public library account. As per the wishes of those funding the project, and because the copyright for the series was included as part of the donation, the *In the Life* collection is available online to anyone with access to the internet. Through the research portal provided by the UCLA Film and Television Archive, *In the Life* becomes an unrestricted, publicly shared archive, accessible around the world.

Making the materials accessible is, of course, only the first step. The fact that archival materials are available does not necessarily mean that people will find and use them. Alexandra Juhasz argues that archival materials can be repurposed and put to use in a process that she refers to as "queer archive activism."[55] Building on this idea, Cvetkovich says, "Queer archive activism insists that the archive serve not just as a repository for safeguarding objects, but also as a resource that 'comes out' into the world to perform public interventions."[56] Activists can use archival materials to remind people of past struggles and triumphs, to fight against historical erasure, and to inspire change for the future. But content cannot be used toward activist ends if it is not easily found, which makes visibility very important.

The placement of *In the Life* at the UCLA Film and Television Archive is helpful in this regard. UCLA is a prominent institution within the realm of film and television studies, and its archive is a well-known and respected resource for media research. But this placement is just the first step. Mark Quigley, the manager of research and study for the archive, says, "You can't just build it and hope that people will come." He goes on to note how important it is to engage in outreach to encourage users to explore the archive.[57] As Don Romesburg discusses, some LGBTQ archives partner with museums or make use of an in-house gallery space to create an exhibit that highlights some of the holdings of the archives, a process that "brings the archives into interaction with many publics."[58] By curating and publicizing a selection of materials, exhibitions help bring new audiences in while pushing the content of the archive out into the world in a very public way. The format of the *In the Life* collection may not lend itself to a museum or gallery exhibition, but there are other ways to share the content of the archive. Quigley notes that UCLA archivists are working to make more pieces of the collection—including production documents, publicity materials, and video outtakes—available online. They are also working to make the materials more searchable so that users can easily find individual clips that feature specific people or topics, and they plan to curate selections from the program and highlight them in a featured section of the website. This will be labor intensive and therefore costly, and Quigley stresses that archivists see the collection as "an ongoing concern" that will be developed in stages as time and funding permit. Video clips or links to those clips are easily shared via social media, and with increased curation and improved searchability, the collection becomes more likely to reach a broad audience, thereby increasing its potential for use in acts of queer archive activism and increasing its value to the future of the LGBTQ movements.

The Future of the Past

When *In the Life* first hit the airwaves in 1992, the program stood out just by daring to present positive images of real LGBTQ people who were not being used for shock value or comic relief. As the show developed, its counterstorytelling efforts shifted from educating viewers about the mere existence of queer people to educating them about the myriad forms of social and political oppression faced by LGBTQ communities, addressing the personal and emotional side of political issues as a way of encouraging positive social change.

In the Life was a valuable resource not only for general audiences wanting to learn about LGBTQ people but also for queer viewers looking for connections to and inspiration from others like them. Despite a lack of support from PBS and the CPB, the program helped public television inch closer to reaching its potential as a source of high-quality, educational, public-affairs programming that could support and enrich a diverse democratic society. However, *In the Life*'s greatest value may lie in its future.

As a publicly accessible collection in the UCLA Film and Television Archive, *In the Life* serves as a unique historical record of a very active and successful period in the LGBTQ rights movements. The many hours of audiovisual footage capture not only landmark events and discussions of sociopolitical issues but also the emotions of the people living through them—an archive of facts and an archive of feelings. But this record is of little value if nobody uses it. Used in conjunction with other historical accounts, it could be an important tool for activists, teachers, and scholars seeking to understand developments in the LGBTQ rights movements as well as those wanting to strategize for future social justice efforts. In the Life Media has therefore created a resource with the potential to benefit LGBTQ communities and the rest of society for decades to come.

3

Training Filmmakers and Educating Audiences

POWER UP

In 2004, Jennifer Beals received the Artistry Award from the Professional Organization of Women in Entertainment Reaching Up (POWER UP) at their Power Premiere, an event honoring the achievements and contributions of gays, lesbians, and their allies in the entertainment industries. In her acceptance speech, Beals said, "In a country and culture so dominated by media, by the manipulation of words and stories, telling the tales of people whose stories have historically not been told is a radical act, and I believe an act that can change the world and help rewrite history." Her comments were primarily in reference to the television series *The L Word* (2004–2009), on which she was appearing at the time, but they also speak to the work of the organization giving her the award. POWER UP is a nonprofit film production company and educational organization dedicated to the advancement of women and LGBTQ people through film. As demonstrated by the previous chapter's discussion of In the Life Media, media storytelling is a crucial component of the movement to achieve social equality for LGBTQ people. The work of POWER UP demonstrates how queer storytelling can advance the LGBTQ movements by strengthening communities through education.

All the organizations discussed in this book create, distribute, and/or exhibit stories that educate viewers by expanding and countering the images of LGBTQ people offered by mainstream media outlets. POWER UP takes things a step further, educating women and LGBTQ filmmakers about the filmmaking process itself. Given their marginalized status in society as a whole, it is perhaps not surprising that both women and queer people are underrepresented in the film and television industries, and this is something that POWER UP seeks to change by training them to work as producers, directors, and crew members. So in addition to telling stories about the LGBTQ experience, as In the Life Media and others have, POWER UP nurtures queer storytellers, enabling them to produce media in the present and preparing them to continue that work well into the future. By educating both storytellers and audiences in a way that challenges heteronormative and phallocentric world views, POWER UP diversifies the media landscape and the industry that creates it, ultimately strengthening the efforts of both feminist and LGBTQ movements.

POWER UP Films

Scholars and critics have long lamented the fact that the vast majority of behind-the-scenes professional positions in film and television are occupied by straight white men. Recently, a few projects and organizations, including Ryan Murphy's Half Foundation and Lifetime's Broad Focus initiative, have taken significant steps toward training and hiring more women, queer people, and people of color to write, produce, direct, and crew films and television programs. POWER UP has been doing similar work for more than fifteen years.

POWER UP was founded in 2000 by writer and producer Stacy Codikow, who recognized the underrepresentation of women in media industries and the lack of high-quality lesbian-oriented media products. "I had a realization that I didn't know anyone gay because I'd been making movies," says Codikow of her time working in the mostly male and mostly straight film industry. In response, she says, "I decided to start an organization where gay people can tell their own stories."[1] The original mission of the organization was "to promote the visibility and integration of gay women in entertainment, arts, and all forms of media."[2] Over the years, the group expanded its reach to include all women and LGBTQ people.

POWER UP is primarily an educational organization that uses the production of high-quality films as a training ground for women and LGBTQ filmmakers who are looking to get a foothold in the industry. The organization provides seminars, workshops, career counseling, and a mentorship program that gives college students and recent graduates a chance to work on a film set in a queer- and women-friendly environment that prepares them for many kinds of jobs in Hollywood. Through its various educational programs and the production of films and public service announcements, POWER UP works to achieve its goal of "challenging perception through film."

POWER UP has much in common with other groups seeking to make significant changes to and through visual media, drawing on the spirit and ideals of movements and organizations variously described as alternative media and community media. A precise definition of *alternative media* is difficult to pin down, given the various ways that scholars have explored the concept in fields like journalism, media studies, and communication studies. Joshua D. Atkinson pulls some of those discussions together to offer a framework that defines media as alternative if it provides some kind of resistance or challenge to dominant, mainstream media by way of content, production, or audience interpretation.[3] This might involve media that openly questions the content provided by mainstream outlets, is produced outside the structures of corporate media conglomerates, and/or is "used by traditionally marginalized groups to understand oppressive power structures or to gain voice in society."[4] Nick Couldry and James Curran add that alternative media "challenges, at least implicitly, actual concentrations of media power."[5] Prominent examples of alternative media include the social justice–oriented radio / TV / internet news program *Democracy Now!*, the radical feminist journal *Off Our Backs*, and the anticonsumerism magazine *Adbusters*. While POWER UP maintains certain ties to the mainstream world of Hollywood, the company models characteristics of alternative media through its efforts to reject norms of both production and content and thereby challenges the industry's phallocentric and heterocentric power structures.

POWER UP also draws heavily from the tradition of community media. Often viewed as an equivalent to or a subset of alternative media, community media generally refers to "media that originates in civil society, outside of commercial and governmental control."[6] Based on the belief that the skills, technologies, and resources involved in the production and dissemination of media should not be limited to large institutions, community media aims to give amateurs and individuals with minimal resources access to media communication. Scribe Video Center in Philadelphia is just one example of a community media facility that offers training, equipment, production space, and networking opportunities for aspiring media creators of all ages.[7] Ellie Rennie argues that community media is about more than just access, noting that participants choose community media outlets "because of the values they uphold"—values that often differ from those of mainstream media institutions.[8]

Groups that have traditionally been excluded from mainstream media production and representation have often used community media as a way of accessing means of communication that otherwise shut them out. And as Dee-Dee Halleck argues, "Community media is often part of a larger process of community activities that can include environmental organizing, alternative health care, community self-defense, labor union mobilization, and hundreds of other activist projects."[9] POWER UP draws inspiration from community media organizations in that it aims to help women and LGBTQ media makers overcome long-standing barriers and access the production industries that have traditionally marginalized and excluded them.

In addition to alternative and community media traditions, the work of POWER UP builds on the legacy of the lesbian-feminist filmmakers who first made a name for themselves in the late 1970s. Drawing energy and ideas from the surging feminist and gay liberation movements, a handful of women filmmakers—including Barbara Hammer, Jan Oxenberg, and Su Friedrich—challenged representations of women that they found limiting and oppressive. Feminist scholars and activists at the time were arguing that mainstream cinema was built on eroticized visions of women, designed specifically for the heterosexual male gaze.[10] As a result, many filmmakers of the era sought to articulate a new cinematic language, experimenting with "the possibilities of film form in order to represent lesbian-feminist concerns, often while simultaneously questioning the very nature of representation itself."[11] POWER UP expresses a similar dissatisfaction with mainstream representations of lesbians and other women, thereby continuing some of the work of the earlier lesbian-feminist filmmakers. In comparison to these earlier filmmakers, however, POWER UP's approach is more liberal than radical. There is no attempt to alter the language of cinema itself. Instead, the organization strives to use the existing language of cinema, placing it in the hands of women who will tell untold stories from perspectives not typically explored.

POWER UP's mission and goals are heavily influenced by the legacies of alternative media, community media, and early lesbian-feminist filmmakers in that the organization works to give marginalized voices access to the tools of media production while creating content that differs from that of mainstream Hollywood by expanding the possibilities for representing women and queer people. However, POWER UP differs significantly from these groups and movements because rather than distancing themselves from Hollywood to create something entirely new, members actively maintain connections with the industry. POWER UP may not be dismantling the existing media industries, but by using media to bring about positive social change, its efforts make an important contribution to the LGBTQ movements.

Since its founding, POWER UP has produced more than fifteen films, including such short films as *D.E.B.S.* (2003), *Little Black Boot* (2004), and *Billy's Dad Is a Fudge-Packer!* (2004) as well as the feature films *Itty Bitty Titty Committee* (2007) and *Girl Trash: All Night Long* (2014). These films have won awards at festivals like Sundance and South by Southwest, and their production has helped launch and promote the careers of many successful industry professionals, including Angela Robinson (who would go on to write and produce for *The L Word* [2004–2009] and *True Blood* [2008–2014]), Jessica Sharzer (*American Horror Story* [2011–]), and Colette Burson (*Hung*

[2009–2011]). In addition to producing films and training mentees, POWER UP also seeks to highlight the accomplishments of lesbians and gay men working in the media and entertainment industries. The organization has frequently hosted an event called the Power Premiere, a celebration of openly gay women and men who have made outstanding contributions to and achieved success within the industry.

The goals of POWER UP reflect its dual roles as both a film production company and an educational nonprofit. According to the organization's former president of film production and distribution Lisa Thrasher, one of the goals in creating the group was "to pull together real Hollywood filmmakers who are gay to collaborate and tell authentic stories that we want to see ourselves represented in . . . true, complex stories of characters that embody good and embody bad but that are interesting and not contrived and not clichés."[12] Thrasher also notes that while POWER UP is open to producing a project that is not queer in nature and does not come from queer creators, "there has to be something in it that has value to [the organization], creatively and socially." Similarly, executive director Stacy Codikow says that she looks for certain qualities when considering which project to pursue: "I want to do something I'm passionate about. I want to make and tell stories that hopefully create change."[13] This desire to create change is balanced with a need to appeal to an audience, as Thrasher points out that in addition to encouraging social change, any film made by POWER UP also "needs to work by itself as an entertainment piece."

Beyond creating socially relevant, entertaining films, POWER UP is dedicated to education. Lisa Thrasher notes that one of the organization's main goals is to "unite and educate and empower a community by empowering talented individuals." This is accomplished on two levels. On one hand, POWER UP funds and supports projects and ideas brought to them by individuals (writers, directors, and producers) who have demonstrated significant talent and potential. Thrasher notes that the organization works with filmmakers who are already on the path to success and "gives them wings to go farther." She says, "We're creating a spotlight for them. We're highlighting them. We're creating a community." At the same time, POWER UP's mentorship program provides mentees with access to the industry, allowing them to work on set with professionals and learn the process while producing a film. By providing basic training for mentees and professional development opportunities for those with more experience, POWER UP aims to educate and train at the same time that it produces entertaining and socially significant films. Building on all this, Thrasher notes that "the most important thing is that POWER UP stays connected with mainstream Hollywood" rather than separating from it. Unlike the lesbian-feminist film movement of the late 1970s, which aimed to work outside mainstream cinema and create an alternative to it, the long-range goal of POWER UP is to get more women and LGBTQ filmmakers into the mainstream industry so as to change it from within.

To achieve this larger aim, POWER UP focuses on reaching its short-term goals of educating and promoting women and LGBTQ filmmakers while telling queer stories that can bring about positive social change. This unique combination of goals played a significant role in the decision to form POWER UP as a nonprofit organization. Thrasher argues it is the drive for profit, rather than discrimination or homophobia, that prevents most studios from producing much in the way of queer content. As she points out, "Private corporations don't have to represent everybody. They don't have to represent people fairly. They don't have to represent people positively. . . . Their only legal duty is to make a profit for their shareholders." So even if a company wants to tell accurate stories about LGBTQ experiences, if company executives do not see significant potential for a profit, they are unlikely to produce such a film.

Freed from the need to make a profit for investors or shareholders, POWER UP can focus on its goals of social change and education. And because it is a registered nonprofit organization, it is supported through donations rather than investments. In addition to individuals who support POWER UP through donations and annual memberships, for-profit companies provide both cash contributions and in-kind donations that are tax deductible. Companies like Showtime, Sony, and Panavision have provided significant support for POWER UP's work over the years. According to Thrasher, the feature films POWER UP has produced would likely have cost around $2 million each if everything had been paid for in cash, but after substantial donations of goods and services, the cash outlay has been closer to $200,000. As another way of keeping the organization financially lean, Stacy Codikow and other staff members have worked as full-time volunteers for the organization rather than drawing a regular paycheck.

Christopher Racster, who produced the short film *Little Black Boot* for POWER UP before cofounding the for-profit production company Mythgarden, notes that POWER UP's nonprofit status allows it to accomplish things that are not possible in the for-profit environment. He says, "They can nurture new voices and up-and-coming talent and take chances that a lot of for-profit people won't."[14] Describing his experience working with POWER UP, Racster notes that it was his first time taking a film to the Sundance Film Festival and that POWER UP provided resources and training to help him navigate and learn about the festival circuit and distribution. So the work of POWER UP supports new filmmakers through the entire process, from writing and development through distribution. Racster argues that what POWER UP does is "absolutely crucial in nurturing voices in a way that most of us can't." He notes that producers seeking a profit "don't have the time or the funds to nurture a bunch of small voices that aren't tied to a return at some point, simply because [they] have to keep the cycle going in order to stay employed." Unlike production companies that have to generate profits to survive and are therefore driven by commercial success, POWER UP's nonprofit status allows the organization to make social change through education its top priority.

Educating for Change

As Christopher Racster's earlier comments suggest, the work of POWER UP is especially valuable and unique because of its educational components. Most film production companies expect a level of professional knowledge on the part of their workers and offer little in the way of training, but POWER UP's status as both a production company and a nonprofit educational organization leads it in a very different direction. And while some of the organization's programming does emphasize the nuts and bolts of day-to-day survival on a film set, its work goes well beyond vocational training. POWER UP's educational programming is driven by a critical perspective that is concerned with challenging inequality and working for social justice.

In many ways, the efforts of POWER UP draw on the ideals and approaches associated with critical pedagogy. Rooted in the academic study of educational structures and practices, critical pedagogy is driven by the belief that schools and educational programs can be agents of positive social change. As Seehwa Cho describes, critical pedagogy "attempts to build more egalitarian power relations, to strengthen the voices of learners, and to inspire critical consciousness, in order to promote social change."[15] The ideals of critical pedagogy are rooted in the critical theory work of the Frankfurt School, which examines the relations of domination and subordination that define life in supposedly democratic, capitalist societies.[16] Feminist, poststructural, postcolonial, and queer theory have all influenced the development of critical pedagogy as it works to address the many different types of oppression that exist in society. As a movement interested in challenging the status quo, critical pedagogy rejects some of the premises that have historically defined mainstream education. In particular, the movement rejects the mainstream view of education as a "great equalizer" that offers every person the same opportunities to succeed. Instead, proponents of critical pedagogy work to identify and remove the barriers that limit the success of marginalized groups.[17] In this way, critical pedagogy imagines education as a way of working toward social justice.

John Smyth argues that one of the greatest strengths of critical pedagogy is its ability to support community capacity building. The concept of capacity building, often used in discussions of economic development, refers to strategies that give a particular group (a nation, a tribe, a community) the knowledge and tools to improve its own situation, as opposed to relying on outsiders who might not have the group's best interest in mind when working to "solve" problems. Smyth describes community capacity building as "a *learning space* or an *arena for possibilities* within which to work towards leveling a playing field that has been inequitably constructed in terms of access to opportunities."[18] Building the capacity of a given community empowers members to challenge inequality and make positive changes. As Smyth points out, capacity building rejects the tendency to pathologize marginalized groups by identifying what is "wrong" with them. Instead, "capacity building starts from the viewpoint that all communities have assets, skills and resources, but they also have constraints that limit what is possible."[19] POWER UP puts the ideas of critical pedagogy into practice to help build the capacity of women and LGBTQ communities through educational programs that (1) question, challenge, and change structures of domination and subordination and (2) develop the potential of women and LGBTQ filmmakers while helping them overcome institutionalized barriers in the media industries.

Additionally, POWER UP's programs and content exemplify the four forms of antioppressive education described by Kevin Kumashiro: "Education for the Other, education about the Other, education that is critical of privileging and Othering, and education that changes students and society."[20] Although Kumashiro argues for the incorporation of antioppressive education in primary and secondary schools, his framework can be applied to any educational initiative, including the storytelling and filmmaking work of POWER UP. In laying out his categories, Kumashiro uses the term *Other* to refer to "those groups that are traditionally marginalized, denigrated, or violated (i.e., Othered) in society."[21] Across its programming and activities, POWER UP addresses each of these categories in one way or another.

POWER UP's mentorship program is the clearest example of Kumashiro's first category, education for the Other. As demonstrated by much of the work in the field of critical pedagogy, most educational institutions do not adequately serve and protect members of marginalized groups or provide opportunities for them to succeed and overcome the oppressions that exist in society as a whole. It therefore becomes necessary to provide educational programming designed to reach these groups to help them overcome the constraints they face. POWER UP's mentorship program provides education and support for two groups that have traditionally been marginalized within the film and television industries: women and LGBTQ people.

POWER UP's mentorship program was initially centered on the production of short films but ultimately shifted to an emphasis on feature films. In either case, the idea is to bring in mentees to work as part of the crew for the film or films being produced so that they can work with and learn from more experienced professionals while contributing to the production of a festival-quality film. According to Lisa Thrasher, ten to fifteen mentees are accepted to participate in each cycle of the program. Most participants have completed or are working on bachelors or master's degrees in film or media production but have little to no professional experience on a film set. Mentees go through a couple weeks of training and classes as part of preproduction, then work on set as production assistants, grips, wardrobe assistants, location scouts, and so on while the film is being shot. This is followed by a week or so of wrap-up work and a summary class. Those who are interested in postproduction may stay for that part of the process as well. Throughout the process, participants work with mentors who have professional credits and active careers, so as Thrasher notes, they are "making alliances and networking with people who would theoretically be able to hire them or recommend them for being hired after the program's done." Given the importance of professional connections and networking in the film and television industries, the opportunity to establish such relationships is as valuable to mentees as the chance to learn the logistics of the production process.

Discussing the professional value of POWER UP's mentorship program, Stacy Codikow notes that "the Film and Television industry is one of the most competitive industries in the world. To succeed in this industry is especially difficult, since it remains an apprentice industry where 98% of what you must know to succeed can only be learned on the job."[22] Lisa Thrasher concurs, noting that there is "a lot of jargon that's used that's only known in the industry. There's a lot of protocol, a lot of rules. And like the military, there's rank, and you have to stay in your rank." In order to navigate the rigid rules and hierarchies that define the industry, Thrasher says, "You have to find someone who's willing to take you under their wing and train you." However, as she goes on to say, finding a mentor can be very difficult "because nobody has the time and you're everybody's competition, and so it's not in anyone's best interest to help you." The surplus of workers competing for a limited number of production jobs available in the industry means not only that people are potentially less likely to mentor others but also that replacing workers is easy. As a result, people are likely to get fired (or at least not hired again) if they make a mistake. Codikow says, "Most failures—at all levels—primarily stem from . . . blunders of industry politics, social skills and missteps on the unmapped hierarchical ladder of respect, deference & politics. Most people who blunder in this industry never get a second chance."[23]

The mentorship program is designed to be more collaborative than competitive, and it gives mentees the space to make mistakes and learn from them, rather than being fired for them. Codikow says, "The best gift POWER UP provides to all mentees is pointing out the mentees' mistakes as they are made while incorporating and helping with the redirection necessary for mentees to learn."[24] Thrasher elaborates by noting that mistakes are "pointed out publicly . . . and explained so everyone can learn from them." In this way, the mentorship program allows mentees to learn not only from their own mistakes but also from the mistakes of their peers, increasing the likelihood that they will be able to avoid such mistakes in the future. While this kind of opportunity would be valuable to anyone trying to get established in media production, it is especially valuable to women and LGBTQ filmmakers, who, along with people of color, continue to be underrepresented in the industry. POWER UP therefore uses mentoring as a kind of activism by working to level the playing field for marginalized groups within the industry. As an example of what Kumashiro describes as "education for the Other," POWER UP's mentorship program goes beyond classroom education that merely teaches marginalized groups how to recognize and critique their own oppression. Regarding such academic treatments of oppression, Christine Sleeter says, "The problem with academic discourse is that it often consists of little more than words and often contributes nothing to improving the real conditions of life for disenfranchised peoples."[25] POWER UP's mentorship program provides an education that is both political and practical, realizing critical pedagogy's potential for community capacity building and challenging social hierarchies by giving disenfranchised groups skills and tools to help them overcome barriers that have traditionally reinforced oppression.

While the mentorship program offers "education for the Other," many of POWER UP's programs demonstrate Kumashiro's second category of antioppressive education, "education about the Other." Kumashiro argues that there are two main types of oppressive knowledge that antioppressive education must work against. The first type is knowledge about only what society has defined as either "normal" (the way things generally are) or normative (the way things should be).[26] In these cases, Otherness is merely implied as the opposite of or a departure from the norm. Narratives that omit LGBTQ people, as has been the case for much of film history as well as the stories circulated by schools and other institutions, contribute to this kind of oppressive knowledge by making queer people invisible and reinforcing cisnormative and heteronormative ideals. The second type of oppressive knowledge "encourages a distorted and misleading understanding of the Other that is based on stereotypes and myths."[27] Stories that present stereotypical images of queer people—either for laughs, shock value, or merely as a contrast to those representing dominant norms—contribute to this type of knowledge by circulating inaccurate meanings that may become accepted as truth. Many of the harmful myths circulated by religious institutions, government agencies, and mainstream media over the years fall into this category. Education about the Other seeks not only to fill in gaps left by incomplete or misleading stories but to actively disrupt existing oppressive knowledge by providing more accurate information about and representations of marginalized people.[28] The work of In the Life Media, discussed in chapter 2, was driven by the need to minimize oppressive knowledge. Similarly, as suggested by their slogan, "Challenging perception through film," POWER UP seeks to disrupt the oppressive knowledge that mainstream media storytellers have contributed to for decades.

In addition to educating aspiring filmmakers through the mentoring process, POWER UP's film production program also serves as the company's most obvious example of education about the Other. The shorts and feature films that emerge from this program (see the following section) circulate to audiences by way of film festivals, broader theatrical distribution, DVD releases, and online outlets. As films produced by, for, and about women and LGBTQ people, they offer representations that seek to counter the invisibility and stereotypes that have traditionally dominated mainstream film.

Although smaller than the film production program, POWER UP's public service announcement (PSA) program also aims to educate viewers about LGBTQ people, but with a more focused agenda built around social issues such as domestic violence and marriage equality. PSAs are generally understood as media texts intended to educate and persuade, as opposed to the entertainment-oriented goals of most short and feature films. As discussed later in the chapter, they are vehicles that allow POWER UP to offer information and encourage additional information seeking without the need to wrap the educational material in an entertaining package.

A third POWER UP program that offers education about the Other is their Power Premiere, a celebrity gala that includes awards for those who make POWER UP's list of "10 Amazing Gay Women (and Men) in Showbiz." The event, along with the awards handed out, aims to highlight the achievements of women and men who are openly gay and "working, creating, and changing lives as they continue their way up the ladder of success in entertainment."[29] Award recipients include celebrities like comedian Lily Tomlin, singer/songwriter Melissa Etheridge, singer/actor Lance Bass, and director Gus Van Sant as well as less publicly visible professionals like media executive Angela Courtin and publicist Howard Bragman. Thrasher notes that highlighting openly queer professionals who may work somewhat outside the spotlight is just as valuable as celebrating more recognizable on-screen performers. Referencing an entertainment attorney who received the award, Thrasher says, "I think it's tremendously important when we highlight and honor people like Jamie Mandelbaum, who's a regular guy with a regular job, and he's living a regular family life. He's not a jet-set celebrity. He's a named partner at his law firm. We forget that living 'out' is a big deal still." While the winners are publicized via POWER UP's website, which would be available to anyone who might care to look, the primary audience being educated by this event is the community of professionals and aspiring professionals in Hollywood, as they are the ones most likely to be connected to and hear about the event and the awards. By shining a light on the award recipients, POWER UP educates those in the industry and beyond about the contributions made by queer professionals working in entertainment, offering role models and positive examples for those who might not otherwise knowingly have contact with successful, out queer people.

Education for and about the Other may help remedy some of the harmful effects of social oppression, but as Kumashiro argues, antioppressive education can have a greater impact if it goes a step further to address the processes through which some groups are oppressed while others are privileged. Kumashiro's third and fourth categories, "education that is critical of privileging and othering" and "education that changes students and society," extend his first two categories to move from knowledge to action, and POWER UP's programs attempt to do the same. By publicly announcing their intent and the reason for their existence, POWER UP embeds a certain critique of privileging and Othering in all its programming. The POWER UP website announces the motivation for founding the organization, noting that "women have been, and remain, terribly underrepresented in all levels of the industry; lesbian content is the least financed entertainment product; and we can't forget that women have never been granted legal equal rights in this country."[30] With the very foundation of the group highlighting the inequities that define the media industries, POWER UP's programs challenge those inequities by offering a different model for producing media. And by highlighting the successes of women and gay men in entertainment, as well as giving aspiring filmmakers tools to create their own success, POWER UP takes a step toward changing the industry and, by extension, society. As more women and LGBTQ filmmakers move through POWER UP's programs, more of them will hopefully work their way into decision-making positions with the power to change the trajectory of the media-production industries. Modeling various forms of antioppressive education, POWER UP demonstrates how the ideals of critical pedagogy can be implemented beyond the traditional classroom and how film can be used to educate society in unexpected ways.

POWER UP's Short Films

In addition to supporting women and LGBTQ filmmakers behind the camera, POWER UP tells stories that depict images and experiences that are often ignored by the creators of popular media. By telling stories about queer people and their lives, the films produced by POWER UP make the imagined LGBTQ community more visible and, in a sense, more real for both those who identify as part of the community and those who do not. The short and feature films produced as part of POWER UP's mentorship program offer diverse images and stories of women and LGBTQ people, thereby challenging popular perceptions, educating audiences, and opening new possibilities for understanding the human experience.

Among the POWER UP short films that move away from mainstream representations to offer more diverse images of women and LGBTQ people are *Stuck* (2001), *Give or Take an Inch* (2003), *Chicken Night* (2001), *Intent* (2003), and *Starcrossed* (2005). *Stuck* focuses on an elderly lesbian couple that reaches a breaking point in their forty-five-year relationship. *Chicken Night* explores the relationship between a young girl and her pregnant single mother, examining the desires and dreams of two women at different stages in their lives, both trying to get by in their poor, rural, and largely isolated existence. In *Intent*, a female police officer tries to stop a serial killer who is targeting lesbian couples. *Give or Take an Inch* tells the story of a family in which a lesbian woman struggles to accept the plans of her sister, who has announced that she will be undergoing gender confirmation surgery. And *Starcrossed*, perhaps POWER UP's most controversial film, tells the story of two brothers who develop and explore a sexual attraction to one another. These and other films offer a wide range of images to demonstrate a richness and complexity rarely captured by mainstream representations of women and queer people. And unlike In the Life Media, which remained fairly conservative in its representational strategies in order to accommodate the expectations of public television, POWER UP's primary outlet of queer film festivals has allowed more freedom to include content that mainstream viewers might find objectionable.

Just by challenging the invisibility and stereotyping that have dominated representations of LGBTQ people over the years, the aforementioned films engage in a kind of counterstorytelling that seeks to disrupt the oppressive knowledge created and sustained by popular media over the years. A few of POWER UP's short films, however, take a more direct approach to counterstorytelling, revisiting very familiar (and typically heteronormative) narratives and genres and queering them, frequently by placing queer individuals in situations and locations where they have traditionally been invisible or vilified.

Billy's Dad Is a Fudge-Packer! (2004), for example, is a parody of 1950s educational films that challenges the normative stories told by such texts. *Billy's Dad* adopts the style of these earlier films (black-and-white images, upbeat music, a friendly but authoritative voice-over narrator) to tell the story of Billy, a young boy preparing for his school's career day and wanting to learn more about what his father does for a living. Actual sex-education films of this era generally avoid any references to homosexuality or gender nonconformity.[31] If such topics are mentioned, it is generally in order to offer warnings about what not to do. For example, the film *Boys Beware* (1961) urges boys to stay away from gay men, who are presented as predatory deviants who lurk in public bathrooms and under piers, waiting to assault unsuspecting young boys. In general, the knowledge imparted by these films is an oppressive form of knowledge, as it teaches only a narrow view of what is acceptable and either ignores or demonizes any behaviors that fall outside the norm.

As a way of mocking these films and their efforts to obscure the realities of human sexuality, *Billy's Dad* uses visual and verbal innuendo to inject queer sexualities into the outwardly heteronormative existence of Billy and his family. The film's title, referencing a slur used to denigrate gay men, actually refers to Billy's father's profession—he oversees the packing of fudge at the local candy factory. The title is just the first of many examples of suggestive wordplay that appear throughout the film. As Billy's dad tells his son about a typical workday, the narrator says, "As a head supervisor, Father has several men under him and likes to stay on top of things." When the grocer's wife, Betty, arrives with some items from the store and Billy's mom gives the woman a longing look, the narrator says, "She always knows just what Mother needs," and later says, "Betty is good at her job. She has a knack for fulfilling the needs of each and every housewife on the block." The film also uses visual innuendo, such as a shot of a factory worker kneeling to pick up a box of candies in front of Billy's dad, framed in such a way that the worker initially appears to be performing oral sex on his boss. Using humor to inject queer sexualities into a format that has traditionally avoided them, *Billy's Dad* calls attention to the ways that so-called educational films have oppressed nonnormative sexualities by making them invisible or presenting them as morally wrong.

Moving away from classroom films and into more popular entertainment, *D.E.B.S.* (2003) offers an unusual take on the espionage drama. The film mimics an episode of a television series, complete with a recap of previous episodes and an opening credit sequence that introduces the main characters. *D.E.B.S.* focuses on a group of young women, selected based on aptitudes revealed by a secret test hidden within the SAT and trained to be spies. Although they maintain their lives as students as a cover for their spy work, the film suggests that their talents are being wasted in high school, a subtle critique of the limitations placed on women by traditional (often oppressive) educational institutions. In this particular episode, one member of the group, Amy, has been abducted by a villain known as Lucy in the Sky, and the three remaining women in the group work to rescue her. What the group does not know is that Amy and Lucy are secretly lovers, and the abduction is an elaborate scheme to allow the two women to be together. When the D.E.B.S. "rescue" Amy but fail to capture Lucy, Amy says, "We'll get her again . . . next time," hinting that the relationship between the women will continue to develop.

With few exceptions over the years, espionage dramas in both film and television have traditionally been male dominated and heteronormative.[32] Women in spy stories often play the role of the helpless victim, the sidekick to the male hero, or the sexy villainess who is either converted or killed by the

FIGURE 3.1 *D.E.B.S.* (2003) introduces lesbian characters into the typically male-centered, heteronormative espionage genre. Frame enlargement.

story's hero.[33] Rather than leaving women to these secondary roles, *D.E.B.S.* places women in the central positions of heroic leads and primary villain. And although the D.E.B.S. go through a lot to rescue Amy, she is anything but a helpless victim, as she is shown to be in on the abduction plot. While many spy stories feature a heteronormative relationship to provide romantic tension and ultimate closure, *D.E.B.S.* foregrounds a lesbian relationship, placing lesbians at the center of a genre where they have traditionally been excluded. Meanwhile, heterosexual men, usually the drivers of this genre, are relegated to the roles of expendable henchmen, emphasizing the film's effort to rewrite the frequently exclusionary espionage narrative so as to open up possibilities for a more inclusive genre.

A narrative genre that has been very inclusive of women, but has limited them to narrowly defined, heteronormative roles, is the fairy tale.[34] *Little Black Boot* (2004) updates and queers the fairy tale by offering a retelling of *Cinderella* with a lesbian teenager in the central role. In *Little Black Boot*, Cindy is a young, somewhat butch lesbian whose stepmother and stepsisters are giving her grief about not attending her school's prom. After Cindy's friend Justin helps her dress up and comb her hair to look like a boy, she goes to the prom and shares a romantic dance and a kiss with a pretty girl named Laurie. When midnight strikes and Cindy remembers that she has to return her friend's father's car, she dashes away from the prom, leaving behind one of her boots. Laurie brings the boot to school on Monday, hoping to return it to the handsome stranger she danced with at the prom. When she discovers that it actually belongs to a young woman, Laurie is initially upset but ultimately realizes that she feels a genuine connection to Cindy. As classmates jeer and shout "Dyke!" the two women kiss again and then run off together, presumably to live "happily ever after."

Some of the earliest stories that young children are exposed to are fairy tales, and when those stories present limited versions of acceptable gender performance and romantic relationships, children can grow up to feel that their own identities are invalid. *Little Black Boot* offers viewers a chance to revisit the stories of their childhood and consider alternative scenarios where it is not just handsome princes who get the girl. Locating the story in a high school highlights the oppression that many queer teens experience in what should be an enlightening educational space.[35] As with all the short films produced by POWER UP, *Little Black Boot* engages in counterstorytelling as a way of challenging norms and offering new possibilities for women and LGBTQ people, pushing back against the limiting, normative, and oppressive educational narratives that have long dominated our society.

Itty Bitty Titty Committee

As the discussion of shorts demonstrates, the content of the films produced by POWER UP frequently reflects the ideals that the organization stands for. Nowhere is this more apparent than in its first feature film, *Itty Bitty Titty Committee*. The characters in the film engage in acts of education, counterstorytelling, community building, and activism, all of which parallel what POWER UP does in the process of producing its films. In this way, the film depicts within its diegesis much of what POWER UP accomplishes in the real world.

Itty Bitty Titty Committee tells the story of a young Latina lesbian named Anna (Melonie Diaz), who, after a chance encounter with a woman named Sadie (Nicole Vicius), is introduced to a group of young feminist activists who call themselves the C(I)A, which stands for Clits in Action. Initially seen as an outsider and greeted with some hostility, Anna overcomes social, political, and romantic missteps to ultimately find her place among the group of outspoken women.

One way that *Itty Bitty* parallels the work of POWER UP is through its focus on education. As with all of POWER UP's films, *Itty Bitty* was produced as part of the mentorship program, meaning that promising filmmakers were learning the ropes of filmmaking while the film was in production. Similarly, the film's storyline emphasizes Anna's education into feminism. Early scenes in the film present Anna as a young woman who is frustrated by her life but generally resigned to accepting many of the norms established by society. The first image after the opening credits shows Anna standing in a small pink room, wearing an ill-fitting dress, and looking at herself in the mirror, an expression of disappointment revealing how she feels about what she is seeing. Offscreen, Anna's mother shouts, "Anna, how are you doing?" and Anna reluctantly walks out of the small room and into the larger space of a bridal dress shop. When Anna's sister emerges from another fitting room wearing her wedding gown, Anna's mother rushes to her and gushes about how beautiful she looks, while Anna stands alone and looks down the front of her dress in frustration. As Anna drives back to work, she sees a billboard advertising a store called Bikini Dee's. The image on the billboard is a close-up of a woman's breasts in a bikini top. The sign is so large that the image of enormous breasts dwarfs a passing car that drives by underneath the sign. Anna eventually makes it back to her job in the office of a plastic surgeon who specializes in breast augmentation. Surrounded by reminders of socially acceptable body types and caught up in her family's celebration of heteronormative matrimony, Anna's frustration and isolation are compounded by a recent breakup with her girlfriend and a rejection by the only college to which she applied, leaving her searching for a new place to fit in.

When Anna catches Sadie spray painting the words "A woman is more than her parts" on the doors of the plastic surgery clinic and Anna does not immediately call the police, Sadie invites her to a C(I)A meeting. This is the beginning of Anna's education into feminism. At the meeting, she is introduced to the other members of the C(I)A, including their leader, Shulamith (Carly Pope), who explains to Anna that "the public arena is entirely dominated by phallocentric imagery, chauvinistic political leaders, [and] male fantasies of women," adding that "most women aren't even aware of how much it affects them." Sadie then shows Anna the C(I)A website and says, "The idea is to create a forum—a teaching space where women everywhere can learn how to fight the system." As Sadie's comment suggests, the C(I)A wants to educate all women, and within the narrative, Anna stands in for those women. She begins with very little understanding of the concerns that the group raises, and though she is willing to learn, she initially frustrates Shulamith with her lack of knowledge of women's issues and feminist history. She actively engages in an attempt to educate herself and eventually impresses Shulamith with her knowledge of the legal history of interracial marriage and its relationship to same-sex marriage. In addition to the personal and emotional growth that Anna undergoes during the course of the film, her education about laws, issues, and histories relevant to feminism are a crucial part of her character development.

Anna is, of course, not the only one being educated during the run of the film, as *Itty Bitty* also seeks to educate the audiences that watch it. As B. Ruby Rich points out, writer/director Jamie Babbit fills the film with references to important predecessors "as though she'd synthesized a mixtape of lesbian and feminist Greatest Hits into the shapes, politics, and subtexts of her screenplay in a bid to make once-powerful ideas live and breathe again."[36] Babbit has frequently described *Itty Bitty* as an homage to Lizzie Borden's landmark lesbian-feminist film *Born in Flames* (1983), which also features fed-up women seeking change through revolution. The leader of the C(I)A takes her name from Shulamith Firestone, an early leader in the radical feminist movement. The cast features supporting performances from Melanie Mayron and Guinevere Turner. Mayron starred in one of the earliest feminist independent feature films, *Girlfriends* (1978), while Turner starred in *Go Fish* (1994) and *The Watermelon Woman* (1996), two of the most prominent New Queer Cinema films directed by women. The soundtrack is filled with music from bands associated with the Riot Grrrl scene, a movement that used rock music, zines, clothing, and other forms of expression to aggressively update feminism for young women in the 1990s. As Rich argues, these and other references to earlier moments in lesbian culture and feminist activism are more than just playful allusions, as they offer "a history lesson and a call to arms, a guerrilla action keyed to audiences fed up with a status quo that seems to have left them behind long ago."[37]

Comments from the producers reveal that this aspect is very intentional. Lamenting the fact that many women and girls "have no idea that they still don't have equal rights," producer Lisa Thrasher compares *Itty Bitty* to a "Feminism 101 class." Producer Andrea Sperling concurs, saying, "I've always wanted the film to be an educational tool for young girls. What I really want to do is teach younger girls that it's OK to be political and to have a point of view and to be a feminist."[38] In this way, the film serves as an example of Kumashiro's "education for the Other," encouraging women of all sexual orientations to reexamine their status in society and to understand the history of feminist struggles. At the same time, for those who do not identify as women or queer, the film offers a kind of "education about the Other," offering a range of queer feminist characters who are rarely visible in mainstream media.

In addition to its focus on education, *Itty Bitty* parallels the work of POWER UP through the characters' use of counterstorytelling. In an attempt to spread their feminist messages and challenge society's patriarchal ideals, the members of C(I)A engage in a series of pranks that can be read as examples of culture jamming. The term *culture jamming* comes from the CB radio slang term *jamming*, which refers to the disruption of existing transmissions. As Christine Harold notes, the practice of culture jamming is a rhetorical strategy that "usually implies an interruption, a sabotage, hoax, prank, banditry, or blockage of what are seen as the monolithic power structures governing cultural life."[39] Culture jammers aim to interfere with society's dominant narratives by offering alternative stories and images, generating "contradictory rhetorical messages in an effort to engender a qualitative change."[40] Culture jamming is generally associated with challenges to and critiques of corporate practices and advertising techniques, but the pranks and hoaxes organized by the C(I)A use similar techniques to challenge messages and stories about women that circulate throughout society.

Soon after joining the C(I)A, Anna is invited to help the group with a prank involving the reimagining of a storefront window display on Rodeo Drive. Late at night, the group breaks into a women's clothing store and replaces the slender mannequins in the store's street-facing display with four sculptures that represent a more realistic range of actual women's bodies. To emphasize their point and challenge the messages sent by the constant use of stick-thin mannequins to display clothing, they paint a message on the window that says, "Women come in all shapes." Later in the film, the women create a statue made to represent African American scholar and activist Angela Davis. They leave the statue on the steps of City Hall with a sign that reads, "Angela Davis never got the props she deserves. Thank you Angela! Women like you changed the world." They also visit the Bikini Dee's billboard that Anna sees at the beginning of the film and place lettering across the model's cleavage that says, "Brains not boobs." For their biggest prank, during the climax of the film, the women take over the control room of a television station that is broadcasting a local talk show. The host and guests are discussing a celebration of the Washington Monument's 125th anniversary, and the C(I)A is angered by the attention being given to what they see as a symbol of male power when so many women's issues are being ignored. They throw the broadcast into chaos when they use special effects to deface and destroy the monument on live television.

FIGURE 3.2 *Itty Bitty Titty Committee* (2007) celebrates feminist activism in a variety of forms. Frame enlargement.

To drive home their point, they finish with an on-screen message that says, "This country has enough dicks."

All the pranks aim to challenge dominant narratives, including those that reduce the value of women to the shape of their bodies or the size of their breasts, those that erase or minimize the accomplishments of women of color, and those that celebrate phallocentric symbols of patriarchy. This entertaining and humorous approach to counterstorytelling echoes the more serious approach that POWER UP engages with in the production of *Itty Bitty* and all its films. *Itty Bitty*'s director, Jamie Babbit, points to the difficulties involved with making a lesbian film. She says, "I think the hardest part about getting a lesbian movie made is just kind of going against the system that's already in place. For me, it's also sexism on every level—it's sexism in the money world, it's sexism in the distribution world, [and] it's sexism in the publicity world, where no one really thinks about women or thinks about lesbians and where you can find them and how to market to them."[41] The challenges that Babbit points to are just part of the larger system that has led to the near invisibility of lesbians in mainstream media. Therefore, just by telling stories that focus on lesbian characters, POWER UP's counterstorytelling seeks to increase lesbian visibility on-screen. And by presenting a range of women with different physical attributes, behavioral characteristics, gender expressions, and sexual orientations, *Itty Bitty* challenges stereotypes of feminists as homely, bra-burning lesbians[42] and of queer women as "masculine man haters."[43]

A third way that the characters in *Itty Bitty* mirror the work of POWER UP is in their efforts to build and sustain a sense of community on multiple levels. Recognizing that their concerns are not those of individuals but of a large portion of society, the women involved with the C(I)A work collaboratively with one another to generate and disseminate their messages. In the process, they become a support system for one another, drawn together by shared goals and a passion for achieving those goals, ultimately functioning as a microcommunity of queer feminists. Not satisfied to interact just with their immediate personal contacts, the members of the C(I)A work to reach a virtual online community by posting photos and videos of their pranks and demonstrations online. Sadie tells Anna, "The idea is to inspire women all over the country to follow our lead," and the C(I)A's resident artist, Meat (Deak Evgenikos), explains that the C(I)A also posts the work of other groups that they admire. They realize that they are just one small part of a larger movement, and by connecting their work to the work of others with similar goals, they position themselves as part of the imagined nationwide LGBTQ community, with the ultimate goal of expanding and strengthening that community.

POWER UP also works to expand and strengthen LGBTQ communities, primarily by bringing them into the film and television industries, which have historically excluded and marginalized women and LGBTQ people. Media industries rely heavily on networking, in part because most jobs are relatively short term. Unlike many fields where individuals may work for years or even an entire career in a single job, film and television are defined by constant job searching. A group of people may be hired to produce a film, but once that film is completed, most members of the crew disperse and have to find other work. As a result, film and television workers are always looking for their next jobs, and they generally rely on professional networks to find those jobs. By pulling together women and queer filmmakers, some new to the industry and some with more experience, POWER UP helps link marginalized storytellers with the media industries, giving those filmmakers access to the networks that are vital to building a successful career. By training gays, lesbians, and allies to be professional storytellers (whether they ultimately work as writers, directors, or producers or in some other capacity) and connecting them to valuable professional networks, POWER UP aims to increase the number of queer voices telling stories in the media landscape. In this way, as Thrasher notes, the organization works to "empower a community by empowering talented individuals," with the hopes that those individuals will create counterstories that challenge misperceptions and educate audiences about women and the LGBTQ communities.

A fourth way that *Itty Bitty*'s content parallels the work of POWER UP is by visualizing and dramatizing activism, which is, in a less overt way, a significant component of all of POWER UP's programs. As previously discussed, the pranks and projects of the C(I)A are intended to educate and raise awareness about patriarchy, misogyny, and their effects on women and society. While recognizing their relatively small contribution to larger social issues (Sadie refers to the C(I)A as a "seed group" that will inspire others), the women are driven by their mission to bring about positive social change. They believe that playing by society's rules will not allow them to accomplish their goals and are therefore willing to break some laws in the name of progress.[44] Explaining their efforts to Anna, Shulamith says, "The only way to make you and people like you understand is to effect change. The most effective way to effect change is to step outside the system and tear it down." While the pranks of the C(I)A never quite amount to anything as revolutionary as tearing down the system, the women involved clearly find them to be inspiring and energizing, and they act as a kind of awakening for Anna. When their Angela Davis statue is referenced in a local paper, Shulamith expresses dissatisfaction, saying, "We need bigger media. Fuck this local bullshit; we need to go statewide." She clearly recognizes that small-scale change is an important first step, but it cannot be the last.

The aesthetics of the film help capture the energy and excitement of the C(I)A's activist efforts, framing them as fun and exciting. Soon after Anna joins the C(I)A, the film offers a montage of some of the group's pranks, including the aforementioned display of their Angela Davis statue and the defacing of the Bikini Dee's billboard. The montage is shot on Super 8 film, with some of the shots in color and others in black and white, giving it a grainy, amateur look. The shots are handheld—with a lot of pans, tilts, and canted angles—and the editing is rapid and includes a number of jump cuts. The movement and pacing raise the energy of the sequence, and the overall visual aesthetic gives the montage a guerrilla filmmaking quality that stands out from the more polished and steady 35-mm footage used in the rest of the film. The montage is accompanied by the song "FYR" by Le Tigre, one of the most well-known bands of the Riot Grrrl movement. Lyrics such as "Feminists we're calling you, please report to the front desk" emphasize the message that the C(I)A is trying to convey, while the punk-influenced music (driving drums and guitars, lyrics that are more shouted than sung) conveys a mix of energy and anger. Throughout the montage are shots of the women laughing and smiling as they carry out their pranks, emphasizing how fun and exciting their activism is. This makes such work seem appealing, as if the filmmakers are hoping to inspire viewers to engage in their own activist efforts.

The overall aesthetic of the film blends edgier, alternative styles like those used in the montage described previously with a more professional style that represents the dominant norms in Hollywood. This combination echoes the different approaches taken by activists. Some, like the C(I)A, aim to work outside the system to make change, while others, like POWER UP, find ways of working within the system to effect change from the inside. As a government-recognized nonprofit educational organization, POWER UP cannot officially present itself as an activist group. Members cannot lobby legislators or actively campaign for changes to laws or statutes, but their work is still activist in nature. Although POWER UP focuses on educational filmmaking programs, as its nonprofit status requires, films like *Itty Bitty* use counterstorytelling to change perceptions of LGBTQ communities and inspire people to take action to bring about positive social change. In this way, *Itty Bitty Titty Committee* is a film that not only depicts activism but also engages in it.

Public Service Announcements

While the shorts and features made by POWER UP encourage and enact subtle forms of activism, its PSA program offers a more overt approach, tackling controversial issues head-on. Most of the PSAs produced by POWER UP have dealt with the issue of marriage equality, specifically responding to California's Proposition 8, a 2008 ballot measure designed to amend the state constitution so as to define marriage as being between a man and a woman. This measure was proposed by opponents of same-sex marriage soon after the California Supreme Court's May 2008 decision that declared the state's previous ban on same-sex marriage unconstitutional and temporarily opened the door for same-sex couples to marry. During the time of the Prop 8 campaign, POWER UP partnered with Feminist Majority to produce some PSAs that featured celebrities, both gay and straight, speaking out in favor of marriage equality. Stacy Codikow encouraged the groups that were running the statewide marriage equality campaign to use these PSAs, but they declined, saying that they already had a campaign plan. As Thrasher notes, many people felt that "the [pro-same-sex marriage] organizations that took the lead on Prop 8 made some very poor decisions with how gay and lesbian families were portrayed in the media." Because the leaders of the campaign were worried that showing actual same-sex couples would scare away possible supporters, their primary campaign spot avoided any images of gay people and instead featured a heterosexual couple on their wedding day. In the video, the bride attempts to make it down the aisle but is tripped up by a variety of obstacles in her way, including a broken doorknob, parked cars blocking her path to the ceremony, and a woman's cane that causes her to trip and fall in the middle of the aisle. As the woman looks to her fiancé in frustration, on-screen text poses the question, "What if you couldn't marry the person you love?" and concludes with a message that says, "Support the freedom to marry." The marriage equality campaign ultimately failed, and Prop 8 successfully limited marriage rights to heterosexual couples only.

The absence of gay people in a campaign about gay rights upset many marriage equality supporters. Thrasher says, "Those of us in Los Angeles in the film community, especially those of us who are gay, were absolutely outraged by the commercial, outraged by the fact that . . . they didn't even reach out to the gay community that was in the film business to try and get our help, when if we had all come together, we could have done a lot better work." Immediately after Prop 8 passed, many organizations began strategizing ways to encourage support for marriage equality with the hopes of improving the outcome of any future campaigns or decisions that might come up. POWER UP decided to make a series of PSAs to contribute to the "Get to Know Us First" campaign, which was designed to reach out to potential allies who did not yet understand the importance of marriage equality. The PSAs feature same-sex couples going about their daily routines, living very unremarkable lives, and asking viewers to get to know them before deciding to take away their rights. The hope was that by presenting honest, accurate, and nonthreatening same-sex couples telling their own stories on-screen, the PSAs could win over viewers who did not have any personal relationships with LGBTQ people.

POWER UP's contributions to the "Get to Know Us First" campaign include five PSAs, each focusing on a particular same-sex couple. The couples include Diane and Robin, Duncan and John, Miguel and Ru, Sonia and Gina, and Xavier and Michael. Two of the five PSAs (Miguel and Ru, Sonia and

Gina) were produced in both English and Spanish in an attempt to reach a broader audience. With the tagline "Get to Know Us First," the overall campaign clearly announced its focus on raising awareness and increasing knowledge about LGBTQ people, another example of what Kumashiro describes as "education about the Other."[45] Many marriage equality campaigns across the country were driven by the belief that people are more likely to vote against LGBTQ rights if they do not know anyone who identifies as part of that group. While a televised PSA cannot create personal relationships, these spots aimed to at least present same-sex couples as relatable people that viewers might want to get to know, hopefully making it harder to discriminate against them. In an attempt to connect with as broad an audience as possible and demonstrate some of the diversity of the LGBTQ population, the spots include a range of couples of different genders, ages, and ethnicities. By allowing the couples to share pieces of their own stories in their own words, the PSAs exhibit a strategy similar to that of *In the Life*, putting a human face on a broader social issue in an attempt to win new allies and thereby strengthen the LGBTQ movements.

Working to educate viewers and connect them to queer communities as allies and supporters, the PSAs rely on strategic uses of counterstorytelling to challenge stereotypes, lies, and misinformation. Although thirty-second spots do not allow for the development of fully fleshed-out narratives, they can offer glimpses of larger stories and encourage viewers to fill in the gaps to paint the bigger picture. As an example, the "Xavier and Michael" spot opens with shots of a group of four young men/boys and an adult man playing basketball while another man and a young girl watch and cheer for the players. This is followed by shots of the same group of people gathered around a dinner table, saying grace and sharing what they are thankful for. In a series of quick shots, one man says, "Dear God, we just want to say thank you," a boy says, "I'm thankful that I passed my finals this semester," and another boy says, "I am thankful for my two dads." This is followed by shots of the two men, Michael and Xavier, sitting on a couch in front of a fireplace, speaking to an unseen interviewer and indirectly addressing the viewer. Michael says, "Twelve and a half years ago . . ." and Xavier interjects, "I had just adopted Manny." Michael then goes on to say, ". . . sitting in a church service and seeing this man speak on what it was like to be a father, and I thought to myself, 'That's my husband—that's him—that is him!'" As Michael speaks about fatherhood, the PSA offers cutaway shots of Xavier helping the young girl with her homework and of Michael braiding the girl's hair. After Michael finishes his last comment, there is a black screen with text that says, "Marriage promotes families. Support marriage equality," and includes the web address "GetToKnowUsFirst.org." The on-screen text is accompanied by voice-overs from the two men, each saying, "Get to know us first."

This PSA challenges a variety of misperceptions, as it uses carefully chosen images and comments to present the story of Michael and Xavier. One myth that the spot tries to change is the belief that queer people are incapable of forming and maintaining long-term relationships. This falsehood has been used as a way to support claims that gays and lesbians are abnormal and should not be treated the same as heterosexuals. In this PSA, when Michael references seeing Xavier for the first time—"Twelve and a half years ago"—and saying to himself, "That's my husband," it suggests that the couple has been together ever since, committed to one another for more than a decade. This emphasis on longevity and commitment runs throughout the series of PSAs. In the "Diane and Robin" spot, Robin says, "Thirty-five years ago, she came over to a birthday party we were having—I always had a crush on Diane." While it is not clear exactly how long the two have actually been a couple, the reference to thirty-five years shows that they have known each other for decades and implies that they have been together for a long time. In "Duncan and John," the couple sits on a couch holding hands and looking lovingly at each other. One of them says, "We met in college in 1991," and the other says, "Pretty much love at first sight." While these comments are taken from different shots at different angles, meaning that they could have come from disconnected moments in the conversation, they are cut together in such a way that the comment about "love at first sight" plays as a response to the statement about when they met and suggests that the two have been together since their first meeting, or roughly seventeen years. In "Sonia and Gina," one woman says, "Even after twelve years, I still admire her." Without directly stating that they have been in monogamous relationships for any specific length of time, all these comments are used to suggest long-term, committed relationships as a defining attribute for these couples. As a counterstorytelling strategy, these comments attempt to refute claims made by antigay leaders who have relied on and re-created a stereotype of gays as being inherently promiscuous.

"Xavier and Michael" also works to disprove the idea that same-sex marriage is in some way harmful to children and families. This is a claim that has been used over the years by antigay conservatives like Anita Bryant and John Briggs to justify discrimination against LGBTQ people, and proponents of Proposition 8 placed the issue front and center in their campaign. Many of the campaign spots opposing marriage equality focused on concerns that schools would educate children about same-sex marriage if the state legalized it. One such ad opens with the statement, "Opponents of Proposition 8 said gay marriage has nothing to do with schools. Then a public school took first-graders to a lesbian wedding, calling it a teachable moment." As the voice-over announcer makes these comments, the video shows a grainy, handheld shot of some people standing on the steps of what looks to be a government building, as suggested by the stone columns and arches visible in the shot. In an apparent reenactment of the wedding, most people cheer and wave as a couple appears at the top of the steps, but one girl turns away, looking somewhat sad and/or confused. The girl appears only briefly, and she is one of five children clearly visible in the shot, making it easy to miss her initially. But as the spot ends, the video clip returns. As the announcer says, "Children *will* be taught about gay marriage unless we vote yes on Proposition 8," a new version of the clip appears, this time zoomed in on the girl and played in slow motion to highlight her look of bewilderment. In this way, the spot presents the little girl as a victim who has been harmed by her brief encounter with same-sex marriage, sending a warning to concerned parents. The message here is clear: even a basic awareness of same-sex marriage will harm children, and they should only be taught about mainstream, heteronormative values—a clear example of what Kumashiro refers to as "oppressive knowledge." Drawing on the strategies of past antigay conservatives, this focus on protecting children from the perceived harms of same-sex marriage became a central component of the campaign in support of Prop 8.

"Xavier and Michael" rejects the idea that same-sex marriage harms children and instead offers a counterstory depicting children who have benefitted from the love and support of their same-sex parents. Aside from Xavier's comment about adopting Manny and one boy's dinner-table comment expressing gratitude for his two dads, the details of the family's relationships, such as who is biologically related and who is adopted, are not specified. The images instead depict two adults and five children/teens playing together, dining together, praying together, and discussing what they are thankful for. In other words, the PSA presents an image of a happy, loving, spiritual family where the children are thriving.

Other PSAs in the campaign also emphasize children and family. All of the spots feature a final screen with text that reads either "Marriage protects families" or "Marriage promotes families," along with the plea to "Support marriage equality." Duncan and John talk about how they "always wanted kids" and are shown playing with their adopted son, Watson, who one of the men describes as "pure joy." Miguel and Ru are shown caring for their three children (apparently triplets) and celebrating the kids' first birthday, surrounded by large numbers of friends and family members. Sonia and Gina's comments about their different parenting styles are paired with images of the family playing in the yard and opening gifts in front of a Christmas tree. In all cases, these PSAs offer targeted comments and images to suggest stories of happy, well-adjusted children who are thriving in the care of their same-sex parents.

In addition to the emphasis on diversity, long-term relationships, and the well-being of children, an overarching element that runs through all of the

PSAs is a clear attempt to present the couples and their families as extremely normal. The families and couples are shown playing games, having meals, celebrating birthdays, and spending time with friends as they talk about love and hope and family. The PSAs go to great lengths to demonstrate that their lives are not that different from the lives of heterosexual couples in the hopes of winning additional allies or at least convincing fence-sitters to learn more ("Get to know us first") before voting to take away people's rights. But as critics like Michael Warner argue, building a campaign on stories of typical, "normal" couples erases those LGBTQ people who might not fit, or want to fit, the mold of the typical couple or family. Warner calls this normalizing strategy a prime example of "antipolitical politics." He says, "The point of being normal is to blend, to have no visible difference and no conflict," which leads to a focus on those who can blend most easily.[46] The campaign thus reinforces an acceptable form of queerness, seeking equal treatment for those who perform the role appropriately but potentially further marginalizing those who fall outside the norms defined by the campaign.

Radical Acts of Storytelling

The shorts, features, and PSAs produced by POWER UP provide images and ideas not frequently seen in mainstream media content. As such, POWER UP, like all the organizations examined in this book, engages in the production of alternative media. John Downing, who argues that the word *alternative* is not strong enough and prefers the term *radical alternative media*, notes that all such forms of media "break somebody's rules, although rarely all of them in every respect."[47] POWER UP breaks many of the unwritten rules of Hollywood by telling stories by, for, and about women and queer people but still plays by some of the rules in an attempt to help filmmakers get access to the mainstream industry. The organization draws on community media traditions by providing groups who have traditionally been silenced an access point to media storytelling. And unlike most queer media organizations, POWER UP draws inspiration from lesbian-feminist filmmakers as they put women front and center both on-screen and off. B. Ruby Rich argues that *Itty Bitty Titty Committee* "has a clear mission to reclaim the specifically lesbian history that can be muffled in the category of queer,"[48] and the same can be said for the bulk of POWER UP's efforts. The spirit of these media traditions is amplified by POWER UP's incorporation of strategies from critical pedagogy, as they work to teach filmmakers and audiences to recognize, resist, and ultimately change the marginalized status of women and LGBTQ people in our society. Striving to remove some of the barriers that limit industry access, POWER UP helps build the capacity of women and queer filmmakers to tell their own stories by making their own films.

Politically, POWER UP's work offers a mix of strategies, sometimes embracing more liberationist tendencies, while other times leaning more toward assimilation. The PSAs embrace the assimilationist strategy that dominated the marriage equality campaign of which they were a part. Given the goal of getting mainstream voters to side with LGBTQ people, and given that the PSAs were essentially delivered into people's homes unrequested, a less-aggressive strategy was likely necessary. POWER UP's films, which are most likely to reach their audience by way of queer film festivals and on-demand home video outlets and therefore reach an already likeminded audience, can afford to be a bit edgier. The in-your-face lesbian feminism of *Itty Bitty Titty Committee*, the highly suggestive double entendres of *Billy's Dad Is a Fudge-Packer!*, and the taboo sexual relationship of *Starcrossed* demonstrate a willingness to tell queer stories without suppressing the differences that define LGBTQ people.

Recognizing that images and stories circulating in media and popular culture are a contributing factor in the oppression of women and queer people rather than just a reflection of that oppression, POWER UP creates alternative images and stories, actively changing the media landscape that has long supported the erasure and marginalization of women and queer people. Recognizing that a lack of diverse storytellers in the media industries contributes to inaccurate and incomplete representations, POWER UP works to change those industries from within, supporting women and LGBTQ filmmakers as they make their way into creative and decision-making positions in media production. By making changes to the media landscape and to the industries that create that landscape, POWER UP engages in activist storytelling, using education as a tool to effect positive social change for women and LGBTQ communities.

4

Connecting Diverse Communities through Film and Media Festivals

Three Dollar Bill Cinema

On a Friday evening in August 2016, I attended a screening of the sci-fi comedy *Codependent Lesbian Space Alien Seeks Same* (2011). The screening took place in Cal Anderson Park, a public park in the heart of the Capitol Hill neighborhood of Seattle, Washington. The event was part of an outdoor summer film series sponsored by Three Dollar Bill Cinema, a Seattle-based nonprofit arts organization. The film was projected onto a portable screen, creating a temporary outdoor theater space surrounded by ball fields, courts, and playgrounds—all nestled in a busy neighborhood filled with apartments, offices, shops, and restaurants. Some people brought lawn chairs or blankets and had picnics before the film, while others sat in the grass, munching on snacks from a vending table. Many had obviously planned to be there, but others seemed to stumble upon the event and then decided to stay. Still others looked on with curiosity as they passed through the park but chose not to stop. Some audience members clearly knew others at the screening, but many were strangers to one another. A handful brought pets with them, which often led to unanticipated interactions between owners. The crowd assembled for the screening represented a wide range of races, ethnicities, ages, gender identities, and socioeconomic circumstances. Across their differences, they united temporarily as an audience for the film, interacting with the images on-screen, with each other, and with their surroundings, embracing a very queer film in a very public space. In so doing, they turned the imagined LGBTQ community into something concrete and visible.

This chapter moves away from considering the production of queer media to examine the exhibition of film and video at LGBTQ film festivals and other similar events, using the programs of Three Dollar Bill Cinema as a case study. As a year-round organization that sponsors numerous annual events, Three Dollar Bill Cinema demonstrates the important role that festival organizers play within the larger landscape of mediated queer counterstorytelling. While production companies like In the Life Media and Professional Organization of Women in Entertainment Reaching Up (POWER UP) create content with the hopes that it will reach an audience, festival organizers like Three Dollar Bill Cinema essentially create and nurture an audience and then provide content for them. The organization does not just represent the queer experience on-screen; they generate new queer experiences by pulling together viewers for events that celebrate and strengthen LGBTQ communities, thereby creating intersections between representation and reality and demonstrating how media exhibition can be just as important as media production when it comes to advancing the LGBTQ movements.

Three Dollar Bill Cinema

The stated mission of Three Dollar Bill Cinema is "to strengthen, connect, and reflect diverse communities through queer film and media."[1] While the organization exists primarily to serve the LGBTQ population in Seattle and the surrounding region, their programming is designed to welcome all interested participants, including allies and potential allies. Executive director Jason Plourde notes that the organization works to welcome everyone to their programs, stressing that "there's a benefit in coming to the events, even if you don't identify as LGBT."[2] The organization was founded in 1995 to produce the first Seattle Lesbian and Gay Film Festival (SLGFF), which took place in October 1996. In the time leading up to the first film festival, the organization's members hosted single-night screenings, concerts, and club events to raise money for and generate interest in the festival. In the early years, the group was led by a board of directors that also took on all the staff roles, including programming, marketing, and outreach. Staff members were all volunteers, working part time to organize the festival, even as most had full-time jobs elsewhere. After a few years, the organization raised enough money that staff members were given stipends, and by 2001, they began having salaried positions for an executive director and festival director.

With the addition of salaried staff members who could dedicate more time to the organization, Three Dollar Bill Cinema started adding programs

FIGURE 4.1 Program from the first Seattle Lesbian and Gay Film Festival in 1996. Image courtesy of Three Dollar Bill Cinema. Program design by Skylar Fein.

beyond the original film festival, eventually developing a year-round slate of queer film and media events. The original festival, held annually in October, has grown to an eleven-day event spread over multiple venues around Seattle, making it one of the largest queer arts events in the Pacific Northwest. In 2016, organizers announced that the name of the festival would be changed from SLGFF to TWIST: Seattle Queer Film Festival, a name that they felt would better represent the diversity of films and filmmakers included in the festival. Translations, Seattle's transgender film festival, takes place each May. During the summer, the organization hosts a free outdoor film series in the city's Cal Anderson Park. It also sponsors a monthly event called Cineoke, a variation on karaoke that allows participants to sing along with favorite musical numbers from films. Reel Queer Youth, the subject of chapter 5, is Three Dollar Bill Cinema's weeklong media literacy and filmmaking program for LGBTQ identified youth. Three Dollar Bill Cinema also provides fiscal sponsorship for queer filmmakers and films with LGBTQ themes. The volume and breadth of programming have increased significantly over the years, but Three Dollar Bill Cinema's film festivals continue to be the organization's most popular and publicly visible events. My examination of these festivals, TWIST and Translations, is rooted in broader discussions of film festivals in general and of queer film festivals in particular.

Studying Film Festivals

Film festivals can serve many purposes, and they are designed to appeal to a variety of audiences. While some emphasize certain aesthetic styles or approaches, others are designed primarily to showcase films in search of distribution and therefore have a business-oriented agenda. Some are designed to draw tourists to a specific location, while others seek to provide a social event for residents of a particular city or neighborhood. Film festivals may be seasonal, aiming to highlight a particular holiday or coincide with a local or regional cultural event. Small campus film festivals highlight the work of students as budding filmmakers, while international film festivals like Cannes or Venice draw established filmmakers and celebrities from around the world. Film festivals are complex events, and to understand them fully, one must take a multifaceted approach to studying them. It helps to consider the functions, logistics, and economics of festivals, but it is also valuable to think about the meanings they generate and the messages they convey.

One way to examine film festivals is to consider their structures and functions, aiming to understand how they operate and where they fit into the domestic and international film industries. To help distinguish between festivals with different goals, Mark Peranson breaks them into two categories: business festivals (those that function as markets, where filmmakers are jockeying for distribution deals to get their films released more broadly) and audience festivals (where the focus is more on the immediate audience of that particular festival).[3] While these categories are somewhat fluid, and most festivals do not fit neatly into just one category, the distinction is helpful in that it highlights the driving forces behind various festivals and suggests different approaches to studying them.

Emphasizing the economic aspects of the business festivals that Peranson identifies, many studies consider them as an alternative distribution outlet to the mainstream channels that funnel blockbusters from Hollywood to suburban multiplex theaters. Marijke De Valck, Thomas Elsaesser, Dina Iordanova, and Ragan Rhyne have recognized that some of the world's larger festivals function not as isolated events but as a complex network or circuit through which filmmakers and distributors negotiate deals and channel films to appropriate audiences.[4] High-profile international festivals like Sundance, Cannes, Toronto, and Venice typically serve as launch pads for films seeking commercial success and critical attention around the world and therefore have a visible impact on the global film industry. While both TWIST and Translations are part of the established circuit of queer film festivals, and both of them do get to premiere new films each year, neither festival serves as a major launching pad for the sale and distribution of films. They are more in line with what Peranson refers to as "audience festivals," as they focus primarily on serving the LGBTQ communities of Seattle.[5]

The exploration of film festival economics is complemented by a consideration of the meanings that are generated by the content, organization, and promotion of those festivals. Julian Stringer, for example, examines the ways that festivals, by curating and presenting specific collections of films, create additional meanings that go beyond the individual texts included in the program. To explore this aspect, Stringer looks at festival programs, marketing, and public relations efforts to investigate "the rhetoric of film festivals—in other words, what the institutions concerned have to say about themselves, and what other people have to say about them."[6] Taking a different approach to understanding the meanings generated by festivals, Daniel Dayon offers an in-depth look at one particular event, examining the Sundance Film Festival as a kind of performance or ritual with rules, traditions, and social scripts that govern the interactions of all participants.[7] He considers the actions that filmmakers, audiences, and buyers go through during the festival and how all of their behaviors (performances) attach meaning to the individual films and the festival as a whole. Analyzing the discursive and performative elements of festivals allows Stringer and Dayon to show that the meaning generated by any given festival is always greater than the sum of its parts.

Frequently, the meanings generated by a film festival are carefully crafted with a particular sociopolitical goal in mind, which highlights a third aspect of film festivals to consider—their broader social and cultural significance. B. Ruby Rich argues that "no film festivals are truly non-political," given that they are always either reinforcing or challenging some kind of social norm, even if only subtly.[8] But many festivals openly announce their political and activist aims. Dina Iordanova and Leshu Torchin examine the potential for film festivals to function as a kind of activism, with Iordanova noting that activist festivals are "engaged in an effort to correct the record on a certain issue by highlighting lesser known aspects for the benefit of improved public understanding."[9] Festivals with an overt political agenda aim to draw attention to such issues as the environment, poverty, and world peace. Sonia Tascón looks specifically at human rights film festivals, demonstrating how they work to balance the tension between universality (rights for all humans) and the local flavor that gives any festival a unique identity.[10]

While festivals with overtly activist agendas tend to focus on specific issues, many other politically minded festivals are built on social identities such as race, nationality, gender, and sexuality. These festivals may not always announce any particular activist aims, but by providing an alternative to the mainstream media images that have silenced or marginalized large groups of people, they certainly point in this direction. As Skadi Loist, Ger Zielinski, and Ragan Rhyne have demonstrated, queer film festivals challenge norms simply by existing, and they have the potential to contribute to positive social change for queer populations.[11]

My examination of TWIST and Translations combines elements of the aforementioned approaches in that it provides details about the inner workings of the festivals in order to better understand how they generate and convey meanings and provide thoughts about the potential social impact of the festivals. After an overview of the evolution of queer film festivals around the world, I will turn to an examination of the festivals sponsored by Seattle's Three Dollar Bill Cinema.

Queer Film Festivals

While queer content has been a part of film since its beginning,[12] festivals dedicated entirely to queer stories and filmmakers are a more recent development. The first major festival of this kind took place in San Francisco in 1977, when a group of gay filmmakers organized themselves into a collective called Persistence of Vision and presented a series of short Super 8 films.[13] Within a few years, queer film festivals began appearing in cities across the United States and around the world. These early festivals were driven by filmmakers and activists who wanted to show accurate and positive images of gays and lesbians, which were otherwise missing from public movie screens. Chicago's first queer film festival was in 1981, Outfest in Los Angeles began in 1982, and in 1987, programmers first presented the London Lesbian and Gay Film Festival and MIX, which is New York's Lesbian and Gay Experimental Film Festival.[14] During the 1990s and beyond, queer film festivals emerged in large cities, small towns, and college campuses around the world.

The emphasis on social identity gives queer film festivals an inherent political agenda in that they are built on stories created by, for, and about a group of people that has traditionally been marginalized in our society. Some queer festivals aim to be overtly political, clearly announcing their desire to engage with the fight for LGBTQ rights, build strategic partnerships with other LGBTQ organizations, and raise awareness about queer issues.[15] Skadi Loist and Ger Zielinski have argued that the radical nature of queer film festivals has diminished over the years, as "later festivals have become part of a film industry or ecosystem specializing in LGBT film."[16] They go on to note that this has led to an increased focus on professionalization and industry acceptance and less focus on dissent and radicalism. But even those that do not espouse an overt political agenda engage with politics in more subtle ways. As Sonia Tascón points out, the earliest film festivals (mostly in Europe) were essentially aimed at subverting the global dominance of Hollywood film. As such, Tascón argues that film festivals in general have a history of being "places of organized unruliness," designed to shake up the system by providing alternatives to the norm.[17] By focusing on a marginalized social group and then giving that group voice and visibility, queer film festivals break many of the unwritten rules of mainstream cinema, drawing attention to social inequalities and the need to correct them. As such, queer film festivals will always be political, regardless of their intent.

Early queer festivals allowed people to see films that they otherwise would not have access to, given that queer films generally did not get wide distribution.[18] These festivals made a statement about the presence of gay people in society, in part by bringing individuals together in a place that made them visible—to each other and to the rest of the world. Queer film festivals became a way for members of queer communities to gather socially, providing an alternative to bars, clubs, and bathhouses. With the rise of home video and the internet and the partial mainstreaming of queer characters and perspectives in film and television, it has become easier to get access to queer content, but festivals have continued to serve a curatorial purpose, as programmers prescreen and evaluate the quality of films, ultimately selecting those that they feel will resonate with their anticipated audiences. Festivals also continue to provide an important social gathering space, connecting individuals in a way that is impossible for home video. And as Dina Iordanova points out, a public event carries more political weight than a series of films distributed online, "supplying legitimacy to what could otherwise still be seen as a marginalized cyberspace project."[19] Festivals draw communities together rather than enabling isolated media consumption.

To build on and encourage the interactive and social nature of film festivals, organizers frequently include additional activities and events beyond screenings. Parties and receptions expand the social dimension of festivals, while art exhibits, musical performances, and other cultural activities provide additional explorations of queer life. Milan's LGBT film festival, for example, has traditionally included book launches and writers' panels as a way of connecting visual and written culture.[20]

Ger Zielinski suggests that a festival fosters "a context, a space for conversations, discussions, and heated debates over issues that matter to its publics."[21] This is most clearly demonstrated when festivals continue the exploration of issues raised in selected films by including panel discussions as part of the festival schedule, inviting filmmakers, scholars, activists, and audience members to engage in conversations and debates. For example, the inaugural Appalachian Queer Film Festival in 2014 included two panel discussions—"A Parent's Journey to Acceptance: Raising an LGBTQ Child" and "Queer Film and Activism"—in support of their stated mission: "To bring queer films and filmmakers to the beautiful state of West Virginia, break down stereotypes and broaden minds in the Appalachian region."[22] These kinds of activities embrace the philosophies of critical pedagogy to help festivals become, as Leshu Torchin calls them, "sites of capacity building," which enhance the content of individual films to share knowledge about history, politics, and ways of making positive changes.[23] By extending activities beyond screenings, organizers increase the opportunities for festivals to bring people together, thereby generating and maintaining a sense of community while educating and inspiring viewers and increasing the visibility of the LGBTQ population.

Some festivals have generated standing organizations that engage in year-round work to offer programs that go well beyond the selection and presentation of films and their associated activities during the run of a festival. Outfest, which runs the Los Angeles LGBTQ Film Festival and the Fusion LGBTQ People of Color Film Festival, also hosts a series of programs under the heading "Outfest Forward." These programs—which include a screenwriting lab, workshops, symposia, and one-on-one meetings with industry professionals—are designed to help develop the next generation of filmmakers through education and mentoring. In 2005, Outfest partnered with the UCLA Film and Television Archive to create the Legacy Project, which preserves and archives moving-image media documenting the LGBTQ experience, including twenty-one seasons of television newsmagazine *In the Life* (see chapter 2). Frameline, the organization that grew out of the filmmakers collective Persistence of Vision, not only sponsors the San Francisco International LGBTQ Film Festival but also distributes films to other festivals and educational institutions, provides grants to emerging and established queer filmmakers, and runs the Generations Filmmaker Workshop, which brings together LGBTQ youth (ages fourteen to twenty-four) and elders (age fifty-five and up) to learn filmmaking and produce their own short films. The activities of these organizations extend their visibility beyond the runs of their respective festivals and carve out a more permanent presence within the cities in which they are located.

TWIST: Seattle Queer Film Festival

Like Outfest and Frameline, Seattle's Three Dollar Bill Cinema offers a wide variety of film-related programs, but the biggest event each year is the one around which the organization was initially built—the Seattle Lesbian and Gay Film Festival, now known as TWIST: Seattle Queer Film Festival. The

FIGURE 4.2 In 2016, the Seattle Lesbian and Gay Film Festival was renamed TWIST: Seattle Queer Film Festival. Image courtesy of Three Dollar Bill Cinema. Program design by Corianton Hale.

first festival was held in October 1996. In the early years, it was a small-scale event, with a handful of films being shown primarily at a neighborhood theater. Over the years, the festival has expanded and evolved in a variety of ways, growing from twenty screenings over seven days in 1996 to sixty-two screenings and nine receptions and parties over eleven days in 2016.

TWIST is coordinated by a festival director who oversees the curation and production of the festival, working with screening committee members (mostly volunteers) to select films for the festival and then assembling those films into a coherent program. Building on Three Dollar Bill Cinema's overall mission to "strengthen, connect, and reflect diverse communities through queer film and media," TWIST has its own goals. According to former festival director Keith Bacon (2013, 2016), the goals for the festival are "to engage, to entertain, to inform, and to evolve so that [it's] always relevant."[24] These goals speak to the festival's potential as an agent for social change. The first two goals, engaging and entertaining, are largely about drawing audience members to the screenings and other events. Once the audience members are there, the screenings have the potential to also inform viewers of relevant situations and circumstances that they might not be aware of, hopefully starting important conversations that continue beyond the festival and may ultimately shape social actions. The first step toward making any of this happen is programming the festival.

As with any film festival, there are various ways that films find their way into the lineup. The process, according to 2014–2015 festival director Kathleen Mullen, involves two possible paths. One path is if the film is pursued by the festival director. Programmers for any film festival will attend and/or keep up with other festivals on the circuit, and TWIST is no exception. Mullen notes that the festival director and the executive director of Three Dollar Bill Cinema attend festivals like Frameline, Outfest, or the Seattle International Film Festival, and if they see a film that they like or is popular with audiences, they then reach out to the filmmaker or their distributor to try to get the film included in the lineup for TWIST.[25]

TWIST also has an open-submission process that begins in late winter / early spring. Filmmakers from around the world are able to submit their films online using popular systems like Film Freeway and Withoutabox. In addition to collecting online submissions, these websites help the festival reach out to filmmakers. Withoutabox, for example, promotes the festival's call for submissions to the "over 350,000 active filmmakers and screenwriters" that are registered on the site, thus raising awareness for the festival within the global filmmaking community.[26] Submitted films go through one of two screening committees (one for features and one for short films), who comment on and score each film using a standardized one to five rating system, before identifying a short list of finalists to recommend to the festival director. The director then makes final decisions by considering the big picture of the overall festival. Describing the factors considered during the selection process, Plourde says, "We really think about what's going to be interesting and challenging and what's important for our audience to see—what has the most artistic merit."

Once films are chosen, they are organized into a coherent festival schedule. This is when the festival director makes curatorial decisions about how to order and arrange the films and other events so as to achieve the goals of the festival. There are many factors that shape the scheduling of films, from logistical needs to creative vision. Opening- and closing-night films and "centerpiece screenings" are generally scheduled first. According to Mullen, films that are expected to have a wide appeal and draw a large audience are more likely to be placed in these slots. These films are typically accompanied by catered receptions and often feature guests in attendance (actors, directors, or others associated with the films). These screenings therefore become higher-profile events than most screenings and are generally accompanied by slightly higher ticket prices. With the bigger events in place, programmers turn to certain routines or traditions that have developed for the festival over the years. For example, each year there is a "Girls Shorts" program, which is a collection of short films featuring and aimed at women. This is typically scheduled during the afternoon on the first Saturday of the festival. Similarly, there is a "Boys Shorts" program on the first Sunday of the festival. Keeping these programs in roughly the same slots each year allows regular festivalgoers to anticipate them, giving those programs a kind of built-in audience.

Some films are scheduled based on their anticipated fit within a particular time slot. For example, Mullen notes that a somewhat mainstream gay comedy will likely play well on a Friday or Saturday night when it can be worked into the audience's weekend social plans, while a serious documentary with an attached panel discussion is more likely to play on a Saturday or Sunday afternoon, when audiences have more time to participate in a discussion and reflect on the topic of the film. Mullen also notes that time slots within a given evening are also considered, as family dramas are more likely to be scheduled early in the evening, while more sexually explicit films are generally placed in late-night slots. Another factor influencing scheduling is the availability of guests. Keith Bacon notes that "if a director or a star is able to attend but they can only come on [a particular] day, then we'll try to accommodate them."

Beyond practical reasons, scheduling can also be an opportunity for creative expression on the part of the festival director. Describing her role as a programmer, Kathleen Mullen says, "Programming a film festival and the work I do is definitely a creative process because it's like a jigsaw puzzle. It's like somehow I'm putting all these pieces together, and I'm trying to figure out the audience and what's a good film and what is going to speak to people but also figuring out the themes and how to place them all together." Mullen notes that the festivals she organizes are recognizable as her work because she has developed somewhat of a signature style: "I have a stamp, definitely, and I would say that my stamp is that I have a reputation for having very diverse festivals . . . having films that speak to a variety of voices. I like the entertaining, I like the mainstream, but I also am known to bring in challenging work and work that is from other countries. It's important to me that there is a variety of work being screened, and I work very consciously to do that, and that's sort of my reputation as a film programmer."

Describing his time as festival director, Keith Bacon says, "I've created some shorts programs that are very much reflective of my personal taste . . . I've done a couple of horror-themed shorts programs. I started a program called 'Saturgay Morning Cartoons' that was a mix of new animated films along with vintage cartoons and toy and cereal commercials from the 1970s and 1980s—things that I grew up watching . . . that was a really popular program." Noting the importance of this creative outlet, Bacon goes on to say, "My favorite thing has traditionally been the shorts programs because that's where I actually get to create something. From the theme to the title to the running order of those shorts, I'm sort of creating—telling a story of my own with other people's work. . . . I want to make these happen because it really is hugely important for me to feel like I'm also flexing some creative muscles." Beyond simply collecting and sharing the stories of others, festival programmers weave together individual films in a way that creates a kind of festival-length metanarrative, offering a second level of storytelling to enhance the creative work of filmmakers.

Translations: Seattle's Transgender Film Festival

Translations was founded in 2006 as part of the Gender Odyssey Conference. Gender Odyssey is an annual event that provides workshops, discussions, and social events for transgender and gender nonconforming individuals, families of trans people, and service providers who work with trans and gender-variant clients. When conference organizers decided that they wanted to incorporate some film screenings into the event, they reached out to Three Dollar Bill Cinema, and the two groups coordinated a small festival as part of the conference. In 2009, organizers established the festival as a stand-alone event, which is how it remains today.

Films produced by transgender filmmakers and featuring stories about trans and gender-variant people have long been included in TWIST, but the history of the transgender movement provides indications as to why it makes sense to have a transgender film festival in addition to the broader festival that happens every fall. In the book *Transgender History* (2008), Susan Stryker offers a detailed discussion of the rise of the transgender rights movement and its relationship to other social movements. Stryker notes that in the first part of the twentieth century, homosexual desire and gender variance were more closely associated than they are today.[27] People generally failed to distinguish between sexual orientation and gender expression, conflating the two to assume that individuals whose gender expression deviated from binary norms must be homosexual and vice versa. As the homophile movement, led by such groups as the Mattachine Society and the Daughter of Bilitis, sought to raise awareness of gay and lesbian issues, advocates often emphasized the ability of gay men and women to perform their expected gender roles and in some ways distanced themselves from those whose gender expressions were a more direct challenge to the normative gender binary.

As gay liberation and the feminist movement (which had its own struggles between straight women and lesbians) gained momentum during the 1970s, they generally continued to exclude transgender people, who were seen as a potential hindrance to fights for equal rights. By the 1980s, as Stryker points out, transgender individuals were largely rejected by all points on the political spectrum, from radical lesbians to conservative politicians.[28] As a result, the transgender movement became more inwardly focused and worked to provide support within the community rather than reaching out. During this time, most transgender communities had small-scale, self-financed, and home-based organizations that rarely extended beyond a local or regional reach.[29] In the 1990s, as queer politics encouraged a breaking down of boundaries and a celebration of more fluid identities, trans and gender-variant people and their concerns were incorporated more fully into a coalitional LGBTQ movement. But despite this inclusion, the relationship has not always been an easy fit, given that the issues and concerns raised by same-sex romantic desire do not always line up with those raised by gender nonconformity. In other words, gays, lesbians, bisexuals, and transgender people may all be united by an opposition to the oppression of a hetero- and gender-normative culture, but the details of how that oppression plays out and how people resist it can vary significantly. As such, there is still a need for events that focus on the unique challenges faced by transgender and gender-variant people.

As with on-screen images of gays and lesbians, representations of transgender identities in mainstream media over the years have been problematic. The history of transgender images in film has been defined largely by invisibility, as such characters rarely appear in mainstream productions. When they do appear, the representations are frequently inaccurate, transphobic, or both. One of the most common ways that transgender imagery has appeared in Hollywood films is in cross-dressing comedies. As John Phillips discusses, these films generally feature characters who dress in drag in order to accomplish a particular goal. In *Some Like It Hot* (1959), for example, two men hiding from the mob disguise themselves as women in order get jobs in an all-female jazz band. And in *Tootsie* (1982), an out-of-work actor dresses as a woman to get a part on a soap opera. The characters in such films do not identify as transgender, and the audience knows that the cross-dressing behavior is motivated by something other than the individual's gender identity, thus creating the comedic premise for the films. As Phillips points out, films such as these use cisgender, heterosexual cross-dressers to indirectly poke fun at transgender people and effeminate gay men.[30] By the films' conclusions, the characters are able to return to their "normal" identities, bringing closure to the temporary disruption of gender norms.

Transgender identities have also frequently been associated with murderous villains in such films as *Psycho* (1960), *Dressed to Kill* (1980), and *The Silence of the Lambs* (1991). While narrative details in these films often make it clear that the characters do not identify as transgender, the films all feature murderers who in some way cross-dress and are therefore often perceived by viewers as being transgender. Phillips notes that as a result of this, "by association if not by definition, transgender is negatively coded, associated directly with castration, madness, murder, and monstrosity."[31] Even films that present more sympathetic treatments of transgender characters often end up focusing on terrible circumstances that cast them as tragic victims, as is the case in *Boys Don't Cry* (1999). There have been films that present well-rounded, nuanced representations of transgender characters that break away from the tropes of villains, victims, and comic relief, but they have been few and far between. And increasing awareness of transgender issues has led to a recent rise in more complex representations, as evidenced by such television programs as *Orange Is the New Black* (2013–present) and *Transparent* (2014–present) as well as such films as *Tangerine* (2015) and *The Danish Girl* (2015). But given the historical lack of such representations and the still relatively small number of contemporary images, Translations has been and continues to be an alternative source for complex, nuanced, and honest portrayals of transgender people and their stories.

The Translations festival is a much smaller event than TWIST, and while there are similarities in the organization of the two festivals, the small size and unique focus of Translations does introduce some differences. Like TWIST, Translations is led by a festival director who coordinates a screening committee and then makes final decisions about which films are programmed for the festival. While the overall quality of transgender films has been on the rise in recent years, Translations festival director Sam Berliner notes that one of the challenges he sometimes faces is being able to get the best films into the festival. Because premieres (world premiere, North American premiere, West Coast premiere) are an important part of a film's marketing campaign, and because Translations is a relatively small festival, some filmmakers decide to hold their films back with the hopes that they can premiere them at a larger festival, like Frameline in San Francisco or Outfest in Los Angeles, where they will achieve greater publicity and a bigger boost for the film. In these cases, Berliner notes, he often has to settle for bringing a big film the following year, after it has already had its big premieres.[32]

Films programmed in the festival tend to fall into two broad categories, which reflect the different audiences served by the event. Berliner says that when selecting films, he is most excited about those that fall into the category that he refers to as Trans New Wave. He says that these are films that work from the assumption that "the audience already has a Trans 101 in their back pocket." In other words, the audience understands the basics of the transgender experience—what it means to be trans or gender variant, what it might be like to come out or go through a physical transition, and so on. The films in this category, therefore, do not focus on gender variance as their main theme or storyline but instead incorporate transgender and gender-variant identities into stories about adventure, crime, love, family, or any other topic that might support an engaging narrative. Gender identity is not ignored, but it is included as part of the story rather than being the entire story.

While many films fall into this category and present images of fully developed people who are not defined solely by their gender identity, Berliner acknowledges the importance of programming some films that will reach out to audience members that do not yet have a broad base of knowledge about the experiences of transgender people. He notes that each year, the festival will include at least a few films that present a more traditional narrative (coming out, physically transitioning) but says that he still looks for films that present "the traditional narrative but with a slight spin." He offers as an example *A Self-Made Man* (Lori Petchers, 2013), a documentary about transgender youth advocate Tony Ferraiolo. In the film, Tony talks about his own experience—including showing baby pictures, discussing how he never felt right in his body, and undergoing hormone treatments—thus offering the educational piece that some audience members might need. But the bulk of the film focuses on his work with transgender youth and their families, moving the story from being about one person's gender identity to being about a person who has dedicated his life to making the world a better place.

Balancing the festival program so that it includes some "Trans 101" films along with the "Trans New Wave" films is not an easy task, but approaching the festival in this way allows it to reach the broadest possible audience, which is something that Berliner identifies as a key goal for the festival. While the "Trans 101" films serve a more pedagogical function for allies, potential allies, and those coming to terms with their own gender-variant identity, the films that lean more toward the "Trans New Wave" provide even greater validation for trans and gender-variant individuals, as they show the range of possibilities open to them and their lives.

According to Berliner, his primary personal goal for the festival is to create "beautiful moments or meaningful moments for the transgender [and] gender-variant communities and our allies." He notes that the hard work and stress that goes into the festival can at times be discouraging but that significant emotional moments make the work worthwhile. He relays a story of one such moment in which a woman that he read to be a transwoman approached him after a screening, struggling to speak through tears. As Berliner describes it, "She was saying how she had been living in a rural community for a long time and recently made it to Seattle and that this is beyond what she thought was possible in terms of representations and community support and acceptance." While most people take it for granted that they will see others like them on-screen when they watch films and television programs, the same cannot be said for trans and gender-variant people. Translations provides these individuals with an opportunity to see their identities and experiences reflected. This can be particularly powerful for those who might still be exploring or coming to terms with their gender identity, as film can help people "construct new conceptions of personhood,"[33] which sometimes includes a "change of sex/gender consciousness"[34] as they see something they have had trouble articulating about themselves.

In addition to making these kinds of emotional connections, Berliner identifies the telling of global stories as a secondary goal for the festival. He says, "We live so focused on where we live and on what we're doing—and especially with these kinds of stories, it's important to know what's happening in the rest of the world." By bringing together transgender and gender-variant people and their allies to see the stories of their communities and stories of people around the world, the festival creates opportunities for education, understanding, and creating valuable personal connections and experiences, making the abstract LGBTQ community a lived reality for those who participate.

Inclusive Programming for Diverse Audiences

The lineup of a festival may reflect the personal preferences of the festival director or the goals of the parent organization, but it is always also a public statement about queer media, queer communities, and queer experiences. Intentionally or unintentionally, the programming of a festival can serve a kind of agenda-setting function in that certain topics, themes, and images are selected for inclusion, and thus made visible, while others are excluded and made invisible. As Sonia Tascón notes, in the world of film festivals, "programming is a form of discursive gatekeeping."[35] The choices made by a festival's programmer establish the identity of the festival itself, but they also present a particular aggregate image of queer communities, reflected back to those communities and to a more general public. As Richard Fung says, "In the work that is selected and the way in which it is grouped and promoted, one not only represents but also produces specific instances and interpretations of queerness."[36] This production of queerness has the potential to create images that may be read as positive or negative, and programmers who show films share a certain burden with those who create the films. As Roya Rastegar argues, "It is not only filmmakers who must be accountable to the meaning their images make—organizers must also be responsible for the meaning they make through film festivals."[37] When it comes to shaping a public image of diverse queer communities, the act of programming the festival carries just as much weight as the production of individual films.

As festival programmers work to reflect the diversity of the LGBTQ population, they must first address the issue of inclusion. Early gay and lesbian film festivals generally cohered around the fact that they featured nonheterosexual stories and/or filmmakers, and because this was such a departure from mainstream cinema, this handling of same-sex desire was seen as enough to unify all members of the LGBTQ community into an audience. But as festivals grew and LGBTQ activism progressed, individuals and organizations became increasingly vocal about the need to recognize differences within the LGBTQ population rather than imagining it to be a coherent, homogenous group. Films about middle-class, white gay men, for example, did not necessarily reflect the experiences of lesbians of color, poor bisexual men, or transgender individuals. As Skadi Loist notes, many festivals responded to these shifts with name changes. Festivals that originally pitched themselves as "gay film festivals" expanded their names to become "gay and lesbian" or "LGBT" film festivals, and many of the most recently launched or renamed events, like TWIST, announce themselves as "queer" festivals.[38] While these shifts in nomenclature indicate recognition of the need for broad inclusion, fully incorporating diversity involves more than surface-level changes.

As Joshua Gamson notes in his study of the organization of film festivals in New York City in the late 1980s and early 1990s, "Any organization attempting to culturally represent such a diverse population faces the political challenge of inclusiveness ... it is extremely difficult to retain legitimacy as a lesbian and gay community organization without demonstrating a commitment to gender, racial, and ethnic diversity."[39] Gamson discusses the struggles that organizers of New York's New Festival and MIX festival faced as they tried to incorporate diversity into their lineup while also trying to strengthen ties between the LGBTQ community and the art film world. In some ways, the festivals were limited by what was available to them. Independent and experimental filmmaking of the era was dominated by white men, so finding work that reached beyond that group was difficult. Organizers of these festivals responded by incorporating more video work into their festivals, since video as a medium had a more diverse pool of producers than did film. They also actively assembled racially diverse programming committees and invited artists of color to act as guest curators to provide a wider range of voices in the process of selecting films.[40]

Other festivals have also struggled with representing the diversity of the community. For example, the perceived lack of diversity in the lineup of Outfest contributed to the creation in 2004 of a separate event called Fusion, envisioned as a film festival for queer people of color. And as Rastegar points out, this festival still faced criticism for the perceived assumption that lumping all queers of color together would create a unified program. As she notes, "Automatic coalition among people of color cannot be assumed, given the many differences that exist."[41] Others raised concerns about the fact that those in charge of programming the festival were not sufficiently connected to the segments of the community that they were setting out to represent or attract.

Even when festival organizers successfully find or attract a diverse array of filmmakers and subjects, they face a second issue—namely, the process of grouping and then advertising films in a way that appropriately highlights the diversity of the lineup. One approach is to group films together based on the ethnic or gender identities of those represented on-screen. For example, some festivals include programs of "Latino Shorts" or "Women of Color" films. This approach may help target particular niches within the larger audience, but it also assumes that festival attendees are primarily or only interested in seeing films about people who are "like them." Drawing on his experiences as a filmmaker and programmer, Richard Fung notes that sometimes, artists of color resent having their films filtered into such narrowly defined programs, in part based on concerns about a kind of "ghettoization" of the festival, where films by or about marginalized groups are further marginalized by being lumped together in one program and then being absent from the rest of the festival.[42]

An alternative approach is to create more mixed programs, grouping films by theme or topic rather than the identities of the individuals on-screen or behind the camera. For example, programmers might pull together a collection of short films that deal with family struggles, or films about sports, or films with overt messages about social activism. Within these collections, one could find films featuring people of varying social backgrounds and identities. This approach is one example of what Loist refers to as "queer programming strategies." She argues that such approaches are more in line with contemporary queer politics in that they help reflect and cultivate a "truly inclusive and diverse counterpublic."[43] Rather than splitting the LGBTQ community into its component parts and then further separating them based on racial and ethnic identities, a mixed-program approach encourages attendees to find the commonalities that unite them as people.

Organizers of TWIST and Translations incorporate diversity into their programs in support of Three Dollar Bill Cinema's stated mission to serve "diverse communities." Keith Bacon acknowledges the challenge involved with this, saying, "Within one large umbrella, there're a lot of very disparate elements, so it's a challenging job to bring all those together for one event, but with the festival, we have eleven days to do it." He goes on to note that "diversity in our programming is really important, and that's definitely something that we look at when we're looking for films—when we're building the schedule. We want to make sure that we are showing [not only] great films but also films that reflect all these different parts of the queer community." Sam Berliner notes that the selection process for Translations is driven by a desire to present high-quality content as well as the most diverse slate of films possible. Berliner says that he looks for films that represent all different kinds of diversity, including race, geography, age, culture, and "all the different kinds of genders that you can have . . . as many representations of gender as we can get." Jason Plourde points out that even if programmers are actively seeking a diverse slate of filmmakers and subject matter, there are limitations based on what is being generated by those who are producing films. He says, "We're working with the films that are available in that year. We sometimes get comments like, 'Why aren't you showing more films about black lesbians?' or some other group, and we say, 'Well, there wasn't a film made this year about that specific group.' But we do try and program so that people will find a film that is directly relevant to their experience, whether that is their ethnicity or their age or something else."

The lineup for TWIST 2016 reflected organizers' efforts to create a diverse and inclusive program, with films from countries around the world, including India, France, Austria, Sweden, Trinidad and Tobago, and South Korea. The festival lineup included documentaries on subjects such as a group of queer women of color performance artists (*The Revival: Women and the Word*), senior transgender women in the Pacific Northwest (*The Pearl*), the animal costume–wearing subculture known as "furries" (*Fursonas*), and Korea's first amateur gay chorus (*Weekends*). Scripted films told stories of young Indian women at a bachelorette party (*Angry Indian Goddesses*), girls who are temporarily turned into boys by a magical plant nectar (*Girls Lost*), murderous pornography producers (*King Cobra*), and a black lesbian filmmaker (the twentieth-anniversary screening of *The Watermelon Woman*). Through comedies, dramas, documentaries, and experimental pieces, the films in this festival presented a wide range of LGBTQ imagery, showing differences in race, ethnicity, class, sexual orientation, gender identity, ability, age, religion, and geography. Taken together, the festival as a whole sought to do what no single film can ever do—namely, capture much of the complexity and difference that defines the experiences of the LGBTQ communities.

When it comes to shorts programs, TWIST organizers use two approaches, presenting some programs that are likely to appeal to a particular subgroup of the larger community and others that will draw a broader audience. For example, both the 2015 and the 2016 festivals included "Boys Shorts," "Girls Shorts," and "Trans Shorts" programs, and the 2016 lineup included the shorts program "QTONE," which focused on queer people of color. While all screenings are open to anyone with a ticket, these programs did announce themselves as focusing on particular subgroups within the larger community, potentially contributing to the concerns that Fung and Loist raise about the "ghettoization" that such programs might encourage. However, these programs were balanced by the mixed programs that Loist calls for. The 2015 festival included a collection of films about queer performers in a program called "Movers and Shakers" as well as "Queer Out!," a collection of films about coming out. The 2016 festival included a collection of queer thrillers called "In the Dark" and a collection of dance-themed films called "5-6-7-8!" These programs, built on themes and issues rather than the identities of the characters on-screen, are more along the lines of the "queer programming strategies" that Loist encourages. They are more likely to bring together people who have shared interests and concerns that cross lines of race, gender, age, and other identity categories, thereby bringing diverse audiences into contact with the diversity on the screen.

Programming a diverse slate of films will not automatically attract a diverse group of spectators to all screenings, and to increase the likelihood of connecting the festival to a broad audience, organizers often partner with community copresenters. According to Plourde, festival organizers have "actively sought out organizations that serve specific niche groups that we can connect with programming in the festival. So if we're showing a film that's from China, we might connect with the Asian Counseling Service. We might connect films that deal with African Americans with the Langston Hughes Performing Arts Institute. When we do our programming, we're constantly thinking about which communities films will reflect and connect with." Describing how such a partnership might work, Bacon says, "We ask them to help get the word out . . . and then they'll come to the screening and say something to the audience beforehand and talk about who they are and what they do, because the people who are interested in this film are probably interested in this copresenter." The copresenting organization is given some free passes to the screening as well as a discount code that they can share with their members or clients, and they will often set up a table with printed literature about their own programs. By working with copresenters, festival planners make direct connections to other local organizations serving similar or overlapping portions of the population, providing many new audience members with an incentive to explore the festival and introducing attendees to services and opportunities available to them in Seattle and the surrounding region. Berliner describes the relationship between the festival and its copresenters as "symbiotic." He says, "We're getting more audience members . . . to see these films and be impacted, and on the flip side, their communities are getting the opportunity to see really cool things, and also they can reach more people about their organization."

As an example, Translations 2014 included a documentary called *Intersexion* (Grant Lahood, 2012), in which intersex individuals share their stories about navigating the gender binary. The copresenter for this film was Advocates for Informed Choice, an organization that advocates for "the legal and human rights of children born with intersex traits."[44] A representative from the organization led a discussion after the film to help audience members understand the relationship between transgender and intersex experiences and to discuss what the organization does and how they might be of help to those in need. In this way, the presence of a copresenter helped turn the screening into a more in-depth educational experience for audience members in search of support as well as those interested in offering support. These kinds of connections help transform the festival from an entertaining event into something that supports Three Dollar Bill Cinema's mission to "strengthen, connect, and reflect diverse communities through queer film and media." In the case of both festivals, the films represent the diversity of the imagined global queer community, and the copresenters help connect audience members to lived communities in and around Seattle.

Festival Time and Space

While individual media texts have the potential to circulate freely over long periods of time and to exist as sounds and images displayed in a range of locations, film festivals are events rooted in specific moments with clearly defined venues. As such, temporal and spatial issues become key components to consider in the examination of any film festival.

Janet Harbord notes that as film viewing practices have changed over the years due to home video and online media access, film festivals have maintained an institutionalized version of viewing where the time of projection remains a fixed, live event. She notes that the "choreography of a dance between the live event on one hand and the recorded, pre-fixed film on the other is the manufactured time of the festival. The alchemy resulting from these different temporalities, the now and the then, characterizes the potency of the film festival as event."[45] Thus festivals present a convergence of the past and present—and I would also argue the future in many cases—during the event that festivalgoers experience. These different temporalities can be seen coming together in many ways during both TWIST and Translations.

The year 2015 was a milestone for both festivals, as it marked the twentieth Lesbian and Gay Festival (the last before organizers changed the name to TWIST) and the tenth Translations festival. As one might expect, this led to many explicit acknowledgments of the histories of the festivals, visible in the programming decisions, statements from festival directors, and the promotional artwork used in printed programs, posters, and other materials. The artwork for Translations 2015, for example, features a series of ones and zeros assembled from individual lines and circles in a rainbow of colors. The overall use of ones and zeros suggests binary code, and the rainbow colors used the present the numbers point to the festival's concern with queering binary understandings of gender. Among the various lines and circles, a prominent one and zero are centered in the image and placed just above the Translations title, clearly referencing the number of years that the festival has been working to challenge binary thinking. The promotional artwork for the 2015 Lesbian and Gay Film Festival features the festival title surrounded by a bouquet of flowers that is dominated by daylilies, a traditional twentieth-anniversary flower.

While the artwork for the festivals may suggest a look back to the past, comments from festival organizers (included in printed programs) explicitly reference history as a way of introducing the new festivals. The first page of the program for the 2015 Translations festival features a letter from the festival director, Sam Berliner, which references the modest origins of the festival in 2006 before asking, "Who could have known that ten years later it would become the internationally recognized event it is today?" Similarly, the program for the 2015 SLGFF includes a statement from Three Dollar Bill executive director Jason Plourde, in which he notes that "a lot has changed in twenty years, and we will continue to evolve and grow." Both comments point to the many years' worth of development that led to the present festivals to make them what they are, asking audiences to reflect on this growth and change. Plourde's statement also encourages audiences to visit a small gallery of posters and ephemera collected during the organization's first two decades and notes that the juries of festival judges include the organization's founder and many other "folks that have helped create and lead our organization over the years."

Reflecting on the past does not end with the statements from organizers but instead carries over into the programming of the festivals. Translations's 2015 lineup includes a "Tenth-Anniversary Retrospective Shorts Program," described as a "dive into the archives" that features "our favorite short films from years past." The slate of films for the 2015 SLGFF includes a free screening of *The Celluloid Closet*, the landmark queer documentary also celebrating its twentieth anniversary, as well as "Thrive at Five: Know Your History," a

FIGURE 4.3 The program from the 2015 Translations Film Festival celebrates the festival's first decade of existence while referencing the binary understandings of gender that the festival seeks to challenge. Image courtesy of Three Dollar Bill Cinema. Program design by Corianton Hale.

series of five documentaries about queer history, all shown at five o'clock with tickets costing $5.

The references to the past are not typically as explicit and foregrounded as they are during milestone anniversary years, but the past is always a part of any festival. As Harbord notes, the live screening (present) of prerecorded films (past) already brings different temporalities together, but these festivals go beyond that. Given that both festivals are aligned with issues of social justice and the desire for progress and positive change for the LGBTQ communities, every year of the festivals' existence is an accomplishment and a testament to the increasing acceptance LGBTQ people have seen in recent decades. This progress is often made strikingly clear by way of films that depict past events, whether real or fictional. For example, films presented in recent festivals include the 2013 film *Test*, directed by Chris Mason Johnson, which is a drama about the members of a modern dance troupe dealing with the AIDS epidemic during the mid-1980s, and Robert Camina's 2015 film *Upstairs Inferno*, which documents the 1973 firebombing of a gay nightclub in New Orleans. For older viewers, these and other films serve as a reminder of more dangerous, less open times. For younger viewers, they serve as important LGBTQ history lessons that are unlikely to appear in textbooks. For all festivalgoers, they encourage reflection about the struggles that LGBTQ people have overcome in the ongoing journey toward equal rights and inclusion.

As films like these encourage festivalgoers to appreciate the positive changes that have led to the present moment in LGBTQ politics, other films encourage viewers not to rest on their laurels as we head toward the future. For example, the 2015 SLGFF included *Stories of Our Lives* (Jim Chuchu, 2014), a Kenyan film (banned in its country of origin) about the struggles that LGBTQ people face in that country, along with *The Pearl of Africa* (Jonny Von Wallström, 2015), a documentary about a transwoman struggling to live authentically in Uganda. Films like these serve as a reminder of the progress that still needs to be made, encouraging viewers to take a stand and speak out in favor of positive change. By bringing live audiences together for shared screenings, documenting and dramatizing history, and encouraging viewers to think about what lies ahead, TWIST and Translations make the past and future converge in the present. This dynamic temporality is a defining feature of these and other festivals, creating unique and fleeting experiences for audience members.

As the temporal aspects of the festivals situate them within the evolving history of the LGBTQ experience, the spatial elements of the festivals locate them within the physical, social, and cultural geography of Seattle and its surrounding region. The festivals both shape and are shaped by the environments in which they occur, ultimately helping establish a visible presence for the events and for the LGBTQ communities that they celebrate.

In its early years, SLGFF was a small-scale event, with a handful of films being shown primarily at the Harvard Exit Theater. This small, now-defunct neighborhood cinema was located in Capitol Hill, an area that has long been a hub for Seattle's queer population. This location rooted the festival in the heart of the community that it aimed to serve, but its small size and somewhat out-of-the-way location did little to bring visibility to the event. Over the years, as the festival expanded, it moved to various venues around the city, and in recent years, it has taken place primarily in three venues: two neighborhood cinemas (the Egyptian Theater and the Northwest Film Forum) and one multiplex (AMC Pacific Place). The more recently founded Translations festival has used a range of venues over the years, including the public library and spaces on college campuses, but its primary location has been the Northwest Film Forum.

The Egyptian Theater was built in 1915 as a Masonic temple, converted to a silent movie house in the 1920s, and amid various changes in ownership and management over the years, it established itself as a home for independent, foreign, and art films.[46] The Northwest Film Forum, which bills itself as "Seattle's premier film arts organization," is dedicated to both film production and film exhibition, offering training and financial support for local filmmakers and screenings of new and classic films.[47] Both of these venues are located in the Capitol Hill neighborhood, physically linking them to the large queer (and queer-friendly) population in the area as well as the generally artsy and progressive vibe that defines this section of Seattle. Both are located on busy streets in high-traffic areas, enhancing the visibility of the festivals, particularly by way of the marquees and other signage advertising the event as well as the crowds and lines that form on the street outside each venue just before the beginnings of more popular screenings.

The third commonly used venue for TWIST is the AMC Pacific Place Theater, which is located in Pacific Place Mall in Seattle's downtown commercial district. In addition to the theater, the mall contains a variety of upscale shopping options as well as a wide array of restaurants, attracting locals and tourists from all walks of life and functioning as a mainstream entertainment complex. Part of the national AMC chain, the theater itself houses eleven screens with stadium-style seating spread over two floors. The festival films are shown in two of the auditoriums, playing alongside more mainstream Hollywood fare. For example, in 2015, the festival entries shared the multiplex with such films as the Steven Spielberg / Tom Hanks Cold War thriller *Bridge of Spies*, Guillermo del Toro's gothic horror story *Crimson Peak*, and family-friendly Halloween films *Goosebumps* and *Hotel Transylvania 2*.

The festivals interact with these spaces in different ways, based in part on the functions of the spaces outside the run of the festivals. The festivals are, after all, limited to a few days out of the year, while the theaters operate year round. Locating the festivals in the Egyptian and the Northwest Film Forum—two venues known for their eclectic mix of nonmainstream fare—positions them as alternatives to mainstream media content. Holding some screenings at the AMC theaters moves in the opposite direction, suggesting that queer content need not be completely separated from the mainstream and that it can coexist with the dominant culture.

Moreover, the small theaters in the Capitol Hill neighborhood exist in what is already a relatively queer space. The large queer and queer-friendly population along with the high number of bars, restaurants, and shops catering to queer clientele create a space where deviating from larger societal norms is not so uncommon. The festivals draw on the existing queerness of the neighborhood, and their presence each year contributes to the maintenance of that queerness. As events, they provide public gathering spaces for the LGBTQ communities and their allies, ultimately reinforcing a public presence for queer people in the neighborhood. Rather than changing the space, the festival events in this part of the city strengthen the existing situation.

The TWIST screenings at the AMC theaters offer something different. By introducing overtly queer content into a generally heteronormative space, the festival helps—at least temporarily—queer the spaces of the theater complex, the mall, and the downtown commercial district. Playing the festival films alongside the theater's regularly programmed Hollywood films gives queer festivalgoers an opportunity to see their stories given equal weight and value as the more normative stories coming from major studios. At the same time, the queer films and the communities that they represent become more visible to those who might not otherwise see them, as anyone wandering the mall or coming to the theater could run across references to the festival. For example, the festival's poster is included in the gallery of "Now Playing" posters displayed outside the theater, drawing in potential viewers or at least making them aware of the event. Similarly, the information tables set up in the lobby are primarily to provide festivalgoers with brochures and other materials about sponsors, but the location of the tables near the shared concession stand make them visible to anyone in the vicinity, even if they did not originally set out to interact with queer media and resources.

While the festival takes some steps to introduce queerness into the mainstream theater, there are some limitations to the visibility and inclusion that the festival creates. For example, tickets for festival screenings are not sold through the theater's main box office. Rather, festival volunteers sell tickets at a table off to the side of the box office—hard for anyone walking through the area to miss, but still separated from "regular" offerings. Additionally, festival offerings are not included on the theater's website. The site lists show times and sells tickets for movies and special events (like live opera performances shown on a big screen), but there is no reference to the festival. While this is likely due to the need to keep festival and AMC bookkeeping separate, the end result is a partial erasure of the festival and its content. Although the event is not fully integrated into the theater or its typical operations, the festival's presence at the AMC theaters still marks a partial queering of a mainstream space, marking the presence of a concrete, lived queer community in downtown Seattle.

The Cultural Work of TWIST and Translations

Beyond being potentially enjoyable diversions for moviegoers, TWIST and Translations do a significant amount of cultural work that has broader implications for the larger LGBTQ movements, including supporting queer counterstorytelling, expanding the meanings generated by individual films, and educating viewers. First and foremost, they encourage, enable, and even improve queer counterstorytelling. By creating outlets for queer films to reach audiences, these festivals contribute to a larger circuit of queer film festivals around the country and around the world. Together, these festivals create demand for more films to be supplied by filmmakers. As B. Ruby Rich argues, "The queer festival circuit has become a production engine as well as an exhibition circuit, driving filmmakers to supply the endless material needed to fill its screens."[48] Similarly, Jason Plourde describes the festival circuit as an "incubator" that supports the development of queer cinema and then acts as "a springboard for it being shown in other places." Early festivals may have had trouble filling out their programs, but increased demand has led to a supply of films that exceeds the amount required to merely fill the screens, and now festival programmers are able to be more selective when organizing an event. This increased competition has generally led to better films (there are, of course, always exceptions), meaning that festivals have helped elevate not only the quantity of queer films being produced but also the quality.

The festivals continue to elevate the quality of queer storytelling by way of the participation of live audiences who are knowledgeable about and invested in the subjects and themes being portrayed. The festival audiences represent what Toni Cade Bambara refers to as the "authenticating audience," described by Rich as "the audience that can really call you out if you've got it wrong or applaud you because they know you got it right."[49] This feedback from festivalgoers encourages accurate, honest, and thoughtful storytelling, which is often a departure from mainstream representations of queer experiences. And for any aspiring filmmakers attending the festival, the increased quantity and quality of films, along with audience responses, inspires them to believe that their own stories will find an audience if those stories are creative, thought provoking, and well executed.

Queer storytelling at these festivals does not begin and end solely with the films. Instead, it spills over into panel discussions, postfilm Q&A sessions, and informal conversations in the lobby. The filmmakers and their films may anchor the storytelling that occurs during the festival, but members of the audience, including specially invited guests as well as regular ticket buyers, often have opportunities to share additional stories. Some of these may mirror and validate stories depicted on-screen, while others provide alternative perspectives to broaden discussions. Some shared stories may even provide the inspiration for future films.

Tied to the notion of storytelling, festivals do significant cultural work by generating and circulating meanings about the LGBTQ population. The individual films of course carry certain meanings that are negotiated between filmmakers and viewers, as would be the case with any media text, but the festival as an event works in many ways to modify the meanings conveyed by individual films. Much of this results from the decisions made by the festival director during the process of curating/programming the films for the festival. The organization of films—their placement and framing within the overall lineup—can activate and highlight certain elements that might not stand out when a film is viewed in isolation. This is particularly noticeable when short films are collected into a themed program. As an example, the film *Myrna the Monster* (Ian Samuels, 2015) mixes animation and live action to tell the story of an alien from the Moon who is struggling with the stress of dating, employment, and the typical challenges faced by young adults in contemporary society. This film played at the 2015 Tacoma Film Festival as part of a collection of shorts spotlighting some of the "25 New Faces of Independent Film" as identified by *Filmmaker* magazine. I saw the film at this screening, and while I felt for the ostracized main character and was amused by her run-in with a fully naked male adult-film star, I didn't read the film as explicitly queer. Three days later, the film played at SLGFF as part of a collection of animated shorts. In this context, the queer elements of the film stood out more, as the exclusion that Myrna experienced mirrored similar experiences depicted in the other films in the program. Unsurprisingly, the film's full-frontal male nudity also stood out more in the context of a queer film festival. As this example suggests, the meanings conveyed by an individual film are shaped by their inclusion within a festival. The curation and organization of films by festival directors can bring out and create meanings across multiple films, creating a whole that is larger than the sum of its parts.

Along with the organization and programming of individual films, contextual meaning is also created by the interplay between the films and the other events and interactions that surround them. Q&A sessions, panel discussions, receptions, and parties give filmmakers and audience members opportunities to think and talk more about the subjects displayed on-screen, and these additional discussions can extend, expand, and otherwise alter the meanings conveyed by individual films. For example, the 2014 SLGFF included a screening of *Out in the Night* (Blair Dorosh-Walther, 2014), a documentary about a group of African American lesbians who fought back after being harassed by a man in New York City and were then prosecuted for gang assault after being vilified by the news media. The film was followed by a panel discussion that included not only the film's director but also community advocates and activists who brought expertise about issues of race, class, and the law. The postfilm discussion started as a conversation about the filmmaking process and then shifted to focus on social structures that have led to institutionalized racism and homophobia in our criminal justice system and in news media. This conversation helped broaden the meanings of the film, shifting it from being the dramatic story of four women in a difficult situation to being just one example that serves as evidence of much larger problems in our society.

By supporting queer storytelling and circulating honest and accurate meanings about LGBTQ people, these festivals serve a critical pedagogical function as they engage in antioppressive education that helps liberate queer identities. This education is not just for allies and potential allies; it is also a valuable component for members of the LGBTQ communities.

One way that the festival educates viewers is through its regular presentation of aspects of queer history. Through documentaries and the occasional historical fiction, the festival reminds and/or informs viewers of the triumphs and struggles that have defined the LGBTQ experience leading up to the present. For example, *We Came to Sweat: The Legend of Starlite* (Kate Kunath and Sasha Wortzel, 2014) tells the story of New York's first black-owned gay bar and the recent attempts to protect it as a cultural landmark, and *Lesbiana: Parallel Revolution* (Myriam Fougère, 2012) documents the North American lesbian separatist movement of the 1970s and 1980s. As previously mentioned, films such as these serve to bring the past into the present during the festival, but more important, they make viewers aware of significant events and social movements that have long been omitted from history books and classes. They define a shared, if little-known, history that establishes a foundation for contemporary struggles to achieve equality.

In addition to educating audience members about history, the festivals introduce them to a variety of perspectives and experiences that may be different from their own. This is as valuable within the LGBTQ communities as it is for those who do not identify with these communities. The experiences of a white lesbian woman will differ from those of a gay man of color, which will differ from those of a teenager exploring their gender-fluid identity. And the experiences of those living in different states, different regions, and different countries will vary based on the laws, customs, and social norms of any given location. Programming films that capture a wide variety of experiences allow these festivals to educate both LGBTQ and straight, cisgender people about the similarities and differences that unite and divide queer communities, encouraging them to understand where they fit into the big picture.

Of course, the lineup of the festivals does not guarantee that all viewers will leave an event more educated than when they arrived. Festivalgoers can pick and choose which films to see during the course of the festival, and their exposure to history or cultural perspectives other than their own will depend on the number and breadth of the films selected. The diverse programs for these festivals therefore provide the potential for antioppressive education—and then it is up to viewers to complete the process.

Making LGBTQ Communities Real

TWIST and Translations present diverse and affirming images of LGBTQ people through storytelling and other forms of meaning making, offering empowerment and education to queer people, their allies, and potential allies. They draw diverse audiences together in a shared time and space, and they make connections between audience members and local organizations and services. In all these ways, the festivals accomplish something very important: they make imagined queer communities concrete and visible, which helps provide an important foundation for local and regional efforts to bring about positive social change through advocacy and activism. As discussed in chapter 1, the concept of a queer community (or communities) is based on the belief that particular shared experiences or identities will create bonds of understanding that will unite people into a community. But without actually knowing one another or interacting face-to-face, such a community is largely imagined and exists only in an abstract way. Concrete, lived queer communities can provide valuable support, access to social services, and the infrastructure for activist organizing.[50] Such communities do exist in many cities and towns, but as some critics have pointed out, these physical communities—often referred to as "gayborhoods"—are shrinking and thinning. Many LGBTQ people are finding that they can no longer afford such neighborhoods (like Seattle's Capitol Hill) as gentrification pushes costs upward, while others are choosing to disperse into more mixed neighborhoods rather than gathering with other queer folks.[51] Like other queer film festivals, TWIST and Translations bring individuals together so they can meet, interact, and share the experience of viewing a film as a lived, concrete, physically copresent group of people. The dispersed community comes back together and the imagined community becomes real, even if only for a short period of time.

The screening of *Codependent Lesbian Space Alien Seeks Same* described at the beginning of this chapter offers one example of this phenomenon, and I experienced a similar sense of community at a screening of *Reel in the Closet*

(Stu Maddox, 2015), a documentary that assembles clips of home movies and other found footage collected from basements, attics, closets, and archives. The clips provide candid, usually amateur glimpses of the real lives of queer people throughout the twentieth century. As I watched the film, I felt surprisingly connected to the rest of the audience (essentially a group of strangers), as if we were all rediscovering some hidden history together. Throughout the film, audience members booed and hissed at clips of antigay figures like Anita Bryant and Fred Phelps and reacted to other images with laughter, sighs, gasps, and spontaneous applause, suggesting that their emotional responses were as strong as mine. For about ninety minutes, the Seattle queer community (as represented by those in the auditorium) became real to me in a way that it never had before, and I felt a sense of validation and strength. My experience is, of course, a single anecdote that does not represent the experiences of all viewers at all screenings. But it does indicate how the social interaction and physical copresence of the festival create meanings that go well beyond the films themselves, connecting people through moments in a shared space and time.

While my experience points to the emotional aspects of realizing an imagined community, there is also a financial side to it. Bringing large groups of people together for a public event makes those people, and the abstract community that they represent, visible to potential sponsors that might support the event. In 2016, sponsors supporting TWIST and Translations ranged from local organizations and companies like the Seattle Counseling Service and Purr Cocktail Lounge to large regional and global companies like CenturyLink, Alaska Airlines, and Xfinity/Comcast. Given that just a couple decades ago, most companies were not willing to be associated with queer communities and events, the mere involvement of these companies might be seen as a victory for queer acceptance and progress in our society. But as many cultural critics have pointed out, a company's willingness to court queer consumers, whether through targeted advertisements or named sponsorship of an event, does not automatically equate to full support of equality.[52] While some companies may, in fact, have excellent track records with respect to diversity and equality, others may be solely interested in attracting more customers to build their bottom line.

But even if some companies are primarily interested in their own profits, the more important point here is that the sponsors allow the festivals to happen. Regardless of the motivation behind their support, without the participation of large and small businesses, the festivals would not be able to pay their staff, purchase supplies, pay screening fees, and so on. As a result, the beneficial aspects of the festivals—including support for storytelling, educational experiences, and community connections—would not happen. So by making the abstract community visible (as an audience and a market), the festivals encourage sponsors to support these and other events, thus allowing the events to strengthen the communities and continue the cycle.

By presenting diverse and affirmative images of LGBTQ people and bringing audiences together for screenings, discussions, and social interaction, Three Dollar Bill Cinema offers an emotionally empowering experience for queer people, brings together individuals and connects them into a concrete and supportive community, and provides educational opportunities for queer individuals, their allies, and potential allies. All this helps build an important foundation for local and regional efforts to bring about positive social change through advocacy and activism.

When TWIST started as SLGFF in 1996, images of LGBTQ people in mainstream media were quite rare, so a film festival was one of the only ways that queer audiences could see themselves on-screen. While queer visibility has grown significantly in the last two decades and there has been great progress toward equality and social justice, there is still much to be done, as highlighted by recent legislation around "religious freedom" and bathroom access. In order to keep pushing for full equality and justice, queer communities need to remain active, energized, and publicly visible. Queer film festivals and events like those presented by Three Dollar Bill Cinema play an important role in "strengthening, connecting, and reflecting" vibrant and diverse trans and queer communities, supporting them in their ongoing fight for social justice.

5

Developing the Next Generation of Storytellers

Reel Queer Youth

In the short film *Out Again* (2014), a teenager named Sam is struggling with his bisexual orientation. After learning that a classmate, Jordan, recently attended a local LGBTQ pride event, Sam sees an opportunity to connect with him by coming out about his own sexuality. He says to Jordan, "I was actually thinking of going to pride 'cause . . . umm . . . I . . . I . . . I have, uh, gay uncles." Jordan responds with an awkward "Good to know . . ." before walking off to his class. Sam, clearly frustrated by his failure to say what was really on his mind, turns to his locker and bonks his head on it. Seconds later, Jordan approaches Sam again as if the previous conversation never took place. After looking at the clock, Sam realizes that he has somehow traveled back in time by a few minutes. He eventually discovers that hitting his head on the locker allows him to rewind time, and he decides to use this newfound ability to make another attempt at coming out to Jordan. His second try does not go much better, as he stumbles over his words and nervously announces that he has "bicurious parents." After a few more failed attempts, he finally manages to tell Jordan that he is bisexual. Jordan responds positively, and the two make plans to meet for coffee after school.

Out Again was produced by participants in Reel Queer Youth, a filmmaking workshop sponsored by Seattle's Three Dollar Bill Cinema. Over the course of one week, LGBTQ youth and allies learn the basics of filmmaking and media literacy, generate ideas and write scripts, and then work in small groups with adult mentors to produce short films. *Out Again* captures the spirit and reflects the values of Reel Queer Youth in many ways. The main character, Sam, struggles to find his voice and explores various ways of expressing himself as he seeks to make a connection with someone else who falls outside the heteronormative boundaries established by society. Similarly, Reel Queer Youth encourages participants to find their voices and figure out what they want to say about the world around them. The program then gives participants media production skills that enable them to make their voices heard. Along the way, the youth are welcomed into a creative community of filmmakers and introduced to peers and mentors who share the experience of being marginalized by a heteronormative society.

This chapter examines Reel Queer Youth to consider its potential impact as an agent of positive social change for the LGBTQ population. The discussion is based on interviews with workshop staff and participants, observations of workshops and public screenings, and analyses of some of the films created by participants. While in previous chapters I have focused on professional storytellers, here I examine storytellers in training. Placing Reel Queer Youth within the contexts of media literacy programs and mainstream representations of queer youth, I consider storytelling and community formation to show how Reel Queer Youth prepares participants to become actively engaged citizens who can improve the world around them. Ultimately, I argue that Reel Queer Youth demonstrates how critical media literacy training with a focus on production can help young people find and use their voices, thereby empowering previously disempowered individuals to become the queer storytellers of the future.

Reel Queer Youth and Critical Media Literacy

Reel Queer Youth is an offshoot of Reel Grrls, which is a year-round media training program where girls and young women between the ages of nine and twenty-one acquire production skills through hands-on workshops and classes taught by female media professionals and educators.[1] Mentors from the Reel Grrls program had the idea to create a similar program for queer youth of all genders. The planning of the program was taken on by Three Dollar Bill Cinema, with Reel Grrls supporting the endeavor by providing work space and equipment such as cameras, light kits, and computers. In 2015, after getting a financial boost from its annual fundraising gala, Three Dollar Bill Cinema was able to acquire the resources to run the entire program on its own.

Reel Queer Youth participants, who are selected through an application process, are between the ages of thirteen and twenty and either self-identify as queer or transgender or consider themselves LGBTQ allies. The groups that

I observed included middle school and high school students of varying racial and ethnic backgrounds, gender identities, and sexual orientations. Organizers do what they can to make the program available to participants from all socioeconomic backgrounds by relying on a "pay what you can" tuition policy. Participants pay between $0 and $295, with donors making up the balance if necessary. Like the participants, the mentors in the program represent a broad range of demographics and come from a variety of backgrounds. According to Reel Queer Youth program manager Danny Tayara, mentors are screened through an interview process and selected based on filmmaking experience and skills, communication style, sensitivity to LGBTQ issues, and experience working with youth. Tayara also works to recruit a group of mentors that will represent a diverse mix of sexual and gender identities as well as ethnic backgrounds. While some mentors work professionally in media production, others are teachers or students, and some just have an interest in working with LGBTQ youth.[2]

The program is structured as an intensive introduction to the basics of filmmaking, with two days set aside for introducing and discussing concepts and techniques and three to five days reserved for production and postproduction of the participants' short films. An early workshop session features a discussion to get the participants thinking about the power and influence of media, particularly when it comes to representations of gender and sexuality. Although this is the only portion of the workshop explicitly labeled by organizers as media literacy, it lays the foundation for the productive/creative

FIGURE 5.1 Reel Queer Youth participants learn how to write, shoot, and edit short films and are mentored by experienced filmmakers. Photo by the author.

forms of literacy training still to come. Additional early sessions in the program include discussions of narrative structure and an introduction to some of the visual techniques used to bring a story to life. Armed with an understanding of the impact of media imagery and a working knowledge of storytelling, participants are asked to return on the second day with an idea for a short film. The second day includes some more workshops about the nuts and bolts of production, but most of the day is dedicated to sharing the story ideas generated by participants, selecting which ideas will be produced as films, and then developing those ideas in preproduction so as to get them ready for the production days that follow.

The content of the films produced by participants varies from year to year and group to group. When participants are notified of their acceptance into the program, they are given some storytelling prompts to get them thinking about stories that they might like to tell. Working from the program's tagline, "Make the film you want to see," Tayara says that participants are encouraged to explore any topic and any style that interests them. Given the nature of the program, its participants, and the early discussions about mainstream media representations, it is not surprising that many of the projects tend to explore similar themes. On the second day of each workshop that I observed (2014, 2015, 2017), all participants shared their ideas for films that they would like to make. The majority of the ideas pitched to the group examined issues of gender identity and/or sexual orientation in some way. After discussing all the ideas that were pitched, the participants chose a small number of ideas to develop into films, and almost all of those tackled gender and sexuality head-on. The fifteen completed films from 2014–2017 include six that deal with the coming out process and/or discovering and adapting to one's sexual identity and six that deal with transgender and gender-variant identities.

The week ends with a "friends and family" screening. This event provides an opportunity for the participants and mentors to show off their achievements from the week, celebrate their successes, and say their good-byes. Parents of the participants see their children as part of a group of peers, which for some of the youth might be a rare occurrence. The event is held at a local cinema, giving participants a chance to see their films on the big screen and get immediate feedback and responses from an audience. After the formal conclusion of the week-long workshop, the films continue to circulate, as all of them are played during TWIST: Seattle Queer Film Festival, and they are entered into other festivals around the world. In this way, even after the conclusion of the workshop, its output continues to circulate and have an impact, just as the experience will continue to have an impact on its participants.

Reel Queer Youth is just one recent addition to a long history of media education programs. Since the rise of mediated popular culture in the early twentieth century, parents, educators, and policy makers have had concerns about youth media consumption. These concerns led to the development of varying forms of media education programs over the years. During the 1990s, schools and communities across the United States embraced an approach to media education that aimed to develop media literacy in young people by teaching them how to analyze media content. On the surface, these popular programs seemed like a great way to educate youth about the impact of media in their lives. But critics of these analysis-only media literacy programs have noted a number of shortcomings. Mary Celeste Kearney, for example, points out that such programs were rooted in socially conservative, middle-class beliefs.[3] They valued high culture over popular culture and aimed to protect children from the sex, violence, and consumerism that seemed all too common in popular media. As David Buckingham argues, this approach was based on "a notion of the media as an enormously powerful (and almost entirely negative) influence, and of children as particularly vulnerable."[4] He goes on to note that such programs consistently cast youth as seriously at risk and unable to resist the power of media, while teachers are seen as being able to stand objectively outside the process.[5] In this scenario, media literacy (as taught by adults) was pitched as something that could protect impressionable youth from harmful media, and it rarely acknowledged the potential for youth to use media to actively respond to and engage with the culture around them.

Reel Queer Youth and many other contemporary media education programs have taken on a more student-centered perspective, respecting youth as intelligent, engaged, and media savvy. This approach recognizes that youth acquire a great deal of knowledge about media on their own, and it values that knowledge as a foundation for further learning.[6] Buckingham notes that this approach views media education "not as a form of *protection*, but as a form or *preparation*."[7] Such programs aim to prepare students to both interpret and participate in the media culture that surrounds them. This leads to the logical conclusion that media production should be incorporated into media literacy training, enabling students to become critical media viewers and critical media producers.[8] After all, in order to be fully literate, one must be able to not only observe and interpret media but also generate alternative media content as a way of responding to and engaging with more mainstream content.

Advocates of production-oriented literacy programs argue that such an approach goes well beyond the attempted protection offered by more traditional programs, preparing students to be active and engaged citizens who can use media to challenge social injustice. Steven Goodman, for example, is the founder of New York's Educational Video Center (EVC), an organization "dedicated to teaching documentary video as a means to develop the artistic, critical literacy, and career skills of young people, while nurturing their idealism and commitment to social change."[9] Goodman says that critical media literacy—including the ability to analyze, evaluate, and produce media—"is

FIGURE 5.2 Reel Queer Youth encourages media literacy by teaching participants how to create media content in addition to interpreting it. Photo by the author.

a prerequisite for self-representation and autonomous citizenship."[10] And Kearney argues that "training in the tools and practices of media production is intrinsic to developing media-literate and critically conscious students whose participation in democratic communication can help to transform media culture."[11] Production-oriented media literacy programs have a value for any youth, but as Goodman points out, youth who are members of groups that are marginalized by mainstream media and culture have even more to gain from such training, as it can give them the tools necessary to speak out against the oppressions of society.[12] Video Machete, for example, was founded with the goal of encouraging the largely Chicano youth population of a Chicago neighborhood to use video as a tool for "sustained involvement in social change."[13] And the Healthy Youth Peer Education (HYPE) program uses digital media to encourage the civic engagement of African American, Latino, and other marginalized youth in Allentown, Pennsylvania.[14]

Reel Queer Youth is another example of a production-oriented critical media literacy program aimed at members of a marginalized community—in this case, the LGBTQ population. According to Tayara, one of the goals of the program is "to teach filmmaking and give people a starting point for potentially a bigger career in filmmaking." As a former Reel Queer Youth participant, Tayara is one example of someone who followed this path. "Without

Reel Queer Youth, I probably wouldn't be doing film," says Tayara. "I'd be in a very different place right now." After participating in Reel Queer Youth, Tayara served as a mentor, a film festival judge, and the programming coordinator for Three Dollar Bill Cinema before taking over leadership of Reel Queer Youth and eventually becoming the festival director for TWIST. Alongside all this work, Tayara has continued to be an active filmmaker. But even for those who have no plans to pursue a career in film, the production-based literacy training is quite valuable.

By focusing on the LGBTQ population, Reel Queer Youth's media literacy training engages with practices associated with critical pedagogy and anti-oppressive education. As with the educational programs of the Professional Organization of Women in Entertainment Reaching Up (POWER UP) discussed in chapter 3, Reel Queer Youth seeks to challenge the status quo of mainstream media by raising participants' awareness of dominant media norms and giving them some of the media tools they need to tell their own stories. The early portion of the program that is officially designated as "media literacy" helps the youth participants understand how they have been marginalized by ignorant and harmful portrayals in mainstream media. The production training builds on this foundation by teaching participants to use the tools of digital media production to tell the stories they want to tell and share their perspectives on the world around them. The program works to challenge oppression by offering both "education for the Other" and "education about the Other."[15] Theo, a participant in the 2015 workshop, points to the relationship between the two components of the program by noting that participants learn "how queers are portrayed in the media and what role we [queer youth] play in changing that narrative."[16] Reel Queer Youth participants are actively engaged as critical media viewers and producers connected to a supportive community and encouraged to find and use their voices to critique and alter the contemporary media landscape.

Representation and Visibility in the Films of Reel Queer Youth

The media literacy discussion during an early session of the workshop focuses on the critical examination of representations of LGBTQ individuals in mainstream media. This discussion helps get participants thinking about the context into which they are entering when producing their own short films. While the discussion does not take a specifically academic tone, it covers much of the same ground as the scholarly literature on the subject, pointing to the general lack of representation over the years while acknowledging recent improvements and potential for additional positive change.

As discussed in previous chapters, positive images of openly gay, lesbian, bisexual, and transgender characters are relatively uncommon across the history of film and television. While some important studies by scholars like Alexander Doty, Harry Benshoff, and Sean Griffin have encouraged readings that illuminate queer content in films and television programs from the earliest days of the industries, more overt depictions of queer characters and experiences have been very limited over the years, with most of those occurring in the past two decades.[17] Writing in the mid-1990s as queer media visibility was on the rise, Ben Gove noted that of the small but growing number of positive queer representations, very few of them were relatable to younger viewers. He pointed out that while queer or questioning youth might be able to find a few positive images and role models in film or television, "the reassuring, enthralling directness of such images is heavily compromised by their basis in frustratingly adult-oriented social environments and predicaments."[18] Queer youth looking for images of people who were their age and dealing with issues relevant to their lives would have to keep looking.

Although the numbers of queer characters in film and television have increased dramatically since the mid-1990s, most of those characters have been adults. There have, of course, been exceptions. Popular television programs like *Dawson's Creek* (1998–2003) and *Buffy the Vampire Slayer* (1997–2003) as well as films like *Clueless* (1995), *Easy A* (2010), and *The Perks of Being a Wallflower* (2012) have included queer teens as significant, though generally secondary, characters. The smash hit *Glee* (2009–2015) foregrounded issues of queer teen sexuality and gender identity throughout the length of its run.[19] But across the full media landscape, images of queer teens (particularly as central characters) have remained relatively uncommon. This is not terribly surprising, given that, as Davis points out, media texts that are "made for a youth audience, and which represent adolescent experience, are (almost exclusively) produced by adults, and for major corporations."[20] The stories, therefore, are filtered through an adult perspective, and their goal is to earn profits rather than tell stories that accurately express the desires, fears, and concerns of queer youth. So despite significant improvements, the world of mainstream mass media continues to be lacking when it comes to providing a broad array of content that engages queer youth by addressing their experiences regarding gender and sexuality.

Unlike previous generations, contemporary youth have access to a valuable alternative to the content created by media conglomerates. They can, and frequently do, turn to the internet—more specifically, to YouTube. As Bryan Wuest has noted, when mainstream media representations fail, youth can search YouTube for images and stories that more accurately reflect their own experiences.[21] YouTube videos involve teens coming out to friends and family, singing and dancing to their favorite pop songs, talking with their friends, sharing fashion advice, and going about their daily lives. Jonathan Alexander and Elizabeth Losh argue that publicly proclaiming one's sexuality online is so common that "coming out videos have become a distinctive YouTube form,"[22] and Matthew O'Neill says that YouTube has become "an outlet for artistic exploration," which "potentially helps the child/teenager come to terms with identity issues."[23] The site, therefore, offers benefits for both creators and viewers, allowing users to express and explore a wide range of queer identities. This freedom is largely due to the fact that users can avoid the corporate media gatekeepers that control the content of commercially driven mainstream film and television. This is not to say that YouTube provides the perfect solution or that it is without its problems. The lack of corporate gatekeepers, for example, might provide certain freedoms when it comes to content, but it also means that there is no quality control, so the technical and aesthetic elements of YouTube content can be hit and miss. And as Sarah Banet-Weiser has noted, there is the potential that users conditioned by the consumption of mainstream media will basically offer a rehashing of imagery that does little to change hegemonic ideals.[24] In other words, offering the freedom to challenge and reimagine norms and conventions does not guarantee that users will take full advantage of that freedom.

Reel Queer Youth offers an alternative to mainstream film and television by drawing on some of the benefits offered by YouTube and other video-sharing outlets while minimizing some of the downsides of those options. Like YouTube, Reel Queer Youth is interactive. Participants are not just consuming media; they are responding to and engaging with media culture by creating their own images and stories. The projects are driven by the youth participants, and stories are told from their perspectives without being filtered through restrictive corporate gatekeepers. The presence of mentors for the workshop helps alleviate some of the problems associated with many online videos. While the mentors do not generally restrict the content generated by participants, they do provide the skills needed to create higher-quality short films, and the workshop's opening discussions help make participants aware of oppressive ideologies that they should avoid reinforcing.

That is not to say that projects are without their flaws—for many participants, it is their first foray into filmmaking, and one week is not enough time for anyone to perfect the skills associated with the process. And even though mentors do not overtly restrict content, they may shape it subtly through their leadership in the workshop. For example, in teaching participants the logistics of filmmaking, mentors offer instructions about three-point lighting, dialogue recording, and the roles and hierarchies of the crew on set. Though the mentors I observed were careful to note that they were only demonstrating one option, and they encouraged the youth to experiment with formal and aesthetic elements, the time constraints of the program do not allow much time to be dedicated to such experimentation or the demonstration of alternative techniques. As such, participants are likely to adopt some of the mainstream approaches demonstrated for them, or they may fall back on their own knowledge about cinematic style, which likely also comes from mainstream sources. Similarly, the literacy workshop does encourage participants to question and challenge mainstream representations, but the brief workshop does not allow for a fully nuanced exploration of every possible representational strategy. Participants may therefore adopt a relatively narrow view of what counts as "acceptable" queer representation based on what is presented in the workshop.

The constraints placed on the workshop by its relatively short running time may limit the technical quality of the projects, and the content of films may stay within certain aesthetic and ideological bounds. However, Reel Queer Youth does encourage participants to question and challenge mainstream images, and many of them push beyond dominant norms. The workshop gives participants the opportunity to tell the kinds of stories that they (and perhaps many other queer youth) would like to see coming from other sources, like the mainstream entertainment industry. Due to the variety of projects made by participants over the years, it is impossible to make any generalizations about the content of all films. However, a closer look at a handful of the films produced during one Reel Queer Youth workshop provides some insights into the most tangible output coming from it. Participants in Reel Queer Youth 2014 produced four films: *Out Again*, *Download My Heart*, *Dysphoric*, and *Thank You Exhibit A*.

Out Again, as described in the introduction, is a coming out story utilizing the science-fiction trope of time travel. As a young man struggles with his attempts to come out as bisexual, he discovers that he has the ability to travel back in time, and he uses this ability to try to improve his coming out experience. *Download My Heart* also borrows from science fiction, as it features robots looking for love and companionship. The two robots at the center of the story struggle to get their relationship off the ground because one robot has trouble accepting the gender-fluid identity of the second robot. *Dysphoric* is an experimental film that uses vignettes and images of various artistic endeavors (including dance and painting) to help express the frustration and stress experienced by the main character as a result of not fitting neatly within society's binary view of gender. The final film, *Thank You Exhibit A*, is another coming out story, this one drawing aesthetic inspiration from documentary films and reality TV. The film features a young woman who has invited all her friends and family to sit down with her one at a time so that she can come out to them on camera, thereby capturing the moment(s) for posterity.

It is perhaps not surprising that the projects draw on some of the genres and forms that have historically invited queer readings and attracted queer filmmakers and viewers. Science-fiction stories, for example, frequently offer characters whose identities and behaviors challenge the strict boundaries of heteronormative society, opening the genre up to various queer readings even when there are no explicitly LGBTQ characters present.[25] *Out Again* and *Download My Heart* draw on elements common to science fiction (time travel and robots) and then foreground queer identities within that context. Within the world of television, queer visibility is perhaps most common in reality TV. The intimate and often confessional nature of reality shows combined with casting directors' desire for diversity in their programs has led to many such shows incorporating or focusing on queer lives and experiences. *Thank You Exhibit A* taps into the conventions of reality TV through its use of direct address, some shaky handheld camerawork, and unsuspecting "real" people who get brought into the production, ultimately turning a series of private interactions into a public performance. Many queer filmmakers have chosen experimental approaches as a way of challenging the norms that dominate the medium. *Dysphoric* takes advantage of the freedom to blend pieces of a narrative with images that help convey emotions and develop themes, breaking the aesthetic norms of mainstream film to question the gender norms of our society. In general, the projects demonstrate the participants' familiarity with many of the conventions of visual storytelling and their ability to use or reject those conventions to express their original ideas. Participants clearly enter the program with a solid base of media literacy, which the program helps expand and refine. After all, they know which genres are amenable to queering, they know the tropes of those genres, and they figure out how to manipulate those tropes to tell their own stories.

Despite their different genres and styles, something that the four films have in common is their emphasis on very personal stories. These are stories about people discovering their identities, revealing private details to others, and building personal relationships. These are not sweeping epics (partially a function of the time and budget allowed, of course) but rather glimpses into the lives of the characters, revealing hopes, fears, dreams, and anxieties. To present the thoughts of their respective main characters, *Thank You Exhibit A* and *Out Again* use a direct address to the audience and a main character briefly talking to himself. Demonstrating an understanding of the language of cinematography, all four films rely heavily on tight shots of main characters' faces (even robot faces) expressing emotions and reacting to situations, all to bring the audience closer to the characters and their experiences. It becomes clear that the producers of the films are sharing personal stories from their own perspectives and inviting the audience to share in those perspectives. This approach is encouraged by mentors, and Tayara believes that "it's good for everyone to speak from their own experience. It's good to have queer youth making the stories about their own selves so they're accurate and more relatable to other queer youth." Reel Queer Youth participants provide a perspective that adult producers reporting to corporate bosses are not able to offer, thereby generating an important alternative to most representations of queer youth.

Another trait that unites all four films is the fact that they all enact fantasies of wish fulfillment. The stories present situations and issues common to most queer youth. Discovering and coming to terms with one's identity, coming out to themselves and others, and building or maintaining relationships are sources of significant tension for most queer youth, and they provide the narrative conflicts in these films. While the filmmakers could have chosen downbeat endings for the films (certainly a reality for many youth in these situations), all of them found happy endings, even if there was some disappointment along the way.

The first half of *Dysphoric*, for example, shows the main character dealing with the frustrations associated with identifying as transgender. He scrutinizes his image in the mirror, visibly dissatisfied with his appearance. He reluctantly responds when his teacher calls him by the name on the class roster—Elizabeth. And after contemplating entering the men's restroom, he ultimately decides to use the women's restroom, as that corresponds with the gender assigned to him at birth. These scenes alternate with shots of unseen or partially obscured artists dancing, reciting poetry, drawing, and painting. The images and sounds of the artists (aggressive dance moves, angry words from the poet, the prominent use of black in the drawings and paintings) reflect the main character's frustration with the situation. The second half of the film is the opposite of the first. The main character is visibly happy with his appearance in the mirror; he responds with a smile when a friend calls him by his chosen name, Alex; and he strides confidently into the men's restroom. The artists are now conveying happiness through flowing dance moves, optimistic words, and bright colors. While the first half of the film represents the life that many transgender youth face, the second half presents life as they wish it could be.

The other films follow similar strategies. In *Download My Heart*, the two central robot characters seem to be hitting it off and truly enjoying one another's company, but when one robot discovers that the other is gender fluid (signified in the film by a rotating head that features the male symbol [♂] on one side and the female symbol [♀] on the other), the first robot rejects the second robot. After much soul searching, the first robot ultimately decides that the second robot's gender identity need not be a barrier to their romantic relationship, and the two wind up together at the end. *Out Again* deals with the anxiety that surrounds the coming out process. While the main character still has a stressful situation to deal with as he comes out to a classmate, his ability to time travel gives him an opportunity to repeat the process again and again until he gets it just right. The main character in *Thank You Exhibit A* is also dealing with stress, but not because she is worried about what people will say or do when she comes out. Her biggest problem is that she quickly realizes that coming out to everyone in her life one at a time will take forever. So she asks the audience to help her spread the word so that everyone will know that she is gay, thus relieving her of the burden that all queer people face—the lifetime of continually coming out in a world that assumes heterosexuality and cisgender identity.

All the films ultimately fulfill wishes that many queer youth have. In the fantasy worlds created by these films, transgender people can feel comfortable with their bodies and identities and ultimately find others who will love them as they are. Individuals can redo the coming out process until it is just right, but once they are satisfied with the outcome, they can set it aside and move on with life rather than having to come out to every person they meet. While these wish-fulfilling narratives might be perceived as escapist, they do acknowledge the difficult situations that queer teens face. In other words, they do not pretend that life is easy for queer youth, but they adopt an optimistic attitude that leads to protagonists overcoming their obstacles. In response to the prompt, "Make the film that you want to see," participants went for happy endings, thereby mirroring the resolutions of most Hollywood narratives while challenging the norm by offering protagonists that Hollywood generally excludes. In this way, they demonstrate one of the values of youth video production identified by Maxine Geene, who notes that when young people create their own videos, they often "find themselves able to 'name' and imagine how they might change their worlds for the first time as they capture it through a scene or narrative, a gesture or dialogue."[26] While these videos focus on small changes in personal situations, they can inspire participants to think about even greater changes with more far-reaching effects.

The alternative representations offered in the completed films are valuable to the participants in that the filmmakers have a chance to see their own stories, desires, and fears reflected back to them on the screen. But the films reach even further when they are distributed and exhibited at a variety of venues. The films are first shown to an audience at the "friends and family" screening at the end of the workshop. The event is often held in the theater of the Northwest Film Forum, a film arts organization that is also located in the Capitol Hill neighborhood. This is a relatively small venue, but it is still a big screen in a darkened theater, and given that the location generally plays well-respected and professionally made films, premiering the Reel Queer Youth films in this space gives them an increased sense of legitimacy and puts them on par with work by far more seasoned filmmakers. The films are also assembled as a shorts program that is included in TWIST, a heavily publicized event that draws a wide range of audience members.

Films from the workshop are also submitted to various festivals beyond Seattle. *Out Again*, for example, screened at Frameline, one of the largest

LGBTQ film festivals in the world and a launching pad for many queer filmmakers. After making the rounds of festivals, the films are made available online via Vimeo, which allows them to reach viewers who might not make it to a film festival. The Reel Queer Youth films, along with the names of the participants, are also included in the Internet Movie Database, publicly crediting all the participants as accomplished filmmakers. Ultimately, the stories and representations generated by the youth filmmakers are disseminated in a variety of ways and to multiple audiences around the world. They may not reach a huge total audience, especially when compared to the content produced by Hollywood, but they do offer an alternative to the few images of queer youth generated by adults in the mainstream entertainment media industries. For audiences searching for just such an alternative, the films of Reel Queer Youth are an important contribution to the media landscape.

Voice and Storytelling

The content of the Reel Queer Youth films and their circulation is only part of the story. The impact the workshop has on its participants is perhaps even more significant, as Reel Queer Youth empowers young storytellers and encourages them to speak up for social change. The critical media literacy training that participants experience during the week initially results in the films produced within the workshop, but the skills and experiences carry over beyond the films and have implications for broader areas of citizenship and social justice. First and foremost, the program helps participants find and develop their voices, which ultimately enables them to tell stories that can contribute to the LGBTQ movements. As discussed in this book's introduction, voice represents "an expression of a distinctive perspective on the world,"[27] and feeling empowered to use one's voice is a vital component of participation in a democratic society. Queer youth are doubly disempowered given that queer voices are marginalized in a heteronormative society, and youth voices tend to be overlooked or trivialized by adults. Youth who do not fit social norms related to gender and sexuality are often forced to hide certain aspects of themselves in order to be accepted. This silencing of queer youth is often exacerbated by hostile school climates and unsupportive families.[28] Regular surveys conducted by the Centers for Disease Control and Prevention have demonstrated that when compared to heterosexual youth, lesbian, gay, bisexual, and transgender youth are at a higher risk for depression, suicide, sexual assault, and drug use.[29] While the precise causes of these risks are not yet known, some researchers have suggested connections between the silencing and isolation of queer youth and the health-related risks they experience.[30] Former Reel Queer Youth program manager Finn Cottom says that a key goal of the workshop is "empowering disempowered voices."[31] By empowering queer youth to find and use their voices to speak up for themselves and to speak out against oppression, and by valuing those voices when they are used, Reel Queer Youth has the potential to improve the immediate well-being of participants and encourage more social engagement in the future.

In his book *Gay Identity, New Storytelling, and the Media* (2009), Christopher Pullen investigates the formation of lesbian and gay identity within the media, focusing particularly on the potential for self-reflexive and out cultural producers to shape new discourses by way of their personal stories. His discussion emphasizes the potential for contemporary storytellers to positively change discourses about gay and lesbian identity and experiences, noting that the majority of these stories generated by religious, medical, and government institutions have pathologized and criminalized individuals and groups so as to contain and distance homosexual identity.[32] He argues that through the revealing and self-reflective practices of queer storytellers, "oppressive myths are challenged, and new stories emerge,"[33] opening up opportunities for community formation and political visibility. Reel Queer Youth participants are engaging in just the kind of storytelling that Pullen describes. During the early portion of the workshop, they are reminded of the kinds of stories that have been told through mainstream channels over the years. Cottom points out that the program encourages participants to "think about how media has been used and is being used to degrade queer and trans people" and then gives youth the skills to create different media that alters that history by changing who is in charge of making media. Participants have the opportunity to tell stories that are a reflection of their own lived experiences and challenge the dominant myths about queer lives by offering new narratives and perspectives.

As discussed in the introduction to this book, Ken Plummer's work on contemporary sexual storytelling identifies four levels over which such stories evolve, moving from the personal level (when an individual works through the motivations for telling a story) to the cultural/historical level (when a story enters the realm of public discourse and reaches an audience).[34] From a social justice perspective, Plummer's fourth level is the most important, as that is when publicly shared stories have the potential to change hearts, minds, and even policies. But not every story makes it to that fourth level without help. Reel Queer Youth enables participants to progress through all four of the levels as they develop their projects.

Most Reel Queer Youth participants come to the workshop with a motivation to tell stories. This is, after all, a big part of why they enrolled in the program. Some may want to tell stories to learn more about themselves; others may want to express their feelings to friends and family or connect to other participants by way of shared stories. The workshop helps participants progress from this personal level, where they are motivated to tell stories, through the rest of the process. Plummer's second level, the situational level, involves individuals turning themselves into storytellers, and the beginning of the Reel Queer Youth workshop focuses on this. As a foundation, the program organizers work to validate the identities of the youth participants to make them feel more comfortable expressing themselves. As an example, Tayara says that program organizers are "really considerate about gender pronouns. Queer youth can walk around at home all day and be misgendered, and then they can come to Reel Queer Youth and we'll validate their identity and not try to push aside part of who they are just so they can participate." The next step is to help participants find their voices. Through the storytelling prompts they are given when accepted into the program, participants are encouraged to dig deep and reflect on what really matters to them. During the initial media literacy workshop, they are shown examples of how others tell stories, and during a pitch session, they practice conveying their story ideas individually to potential collaborators before presenting their ideas to the full group. Describing the relationship between mentors and participants in the workshop, 2015 participant Theo says, "From writing the story to deciding which shots we were going to use . . . I can remember we would look to them and ask, 'What do we do next?' and they were like, 'Well, what do *you* think? What do *you* want to do?'" Rather than being told what to do or how to think, youth participants are asked to do it on their own, hopefully discovering what they want to say and how they want to say it, improving their skills and finding their voices as storytellers.

While the participants continue to develop their voices and stories (first as individuals and then as a group), the workshop helps them move to Plummer's third level, the organizational level, where stories are organized and refined to fit the norms of particular media formats. By providing training and experience with visual storytelling tools such as cinematography and editing, the program enables youth to convert their ideas into narratives and images that can be shared with an audience. This ultimately leads to the fourth and final level, the cultural/historical level, where the story enters public discourse as it is received by an audience. The entire process is validated for participants as the videos are distributed and exhibited at a variety of venues to show the creators that their voices can and will be heard. The overall process of looking inward and outward to find something to say, practicing ways to say it, and then seeing the results of speaking out prepares participants to go through the same process in other aspects of their lives. Once they understand that their voices matter and they know how to use them, they are well situated to use their newly sharpened media literacy skills to advocate and take a stand on issues important to queer communities and other marginalized groups.

Community Development and Collaboration

A solo voice might open a discussion, but a chorus of voices is much more likely to bring about change. Reel Queer Youth encourages participants to join their voices by emphasizing community development and collaboration. As a program of Three Dollar Bill Cinema, Reel Queer Youth aims to support the mission of its parent organization, especially with respect to strengthening, connecting, and reflecting "diverse communities through queer film and media." As discussed at various points in this book, the concept of community, particularly as it relates to the LGBTQ population, is more complicated than it might seem. Individual queer communities based on personal relationships and geographic proximity exist in concrete ways in various cities and towns around the world. But there is also the more abstract idea of a nationwide or even global LGBTQ community—an imagined community defined largely in opposition to mainstream society. Jeffrey Weeks argues for the political significance of an imagined queer community, noting that "the idea of a sexual community may be fiction, but it is a necessary fiction: an imagined community, an invented tradition which enables and empowers. It provides the context for the articulation of identity, the vocabulary of values through which ways of life can be developed."[35]

Whether concrete or imagined, the diversity of the LGBTQ population and its intersections with other groups makes it difficult to define a single community, and this complexity is built into the mission statement of Reel Queer Youth's parent organization. Addressing the pluralization of the word *communities* in the Three Dollar Bill Cinema mission statement, executive director Jason Plourde says, "We recognize that there's a larger concept of the LGBT community, but . . . within that, there's smaller groups that also have specific needs or different affinities."[36] One of those smaller groups is the youth population, which has needs and interests that often differ from those of adults. Reel Queer Youth works to connect participants to a concrete, lived community during the workshop while simultaneously helping them feel connected to the larger and more abstract LGBTQ community long after the workshop ends.

For any community to thrive, it first needs a place to exist. Noting that "a lot of queer spaces are more of a family to queer people than their blood families are," Tayara says that Reel Queer Youth organizers work to create a safe queer space for participants. As Lynne Hillier and Lyn Harrison argue, queer youth are in many ways "space deprived"—that is, they do not always have safe spaces where they can meet one another and interact so as to form a community—and it is partially for this reason that so many queer teens seek out a sense of community online.[37] Reel Queer Youth seeks to develop community connections offline and face-to-face, and therefore the environment in which the workshop takes place becomes very important.

The main Reel Queer Youth program is held in the Capitol Hill neighborhood of Seattle.[38] This location situates the program geographically within an area that is known for its sizable LGBTQ population, thriving arts scene, and generally progressive attitudes. As such, the program is able to draw on these existing characteristics to create a welcoming atmosphere for participants, and the program in turn strengthens the creative, artistic, queer-friendly vibe of the neighborhood. For many years, the program was housed at the space occupied by Reel Grrls, but in 2014, after Reel Grrls moved its office across town and farther away from the Three Dollar Bill Cinema office, the workshop was held at the Bright Water School, a private institution that serves children from prekindergarten through eighth grade. In 2015, the workshop moved again, this time to the 12th Avenue Arts Building, a newly built multifunction facility that had recently become the home of Three Dollar Bill Cinema's main office. In both cases, the interactions between the Reel Queer Youth program and its physical surroundings reveal and highlight relationships between queer youth and the society in which they live.

Although the regular students at the Bright Water School were on summer vacation during the week of Reel Queer Youth, the space itself always carries with it numerous reminders of its usual function, and this gives it a symbolic power that is significant to the overall program. School, after all, is a space where many queer youth feel vulnerable; it is often a space of harassment and bullying.[39] While educational institutions are making substantial advances toward inclusion, primary schools have not historically been a space for youth to understand, experience, or explore nontraditional gender identities or nonheterosexual orientations.

Situated in this location, Reel Queer Youth temporarily queered the traditionally heteronormative space of the school, refashioning it as a queer-positive and accepting environment where participants could be themselves and allow their own identities and creativity to flourish. I do not want to suggest that the Bright Water School or its policies are unwelcoming to queer youth. It is not the specific school that matters here but rather what it symbolizes. With its familiar layout and decor, this school could be any school and therefore subtly evokes the experiences of many students, past and present. By turning a potentially threatening environment into a welcoming and affirming one, Reel Queer Youth 2014 provided participants with an opportunity to reimagine their own relationships to educational spaces. Two of the four completed films from 2014 feature stories set in schools, allowing the filmmakers to actively rewrite the experience of being queer in school.

The 12th Avenue Arts Building has a very different feel from the school. The building opened about six months before the start of the 2015 workshop, giving everything a more modern and up-to-date appearance. The building was developed by Capitol Hill Housing, an organization dedicated to providing affordable housing for low- and moderate-income individuals and families.[40] Designed as a community-centered, mixed-use facility, the building includes eighty-eight apartments, two performing arts spaces, office space for local nonprofits, and retail space for local businesses. Three Dollar Bill Cinema occupies one of the office suites and has neighbors like the Capitol Hill Chamber of Commerce and the administrative office of Capitol Hill Housing. The building includes a handful of shared meeting/conference rooms, and these spaces have become the home of the Reel Queer Youth workshop. The main room used for the workshop includes conference tables arranged in a horseshoe shape, fluorescent lights, exposed ductwork and concrete pillars, beige walls, and short gray carpeting, all of which come together to give the space a generically professional feel. While the physical and visual details of the school gave the previous year's location a direct association with spaces very familiar to the youth participants, this space offers more of a blank slate without such obvious connections to particular experiences. While the rather bland, sterile space might not inspire much creativity, the fact that the meeting space is the same one regularly used by the local nonprofit groups that populate the building suggests that the work of Reel Queer Youth is on par with that of the other organizations. Occupying a space generally inhabited by community-oriented professionals situates the concerns and projects of the youth participants among those of other organizations working to improve the community, suggesting that the ideas and concerns of the youth in the workshop are to be taken seriously rather than dismissed or trivialized.

Within the larger spaces of the school and the arts building—or any other public building, for that matter—one location that can be a significant source of stress for queer youth is the bathroom. Emblazoned with the words *Boys* and *Girls* or *Men* and *Women*, public bathrooms are a constant reminder of society's norms related to gender identity. For an individual whose identity does not fit neatly into the either/or binary of traditional gender definitions, just walking past such a bathroom can be uncomfortable, and entering one can be far worse. For some, the primary conflict is internal, as they do not see themselves as aligned solely with one or the other of the given options, and being forced to choose one induces stress. Others may be comfortable identifying with one gender category, but their self-identity might not match the way others perceive them, and they may therefore be read by others as being in the "wrong" bathroom. This can lead to taunting, threats, or even physical violence.[41] To alleviate the pressures associated with traditionally designated bathrooms, Reel Queer Youth staff covered the permanent signs on bathrooms at the Bright Water School with paper signs that read "All Gender Restroom." The 12th Avenue Arts Building features a gender-neutral bathroom in addition to bathrooms designated as being for "Men" and "Women," perhaps in response to requests from transgender advocates who have pushed for the inclusion of such bathrooms in newly built or renovated public spaces. And while this does alleviate some of the stress that transgender individuals might feel when entering bathrooms clearly designated for a particular gender identity, the permanent signage on the bathroom still features the traditional symbols used to represent men and women, thereby affirming these as the only two choices in a binary system. In response, Reel Queer Youth staff again put up the more inclusive "All Gender Restroom" sign. In both locations, this modification provided a safe space for the participants during their time in the program, but the makeshift/temporary nature of the signs serves as a reminder that the standard in our society is still one of distinct boundaries around clearly defined gender categories.

A welcoming and queer-friendly space helps establish an environment that is conducive to forging connections between strangers, and the structure of Reel Queer Youth builds on that foundation. The nature of the workshop is such that participants come together as a creative community working toward a common goal. Tayara shares a story about a wrap-up session on the first day of the 2014 workshop. During that session, one of the participants told the group that they were happy to be there because they knew that they would not feel so alone anymore. Tayara believes that through Reel Queer Youth, "people are meeting each other and realizing that there are other people similar to them, and there's potential for great friendships to grow from that. Our mission is to teach film to queer youth, but I think the larger mission is really building a community and doing that through filmmaking." Theo concurs, noting that the mentors work hard to welcome youth into the community by establishing the program as a "judgment-free zone, where all ideas are accepted." The newly formed community is particularly important here in that it provides the necessary support for participants to find their voices and share aspects of themselves with one another.

The sense of community created within the workshop is enhanced significantly by the collaboration that defines all aspects of the program. Filmmaking, by its very nature, is a collaborative endeavor, so teamwork is somewhat built into the program. But the organizers of the workshop emphasize and model positive collaboration throughout the week to show that it is about more than just working alongside other people. The workshops that introduce participants to concepts like media literacy, storytelling, composition, lighting, and audio are divided among the mentors, thus giving them shared responsibility for content delivery and modeling collaborative work for the participants.

Collaboration dominates the development and production process as well, as ideas initially generated by individuals are turned into finished short films produced by teams. Participants receive feedback from one another and from mentors throughout the process of developing and pitching ideas for short films. After the ideas are voted on and narrowed down to the four that will be produced, participants and mentors provide more detailed written feedback about each of the selected ideas. Once teams are formed and assigned to the various projects, those teams continue the development process, building on the ideas provided by the entire group and working as a small team to hammer out the details of scripting, storyboarding, and the rest of preproduction. Even during the production process, collaborative decision-making is encouraged by mentors, and members of all the groups help one another by serving as actors, extras, and additional crew members as needed for the various projects. Thus each of the completed films is the result of focused work by a team of three or four participants and two mentors, with significant support provided by participants and mentors from across the workshop. The youth experience the many benefits of collaborative work, including problem solving enhanced by multiple perspectives, and the value of having complementary strengths and weaknesses contributing to the project. This also helps solidify the sense of community in the workshop, as everyone contributes to all of the projects, and therefore each person is invested in each of the films made by the group.

The mentors play an important role in the collaborative process and the development of community, and they have to work carefully to provide the necessary support without imposing their own ideas in a way that would inhibit the autonomy of the youth participants. As Lora Taub-Pervizpour argues in her discussion of youth media programs, "Youth media educators share a responsibility to expand young people's right to communicate, not to impose further limitations upon that right."[42] According to Theo, the word *balance* comes to mind when describing the role of the mentors, as they provided "knowledge and information, skills and new ideas" but allowed the participants to remain largely autonomous in terms of creative decision-making. Shawna, another 2015 participant, agrees, saying, "Even though all of the mentors have great film experience, they weren't like, 'Here's what you're gonna do, and here's how you're gonna do it.' They were like, 'What do you guys wanna do?' and 'We'll support you on it.'"[43] Tobey, a multiyear participant, notes that he appreciates a mentor "who works alongside the youth as opposed to presenting themselves as an authority figure."[44] While the collaboration and support of mentors help empower the youth participants, the mentors do occasionally need to step in to make sure projects stay on track. Commenting on his own work with the EVC in New York, Steven Goodman says, "The teacher bears the ultimate responsibility for ensuring the group meets its deadline and the production results in a finished product."[45] Reel Queer Youth mentors must therefore balance logistical demands with the goals of empowering youth voices and building a collaborative community. This may occasionally mean dampening certain creative impulses, but it increases the likelihood of having a finished project ready to share with an audience.

In addition to forming a community within the workshop, Reel Queer Youth helps connect participants to other communities outside the program. This is especially valuable because, as Suzanna Walters has pointed out, queer people are generally born into and raised by straight families, meaning that they "must actively seek out and construct a community" of other queer people.[46] And as Joseph Goodwin has argued, society is filled with institutions (schools, churches, social organizations) that enculturate individuals into straight communities, but finding equivalents for queer communities is very difficult.[47] By introducing participants to each other and to queer and allied mentors, Reel Queer Youth connects individuals to the lived queer community that exists in Seattle and the larger imagined queer community that links all LGBTQ individuals and their supporters. For some participants who may come from neighborhoods or towns without a visible and active queer community, this connection to members of Seattle's queer community offers access to informational resources and support services that might otherwise be inaccessible. It also provides them with personal connections within the larger community—friends and mentors that they can turn to for support in a variety of situations. The program also connects participants to the sizable Seattle filmmaking community and, by extension, the larger arts community in the region. Some of the mentors work as filmmakers in the area, and participants are encouraged to seek out other filmmaking opportunities after the end of the program. For example, one mentor who regularly participates in filmmaking competitions encouraged workshop attendees to put together teams and enter Seattle's forty-eight-hour film race and other similar programs. To support these and other efforts, Reel Queer Youth offers participants free access to the equipment used in the program for six months after completing the workshop. In this way, the program encourages participants to continue making films as part of the local filmmaking scene, and it gives them the resources to do so.

By encouraging participants to see the power of collaborative work and then helping them build a new community and connect with existing communities, Reel Queer Youth provides access to tools that are vital components of any social activism. As they use their refined media literacy skills to create alternative representations and tell stories that matter to them, participants also learn how to build teams and expand their networks, thus positioning them to contribute effectively to social movements in the future.

Storytelling for a Better Future

While policies and attitudes toward the LGBTQ population in the United States have shifted dramatically in recent years, many queer youth still feel isolated, silenced, and powerless. They often turn to entertainment media to help them cope with their frustrations, looking for positive representations of queer life to counteract the negative experiences of their own lives.[48] But sometimes, even representations that aim for positive portrayals can reinforce harmful stereotypes, and most are lacking the youth perspective that would really resonate with younger viewers. Escaping into media consumption as a way of coping with life may end up frustrating queer youth more than helping them. Traditional media literacy programs aim to help all youth (LGBTQ or otherwise) take a more critical view of the media that they encounter in their everyday lives. Reel Queer Youth takes things a step further by asking participants to apply their critical perspectives to the production of original content that offers something that is lacking in mainstream texts. Rather than trying to protect youth from the negative influences of mass media, Reel Queer Youth uses antioppressive education as a foundation for activist storytelling, empowering participants to respond to mainstream media with their own stories and images. Offering an optimistic take on the potential impact of the program, Danny Tayara says, "It's really going to be great to have young people have tools to make the media that they want to see because they're just going to grow up and teach other people how to do it, and it will make a shift in the kind of media that we're seeing."

Reel Queer Youth does, of course, have its limitations when it comes to changing the media landscape. The festival circuit may generate some attention and visibility, and online distribution can eventually make the films available to many people, but without large promotional budgets, these films are unlikely to reach a comparatively large audience or a cross-section of the population. Rather, they are likely to extend only to those who seek them out at festivals or online and are generally likeminded when it comes to the issues being addressed. Contributing alternative representations and stories is a step in the right direction, and while it provides a response to mainstream media content, the workshop does not have the ability to change the mainstream in any significant way—at least not immediately. The bigger impact comes from the lessons learned and skills gained by participants in the program, as those skills can be used long after the workshop concludes. Some participants may be inspired to pursue careers in media production, and they might eventually work their way up to decision-making positions in mainstream production companies or smaller alternative organizations like those discussed in this book, but it is more likely that they will find uses for storytelling and team-building skills in other venues.

In the end, the experiences of participants in Reel Queer Youth are similar to those of the protagonist of the short film *Out Again*. In the film, Sam works to find his voice, figure out what he wants to say, and then come up with a way to say it. He makes some mistakes along the way, but through trial and error and the magic of time travel, he learns from them and improves himself with each step. Reel Queer Youth participants go through much the same process. They might not have the luxury of time travel, but they are given the freedom to make mistakes in a safe environment where they will be supported in their learning process. By opening up and sharing an important aspect of himself, Sam forges an emotional connection with someone who understands him, an experience that, once again, parallels that of the workshop participants.

During the course of their week with Reel Queer Youth, workshop participants are encouraged to find and use their voices and collaborate creatively with others—all in the service of telling stories that matter. This represents an important shift from queer youth being spoken about by adults to queer youth speaking out for themselves. Even if the content of the films produced during the week is not overtly activist in nature, the process of producing the films develops skills that are vital to serving as an advocate or activist when such a need or opportunity presents itself. Reel Queer Youth and programs like it therefore have the potential to not only change the lives of those who participate but also give participants the ability to make positive changes to the world around them.

Conclusion

Stories of Some of Our Lives

Storytellers rarely set out to be activists. Many of them just want to share an experience, express their feelings, or entertain an audience. But those individuals and organizations who dedicate themselves to making positive changes by telling the stories of marginalized people can play a major role in social justice efforts. I have focused my discussion on In the Life Media, the Professional Organization of Women in Entertainment Reaching Up (POWER UP), and Three Dollar Bill Cinema, but these are just a few of the many organizations involved with generating, preserving, and circulating queer stories to effect positive social change. In addition to other filmmakers, production companies, and festivals dedicated to LGBTQ media, there are groups that have focused their energy on collecting oral histories and herstories, distributing content to the home video market, and monitoring the stories of queer people that populate the media landscape.

The ACT UP Oral History Project is a collection of interviews with surviving members of the activist organization AIDS Coalition to Unleash Power (ACT UP). Coordinated by Jim Hubbard and Sarah Schulman, the project seeks to capture the experiences of those fighting to change perceptions of AIDS and people living with it. Short clips and full transcripts of all interviews are available online, while complete recordings of the interviews are housed at the San Francisco Main Library and the New York Public Library and are available for purchase on DVD. According to the project website, organizers hope that the collection "will de-mystify the process of making social change, remind us that change can be made, and help us understand how to do it."[1] By collecting and sharing these stories, organizers aim not only to preserve history through personal stories but also to offer tools and ideas for activists working in the present and future.

StoryCorps is an organization dedicated to collecting the oral histories of people from all walks of life. Recognizing the power of storytelling as a catalyst for positive change, StoryCorps is driven by a mission "to preserve and share humanity's stories in order to build connections between people and create a more just and compassionate world."[2] As part of their larger project, the organization has special collections focusing on particular groups, including veterans, Latinos, and 9/11 survivors. In 2014, the forty-fifth anniversary of the Stonewall Uprising, they launched StoryCorps OutLoud, a special initiative focused on collecting stories from LGBTQ people. By including a special collection within the larger project, StoryCorps acknowledges the unique experiences and perspectives of LGBTQ people while situating them within a broader framework of storytelling for social change.

Adopting a more narrow focus is the Old Lesbian Oral Herstory Project (OLOHP). Started by Arden Eversmeyer in 1998 and supported by the organization Old Lesbians Organizing for Change, the project collects the personal stories of lesbians seventy years of age and older. The herstories are collected through interviews, transcribed, and then archived as part of the Sophia Smith Collection at Smith College. As a way of sharing the stories beyond the archive, excerpts have been collected in two printed anthologies as well as a live presentation of dramatic readings delivered at conferences and other public events. As its primary goal, the project seeks to preserve the stories of individuals who are silenced in multiple ways by a society that marginalizes the voices of women, seniors, and LGBTQ people. ACT UP, StoryCorps OutLoud, and OLOHP are just a few examples of the many oral history projects working to preserve the stories of LGBTQ people from all walks of life around the world.

While these organizations focus on collecting and preserving queer stories, others focus specifically on distributing LGBTQ film and video. Organizations working to deliver LGBTQ media to theaters, festivals, and people's homes include Ariztical Entertainment, Breaking Glass Pictures, First Run Features, and Strand Releasing. Two of the more prominent companies working in this arena are TLA and Wolfe. Philadelphia-based TLA had its roots in experimental live theater and art cinema before turning to the home video market in the early 1980s. The company first opened a handful of alternative video stores in Philadelphia and New York and then added a mail-order catalog to reach a broader home video audience. In the mid-1990s, TLA launched an online video store and an LGBTQ film festival and eventually added a video on demand service. In 2000, the TLA Releasing wing of the company started acquiring, licensing, and distributing LGBTQ films through theaters, festivals, and home video. Through the company's many endeavors, TLA has positioned itself as a provider of a wide array of alternative and independent films, with a heavy emphasis on LGBTQ content.

Wolfe was founded in 1985 by Kathy Wolfe and has always focused exclusively on LGBTQ content, placing a particular emphasis on harder-to-find lesbian titles. The company began as a mail-order home video service before moving into film festivals and online distribution. Like TLA, Wolfe acquires and releases films under its own label, Wolfe Releasing, and distributes films from other companies via its website and on-demand service. While neither Wolfe nor TLA produces any of the stories that they distribute, they provide an important link in the chain that connects queer stories and storytellers with audiences wanting to see and hear those stories.

In addition to those individuals and organizations creating, preserving, distributing, and exhibiting LGBTQ stories, there is one group dedicated to monitoring and evaluating images and stories about queer people. The Gay and Lesbian Alliance Against Defamation (GLAAD) was founded in 1985 by a group of gay activists who were dissatisfied with the insufficient and inaccurate coverage of the AIDS epidemic in the mainstream news media. Since then, GLAAD has grown into the most prominent media watchdog group focused on LGBTQ representation, keeping an eye on content created by studios, networks, and independents, whether they originate from queer or straight storytellers. Each year, GLAAD hands out awards for what they deem positive or progressive representations, and they regularly issue warnings or complaints about films and television programs that reinforce stereotypes or harmful images of LGBTQ people. Although GLAAD has received some criticism over the years for aligning itself with politically questionable financial partners and for celebrating the assimilation of some queer identities while marginalizing others,[3] they continue to be recognized as the most visible and vocal organization to monitor and provide public feedback about representations in storytelling involving LGBTQ characters.

Advancing the LGBTQ Movements

In the Life Media, POWER UP, Three Dollar Bill Cinema, and all the other organizations and individuals dedicated to sharing the stories of queer people help push the LGBTQ movements forward. Each organization makes its own unique contributions, but all of them support LGBTQ social justice in a few key ways. First, they provide inspirational images that expand the possibilities for what it means to be queer in our society. Second, they preserve and share accounts of the triumphs and setbacks that LGBTQ people face. Finally, they help sustain a discursive queer public that provides a base for further activist efforts.

For individual viewers, particularly those discovering or coming to terms with their sexuality or gender identity, the work of queer storytellers can provide support on a very personal level. Seeing queer characters and stories on-screen often provides glimpses of what psychologists Hazel Markus and Paula Nurius refer to as "possible selves."[4] As described by Markus and Nurius, individuals envision their possible selves by drawing on a perception of their past and present identities and then projecting desires onto future versions of themselves. The envisioned possibilities often shape goal setting and ultimately the development of actual selves in the future.

While possible selves are unique and individualized, they also have a substantial social component in that individuals rely on context for their perceptions of past and present and their visions of the future. Individuals are free to imagine any future version of themselves that they would like, but the world around them makes certain options seem either more or less realistic. Markus and Nurius note that "the pool of possible selves derives from the categories made salient by the individual's particular sociocultural and historical context, and from the models, images, and symbols provided by the media and by the individual's immediate social experiences."[5] In other words, most people imagine possible selves based on who and what they see around them in the present. When queer people are invisible or represented as victims, villains, or social deviants, it becomes harder for individuals to imagine possible selves that are successful and productive members of society.

Queer storytellers like those examined in this book offer a wide range of representations that provide the raw materials for individuals to imagine possible queer selves that are happy, successful, and part of a larger community. *In the Life* offers images of real people, both everyday and extraordinary, while the shorts and features of POWER UP provide fictional characters that reflect wishes and desires along with reality. In addition to the people on-screen, Three Dollar Bill Cinema's festivals include visits by successful filmmakers who offer in-person examples of possible selves. And Reel Queer Youth lets youth participants not only see but also work with mentors who embody new possibilities for their futures. As Robert Benford argues, narratives generated by social movements begin with the status quo but envision developments that lead to more desirable narrative endings for those involved. Social movement actors "seek to insert themselves, individually and collectively, into an extant narrative (the status quo story) to bring about change, to create a new narrative."[6] As part of the LGBTQ movements, the organizations explored here offer alternative endings that suggest possible selves for individuals along with new narratives for society as a whole.

In addition to providing inspirational and aspirational images for LGBTQ people and their allies, queer media storytelling frequently provides a kind of testimony, bearing witness to the social injustices that queer people have faced throughout history and continue to face on a regular basis. While the use of the concept varies slightly across fields such as law, psychoanalysis, religion, and history, testimony has traditionally been understood as "the truthful first-person narration of suffering to transform the world."[7] The Latin American literary genre of *testimonio* is in many ways dedicated to this kind of storytelling. George Yúdice defines such testimonial writing as "an authentic narrative, told by a witness who is moved to narrate by the urgency of a situation" and goes on to note that "truth is summoned in the cause of denouncing a present situation of exploitation and oppression or in exorcising and setting aright official history."[8] Leshu Torchin argues that films with activist aims share many of the same characteristics, saying that the activist film "functions as a truthful narration of a situation, presented with the intention of bringing about beneficial change."[9] Describing various kinds of testimonial narratives as "authentic" or "truthful," as Yúdice and Torchin do, invites additional scrutiny. Truth, of course, is frequently subjective and may vary based on perspective and context. As such, it is helpful to think of testimonial narratives as those that offer truth and authenticity as they are perceived by the person offering the narrative. Such narratives, therefore, express a specific storyteller's authentic truth rather than any absolute truth, but it may still reflect and resonate with the experiences of others in similar situations.

The truth of testimony may be personal and come from a particular perspective, but it should not be seen as private. Roger Hallas argues, "The truth produced by testimony is not the privatized and internalized truth of the subject generated in confession, but rather a truth that locates the subject and his or her experience relationally and historically."[10] The truth of testimony is situated within a particular context, responding to and potentially changing that context through its expression. Individuals providing testimony are generally seen as witnesses, and they may occupy one of two positions. There are external witnesses, who experience events solely as observers and therefore provide seemingly objective accounts of situations. There are also internal witnesses, or those who live through and experience a situation firsthand.[11] If the event or situation in question is a traumatic one, an internal witness is often viewed as a survivor of that trauma, a status that brings emotional authority that the external witness may not possess.

The emotional weight of someone's personal experience will have little impact if not conveyed effectively to listeners, viewers, or some other kind of audience. In order for a witness to relay a personal experience, "an act of perception must be transformed into a speech act; mediated by human memory, visual perception thus becomes verbal enunciation."[12] In other words, the act of bearing witness and providing testimony is always a kind of storytelling, and its purpose is to disrupt oppressive knowledge by revealing truths that will bring about beneficial change. Much of the film and video content produced by queer media storytellers has similar aims in that writers, directors, producers, and festival programmers are seeking to improve the world by sharing truthful (in their eyes) accounts of LGBTQ lives and experiences. As media professionals, representatives of the organizations discussed in this book have the skills and knowledge to act as stewards for the stories of LGBTQ individuals and groups, drawing on the conventions of the film and television industries to transform lived experiences into compelling narratives that hopefully connect with an audience.

Most episodes of *In the Life* feature individuals sharing their personal stories, providing testimony and bearing witness to the injustices faced by LGBTQ people over the years. Jeff Howe, for example, shares his experience as a gay man inspired to fight for his country in response to the terrorist attacks on September 11, 2001. He talks about being forced to go back in the closet in order to enlist in the army and discusses the painful and humiliating experience of being kicked out of the military after someone discovered that he was gay. In sharing his story, he bears witness to the pain and suffering caused by the U.S. military's "Don't Ask, Don't Tell" policy. The producers working on the segment made choices about how to shoot and edit Howe's testimony, ultimately delivering his story to a television audience with the goal of inspiring change.

The act of bearing witness is most often associated with stories of harmful activities, whether that means individual crimes or widespread human rights violations. But we can also think of testimonial narratives that bear witness to achievements and advances as well as the realities of everyday life. POWER UP's public service announcements (PSAs) feature committed same-sex couples sharing brief excerpts of their own stories. They reference their love for one another, the amount of time they have been together, and the joys they share raising children. In doing so, they bear witness to the stability of same-sex relationships and the good that can come from them, challenging harmful myths about LGBTQ people by offering their own truths. When packaged as PSAs, the stories advocate for marriage equality, seeking what producers and participants view as a positive social change.

Even fictional stories can be seen as providing a kind of testimony. They may not directly express the lived experience of a real individual, but fictionalized stories frequently draw on the shared experiences of many people to create composite characters and stories that reflect the lives of large groups of people. POWER UP's *Itty Bitty Titty Committee*, for example, may push beyond the bounds of realism in terms of some of its plot points, but the frustration expressed by the characters, who are tired of being forced to live in a patriarchal and heteronormative society, is very real for many women, including those involved in the film's production. Similarly, the short film *Out Again*, produced by participants in Reel Queer Youth, is built on a premise of time travel, which is clearly not taken from someone's actual experience. But at its heart, the film is a coming out story, which taps into a difficult experience common to most queer people. Fictional queer stories, therefore, may not provide testimony about actual events, but they are often rooted in a shared truth about what it means to be queer in a particular cultural context. They bear witness to feelings and emotions rather than factual events, ultimately sharing a different kind of truth as a way of bringing about positive change.

Providing testimony and bearing witness may offer therapeutic benefits for the individual recounting a personal experience, but for queer stories to have a significant impact, they must reach an audience, and that audience must be moved to act in some way. As Torchin argues, the most effective testimonial narratives "produce a community conducive to listening and responding."[13] Effective testimony, in other words, does not just reach a preexisting group of people; instead, it has a significant role in generating that group and developing in them a willingness to take action. In this way, such testimonial narratives, including those created and disseminated by the organizations discussed in this book, can be viewed as building and sustaining a kind of public or counterpublic.

As Michael Warner has discussed in his book on the subject, the term *public* is used in several related yet distinct ways. References to "the public" generally include a totality of all people and stand in contrast to notions of privacy and intimacy. "A public" often refers to a concrete group of people gathered for an event and bounded by a shared physical space, as in the audience for a concert or the participants in a physical protest. While the audience for a specific film screening would fit into this category, there is a third way of thinking of publics that better aligns with the work done by testimonial queer stories shared through film and video. As Warner explains, this third category can be identified as "the kind of public that comes into being only in relation to texts and their circulation."[14] He goes on to suggest that such a public "exists by virtue of being addressed."[15] Thus when texts of any kind—whether they are speeches, films, television programs, websites, or some other form—address a particular set of individuals, those individuals have the potential to become a public. A single text is not enough to create a public, but when many texts with similar messages combine to generate an ongoing discourse that individuals can draw from and contribute to, that circulating discourse can create and sustain a public. Warner argues that a discourse public is only realized through the active participation of the individuals involved and that publics unite strangers through participation.[16] A fully realized public therefore has the potential to bring about social change by uniting people behind a particular cause.

A public that forms around stories circulating through queer film and media stands in opposition to mainstream norms and therefore can be viewed as a counterpublic. In her discussion of the public sphere and democracy, Nancy Fraser argues that many subordinated social groups in our society—including women, people of color, and gays and lesbians—have found it helpful to create publics that provide alternatives to mainstream ideals. She refers to these groups as "subaltern counterpublics," which she defines as "parallel discursive arenas where members of subordinated social groups invent and circulate counterdiscourses, which in turn permit them to formulate alternative interpretations of their identities, interests, and needs."[17] The generation and circulation of counterdiscourses—or counterstorytelling, as I have generally referred to it—is a key concern for all the organizations and individuals discussed in this book. The pilot episode of *In the Life* had relatively modest goals in that it sought to present a realistic cross-section of gays and lesbians on stage and in the audience, largely for the sake of increasing LGBTQ visibility on television. But just by providing a broad range of queer people in a single episode, the show countered the narrow stereotypes that had long dominated representations on television. As *In the Life* developed over the years, producers offered additional counternarratives that aggressively challenged the lies and myths perpetuated by antigay activists and institutions. Similarly, the fiction films of POWER UP offer a wide range of queer people, particularly lesbians, as a way of countering stereotypes and insert queer characters and concerns into largely heteronormative genres. Their PSAs engage directly in political debates, providing glimpses into the lives of functional queer families as a way of challenging misconceptions about what same-sex marriage looks like. Focusing less on the generation and more on the circulation of counterdiscourses, the programming of Three Dollar Bill Cinema provides a venue for introducing audiences to the wide range of counternarratives created by film and video storytellers from around the world.

The media texts generated and circulated by these organizations are not entirely responsible for creating and sustaining queer counterpublics, but they do make significant contributions to that effort. They combine with political speeches from activists, lobbyists, and government leaders; legislation and policies written by elected and appointed officials; printed stories from journalists, bloggers, and novelists; and various expressive works from musicians, dancers, and other artists. All these texts work together to generate counterdiscourses and sustain queer counterpublics.

Fraser argues that one of the strengths of active counterpublics is their ability to interact with—and change—the shape of dominant discourses. She says, "After all, to interact discursively as a member of a public—subaltern or otherwise—is to disseminate one's discourse into ever widening arenas."[18] In addition to sustaining LGBTQ counterpublics, the work of queer media storytellers helps change dominant discourses by reaching beyond those counterpublics and into the mainstream. Individual segments of *In the Life*, for example, were used to educate legislators and other decision-makers as they debated public policy initiatives that shape how the government views and treats LGBTQ people. The regular program made it into people's homes by way of public television, where it mixed with other topical programs about social issues and culture. POWER UP's PSAs also reached out to mainstream television audiences, specifically asking them to reconsider their views on same-sex marriage. And the training programs of POWER UP and Reel Queer Youth not only generate new queer stories in the short term but also work toward long-term goals by training storytellers to share their ideas with a wide range of audiences.

Queer media storytellers support and advance the LGBTQ movements by providing inspirational images of possible selves, sharing testimony that bears witness to the struggles and triumphs of LGBTQ people, and helping sustain and strengthen active queer counterpublics. As contributors to the larger LGBTQ movements, organizations dedicated to queer storytelling also reflect the tension between liberationist and assimilationist strategies that have long defined those movements. Overall, organizations dedicated to queer media storytelling tend to embrace approaches that reflect assimilationist strategies. This is perhaps not surprising, given that such an approach is more likely to be sustainable for an organization that wants to thrive in the long run. Assimilationist efforts tend to focus on finding common ground with other groups as a way of minimizing perceived differences, and in some cases, this is what provides access to the resources of the mainstream media industries and their distribution outlets. For those seeking to reach a wide audience, access to such outlets is vital, and so it becomes helpful to play by at least some of the rules established by the mainstream. In the Life Media, for example, decided to pursue public television as the primary distribution outlet for their program. What now seems like a very tame and reserved first season of *In the Life* still generated controversy and resistance. Expressing a liberal politics of inclusion was not enough to get the program past gatekeepers and into the nationwide PBS lineup, but producers were eventually able to get the show on hundreds of public television stations around the country, which might not have happened had the show embraced a more radical political sensibility. Similarly, POWER UP's PSAs were designed to strengthen support for marriage equality, a component of the rights movement that was already assimilationist by its very nature.

Films produced with a festival audience in mind have more freedom to take risks, express a more radical political stance, and experiment with the norms of film form, in part because they expect to play for audiences that are expecting and even desiring departures from mainstream storytelling. Some of POWER UP's films, including *Starcrossed* and *Itty Bitty Titty Committee*, push beyond the limitations of assimilation to tell riskier stories and express more radical views. But even these films still generally conform to the norms of mainstream film style, in part due to the fact that POWER UP seeks to prepare filmmakers to enter the industry, and this still means playing by certain rules when it comes to form, style, and the on-set production environment. Three Dollar Bill Cinema has the luxury of programming a broad slate of films for any given festival. One politically or stylistically radical film is not likely to drive anyone away from an entire festival, as the range of screenings is likely to at least come close to offering something for every taste.

Whether organizations or their individual projects lean toward strategies of radical transformation or liberal inclusion, they all help advance the LGBTQ movements by altering the media landscape. Ken Plummer reminds us that "the story telling process flows through social acts of domination, hierarchy, marginalization and inequality."[19] Those with more power and resources are more likely to be heard and are able to set the agendas and frame the questions that guide public media discourse. Queer counterstorytellers strengthen and amplify the voices of the less powerful to help reset agendas and reframe questions so that LGBTQ people are visible and validated in the public sphere.

For many decades, LGBTQ activists worked in an environment where mediated images of queer people were either nonexistent or rooted in stereotypes and lies. Working in an environment that oppressed them, activists struggled to get their messages about equality to mainstream voters, policy makers, and the general public. More recently, as queer storytellers have circulated their own images and ideas through film, television, and other media, they have not only increased the number of such images in circulation but also offered a wider range of perspectives that come closer to capturing the true diversity of the LGBTQ population. With these images circulating more prominently and pushing back against the silence and lies that had previously dominated the media landscape, the work of LGBTQ activists is given a more hospitable cultural environment in which to seek real change with respect to laws, policies, and social practices.

Moving Forward

The organizations discussed in this book, including those examined in depth as well as those mentioned only briefly, all make valuable contributions to the ever-expanding queer media landscape, and as such, they shape the ongoing development of the LGBTQ movements. But the work is not finished. The push for LGBTQ equality has led to changes in policies related to military service and marriage equality, but there is significant conservative backlash threatening to slow progress or even reverse some of the gains of the LGBTQ movements. For those who might have become complacent after eight years of advances under the Obama administration, the 2016 election of Donald Trump as president of the United States served as a wake-up call, particularly as President Trump filled his cabinet with individuals who have been very public with their anti-LGBTQ actions and sentiments. Additionally, states like North Carolina, Tennessee, and Texas have passed or considered legislation that not only allows discrimination against LGBTQ people in areas like employment and housing but goes so far as to make it illegal for individual cities to pass their own antidiscrimination measures if they offer more protection than what is provided at the state level. Some conservative activists and politicians are using questions of bathroom privacy and religious freedom as justification for denying queer people equal rights. Clearly the LGBTQ movements still have work to do, and so do storytellers. In an era when queer people cannot always count on support and protection from their government, this work becomes even more important.

As lobbyists, protestors, and other political activists work on the front lines of the LGBTQ movements, storytellers must continue to collect, generate, and share narratives that express the humanity of LGBTQ people in all their diversity. Unfortunately, one trait that the queer media landscape has in common with the mainstream media landscape is the fact that cisgender white men are overrepresented (with respect to the overall population) both on-screen and behind the camera. Women, trans people, and people of color continue to be underrepresented in both areas, and in order to advance the larger LGBTQ movements effectively, organizations that support queer storytelling must increase their attention to the stories and voices of groups that are marginalized within the larger LGBTQ population.

Even with increasing attention to LGBTQ stories from mainstream media producers—including corporate-run studios and networks as well as straight writers, directors, and performers—there is still a need for queer storytellers to tell their own stories as well as those of other queer people. While the increased acceptance from mainstream creators is valuable, those stories are frequently filtered through a heteronormative lens. Or, at the very least, if they are created by a major studio or network that is driven by the bottom line and must therefore appeal to as broad an audience as possible, they are likely to be packaged in a way that will make them safe and appealing to mainstream audiences. To continue providing a variety of perspectives on LGBTQ experiences, including those that might not be palatable to mainstream audiences or even to all queer audiences, we must continue to encourage storytelling by liberal, radical, and yes, even conservative queer people.

To generate more perspectives from more storytellers, those who already possess storytelling knowledge and skills must work to share their knowledge with others. Following the examples of POWER UP and Reel Queer Youth, skilled storytellers can have a significant impact by focusing on critical pedagogy and community building. A critical pedagogical approach can first help new storytellers understand how oppressive narratives from the past and present create obstacles for queer people and then show them how to generate new narratives to help liberate people from that oppression. An emphasis on community building reminds individuals that they can make a larger impact if they connect and collaborate with others who have similar passions and goals.

The LGBTQ movements must also embrace and support storytelling in a wide variety of forms as made possible by ever-changing media technologies. For many years, individuals were essentially shut out of visual media storytelling by the high barriers to entry that define film and television production. The introduction of consumer cameras, smartphones, desktop editing software, and an array of social media and video sharing platforms have all made audiovisual storytelling accessible to a broader range of people, but there is still the problem of getting content to the right audiences. While videos posted on YouTube are available to almost everyone, the sheer volume of video content posted there makes it difficult for a single storyteller to break through the clutter and connect with an audience. For those who do not have the time or interest to browse and search endlessly through online videos, those stories essentially disappear. The volume of online videos is only going to increase, and finding the best content will get more difficult. Pulling together the work of queer storytellers so that individuals can find it easily will help prevent the disappearance of stories that might otherwise get lost in the shuffle. The It Gets Better Project provides one model of what this curation might look like, as its site pulls together thousands of videos with a shared theme that is likely to resonate with many queer viewers. Collecting and organizing stories of activism, coming out, families, dating, or other topics would help filter the vast offerings of the internet to connect stories with audiences. Making collections searchable and individual items sharable (via social media) will make them even more powerful tools for social change. As digital storytelling proliferates, the careful curation of online stories will be just as important as the generation of those stories.

To continue pushing the LGBTQ movements forward, storytellers—including writers, directors, actors, producers, and visual designers—must continue to tell their own stories as well as those of people who may not have the ability to get their stories on a page or on a screen. Archivists, librarians, and historians must continue to collect and preserve stories in whatever form they exist, finding ways to protect them and make them available to future generations. Critics and scholars must continue to examine and discuss these stories to better understand the processes by which they are created and the impact they may have. In all these ways, we can ensure that creative acts of queer storytelling will continue to highlight and express the humanity of the LGBTQ communities, helping achieve and protect social equality for all queer people.

Acknowledgments

This book is about storytelling and storytellers. Completing the book would not have been possible without the generosity of those who shared their stories and their time with me, helping me understand the work they have done to create, preserve, and disseminate stories that matter. I am forever grateful to Christopher Racster, Robert Gant, Chad Allen, Craig Dougherty, Michelle Kristel, Jacqueline Gares, Chuy Sanchez, Erik Satre, Eleanor Moonier, Ellen Carton, Lisa Thrasher, Jason Plourde, Danny Tayara, Sam Berliner, Keith Bacon, Kathleen Mullen, Finn Cottom, Theo Calhoun, and Mark Quigley. Thanks also to the participants and mentors of the Reel Queer Youth program who allowed me to observe their activities during summer workshops between 2014 and 2017.

I am fortunate to have colleagues who provided support for this project at various stages of its development. Jon Cavallero, Ingrid Walker, and Charles Williams offered suggestions that helped me turn conference papers and rough essays into book chapters. Stephen Tropiano drew on his extensive knowledge of queer media studies to provide valuable feedback on the full manuscript. Zach Curtis helped prepare illustrations for the book. Bill Kunz and Jeny McCray helped me work through a variety of occupational challenges. And the faculty, staff, students, and administration of the School of Interdisciplinary Arts and Sciences at the University of Washington Tacoma—particularly those in film studies, American studies, and communication—provided an intellectually stimulating environment in which to conduct my work. I thank all of them for their valuable contributions to this project.

I thank Leslie Mitchner and Lisa Banning for supporting this book, guiding it through the editorial process, and keeping things running smoothly. I also know that after this acknowledgments section is finalized and the manuscript leaves my hands, many more people at Rutgers University Press will contribute to elements like layout, design, and marketing. I thank all those whose work is yet to come.

I am grateful to my family for supporting me throughout my various personal and professional journeys. And I appreciate the friends who have contributed to my emotional well-being by occasionally pulling me away from my work. In particular, I want to thank Lisa Marchal, Jason Thrasher, Adam Parker, and Rascal.

Most importantly, I thank Ed Chamberlain for being my biggest supporter, my most valuable sounding board, and a constant inspiration to me, both professionally and personally.

Appendix

In addition to the small number of organizations discussed in this book, there are many more that focus on collecting, preserving, and sharing the stories of LGBTQ people. The following is a partial list of media festivals, archives, libraries, and other collections that house LGBTQ stories in a variety of formats. This list is not meant to be exhaustive; rather, it provides a sampling of the many resources available to scholars, students, filmmakers, and audiences.

LGBTQ Media Festivals

Appalachian Queer Film Festival
Lewisburg, WV
http://www.aqff.org

Austin Gay and Lesbian International Film Festival
Austin, TX
http://www.agliff.org

BFI Flare: London LGBT Film Festival
London, United Kingdom
http://www.bfi.org.uk/flare

Bloomington Pride Film Festival
Bloomington, IN
http://www.bloomingtonpride.org

Chéries-Chéris: Paris Gay, Lesbian, Trans Film Festival
Paris, France
http://www.cheries-cheris.com

Connecticut LGBT Film Festival
Hartford, CT
http://www.outfilmct.org

Festival Mix Milano di Cinema Gaylesbico e Queer Culture
Milan, Italy
http://www.festivalmixmilano.com/

Frameline: San Francisco International LGBTQ Film Festival
San Francisco, CA
http://www.frameline.org

Hong Kong Lesbian and Gay Film Festival
Hong Kong, China
http://www.hklgff.hk

image+nation: Montreal LGBTQ Film Festival
Montreal, Canada
http://www.image-nation.org

Inside Out: Toronto LGBT Film Festival
Toronto, Canada
http://www.insideout.ca

Kaleidoscope LGBT Film Festival
Little Rock, AR
http://www.kaleidoscopefilmfestival.com

KASHISH Mumbai International Queer Film Festival
Mumbai, India
http://www.mumbaiqueerfest.com

MIX Copenhagen LesbianGayBiTrans Film Festival
Copenhagen, Denmark
http://www.mixcopenhagen.dk

MIX NYC: New York Queer Experimental Film Festival
New York, NY
http://www.mixnyc.org

Newfest: New York LGBT Film Festival
New York, NY
http://www.newfest.org

North Carolina Gay + Lesbian Film Festival
Durham, NC
http://www.carolinatheatre.org/films/festivals/ncglff

Outfest Los Angeles LGBT Film Festival
Los Angeles, CA
http://www.outfest.org

Outfest Peru
Lima, Peru
http://www.outfestperu.com

Out on Film: Atlanta's LGBT Film Festival
Atlanta, GA
http://www.outonfilm.org

Outshine Film Festival
Miami, FL, and Fort Lauderdale, FL
http://www.mifofilm.com

Paris International Lesbian and Feminist Film Festival
Paris, France
http://www.cineffable.fr/en

QDoc Portland Queer Documentary Film Festival
Portland, OR
http://www.queerdocfest.org

qFLIX Philadelphia
Philadelphia, PA
http://www.qflixphilly.com

Queer Screen Film Fest
Sydney, Australia
http://www.queerscreen.org.au

Rainbow Reel Tokyo
Tokyo, Japan
http://www.rainbowreeltokyo.com

Reel Affirmations: Washington DC's International LGBT Film Festival
Washington, DC
http://www.thedccenter.org/reelaffirmations

Reeling: The Chicago LGBTQ+ International Film Festival
Chicago, IL
http://www.reelingfilmfestival.org

ReelQ: Pittsburg LGBT Film Festival
Pittsburg, PA
http://www.reelq.org

Rio's Gender and Sexuality Film Festival
Rio de Janeiro, Brazil
http://www.riofgc.com

San Francisco Transgender Film Festival
San Francisco, CA
http://www.sftff.org

Tampa Bay International Gay and Lesbian Film Festival
Tampa, FL
http://www.tiglff.com

Translations: The Seattle Transgender Film Festival
Seattle, WA
http://www.threedollarbillcinema.org/programs/translations

TWIST: Seattle Queer Film Festival
Seattle, WA
http://www.threedollarbillcinema.org/programs/TWIST

Vancouver Queer Film Festival
Vancouver, Canada
http://www.queerfilmfestival.ca

Wicked Queer Boston LGBT Film Festival
Boston, MA
http://www.wickedqueer.org

LGBTQ Archives, Libraries, and Collections

ACT UP Oral History Project
Excerpts and transcripts available online
Full videos at San Francisco Main Library and New York Public Library
http://www.actuporalhistory.org

Australian Lesbian and Gay Archives
Melbourne, Australia
http://www.alga.org.au

Barbara Gittings Gay/Lesbian Collection at the Independence Branch Library
Philadelphia, PA
http://www.freelibrary.org

Canadian Lesbian and Gay Archives
Toronto, Canada
http://www.clga.ca

Gay and Lesbian Archive of Mid-America
University of Missouri–Kansas City
Kansas City, MO
http://library.umkc.edu/spec-col/glama/index.htm

Gay and Lesbian Archives of the Pacific Northwest
Portland, OR
http://www.glapn.org

Gay and Lesbian Collections and AIDS/HIV Collections
New York Public Library
New York, NY
http://www.nypl.org

Gay and Lesbian Memory in Action (GALA)
Johannesburg, South Africa
http://www.gala.co.za/archives_research.htm

Gerber/Hart Library and Archives
Chicago, IL
http://www.gerberhart.org

GLBT Historical Society Archives and Museum
San Francisco, CA
http://www.glbthistory.org

Gulf Coast Archives and Museum of GLBT History
Houston, TX
http://www.gcam.org

International Homo/Lesbisch Informatiecentrum en Archeif (IHLIA)
Amsterdam Public Library
Amsterdam, Netherlands
http://www.ihlia.nl/?lang=en

James C. Hormel LGBTQIA Center
San Francisco Public Library
San Francisco, CA
http://www.sfpl.org/gaylesbian

Jean Byers Sampson Center for Diversity in Maine—LGBT Collection
University of Southern Maine
Portland, ME
http://usm.maine.edu/library/specialcollections/lgbt-collection

Jean-Nickolaus Tretter Collection in Gay, Lesbian, Bisexual, and Transgender Studies
University of Minnesota
Minneapolis, MN
http://www.lib.umn.edu/tretter

John J. Wilcox Jr. LGBT Archives of Philadelphia
William Way LGBT Community Center
Philadelphia, PA
http://www.waygay.org/archives/

June L. Mazer Lesbian Archives
West Hollywood, CA
http://www.mazerlesbianarchives.org

Kendall Clawson Library, Q Center Portland
Portland, OR
http://www.pdxqcenter.org

Kinsey Institute for Research in Sex, Gender, and Reproduction
Indiana University
Bloomington, IN
http://www.kinseyinstitute.org

Leather Archives and Museum
Chicago, IL
http://www.leatherarchives.org

Lesbian and Gay Archives of New Zealand
Wellington, New Zealand
http://www.laganz.org.nz/

Lesbian and Gay Newsmedia Archive (LAGNA)
London, United Kingdom
http://www.lagna.org.uk/

Lesbian Herstory Archives
New York, NY
http://www.lesbianherstoryarchives.org

LGBT Community Center National History Archive
New York, NY
http://www.gaycenter.org/archives

Old Lesbian Oral Herstory Project
Print Copies housed at Smith College
Northampton, MA
http://www.olohp.org

ONE National Gay and Lesbian Archives
Los Angeles, CA
http://www.onearchives.org

Outfest UCLA Legacy Project for LGBT Moving Image Preservation
Los Angeles, CA
http://www.cinema.ucla.edu/collections/outfest-ucla-legacy-project-lgbt-moving-image-preservation

Quatrefoil Library
Minneapolis, MN
http://www.qlibrary.org

Rainbow History Project
Washington, DC
http://www.rainbowhistory.org

Schwules Museum and Archives
Berlin, Germany
http://www.schwulesmuseum.de/en/archive/

Skeivt Arkiv—Norwegian national archive for queer and LGBT history
Bergen, Norway
http://www.skeivtarkiv.no/en

Sophia Smith Collection
Smith College
Northampton, MA
http://www.smith.edu/libraries/special-collections

Stonewall National Library and Archives
Fort Lauderdale, FL
http://www.stonewallnationalmuseum.org

StoryCorps OutLoud
Excerpts available online
Full collection housed at the American Folklife Center, Library of Congress
Washington, DC
http://www.storycorps.org/discover/outloud/

Transgender Archives
University of Victoria
Victoria, Canada
http://www.uvic.ca/transgenderarchives/

Williams-Nichols Collection
University of Louisville
Louisville, KY
http://library.louisville.edu/ekstrom/lgbt_studies/primary

Notes

Introduction Telling Stories for Social Change

1 "Digital Storytelling: Spotlighting Same-Sex Couples and Other Messengers Online," *Freedom to Marry*, accessed August 28, 2016, http://www.freedomtomarry.org/pages/Digital-Storytelling-Spotlighting-Same-Sex-Couples-And-Other-Messengers.
2 "Digital Storytelling."
3 See, for example, Vicki Mayer, Miranda J. Banks, and John Thornton Caldwell, eds., *Production Studies: Cultural Studies of Media Industries* (New York: Routledge, 2009).
4 Throughout the book, I use the word *queer* as an umbrella term to refer to individuals, actions, and beliefs that do not fit within heteronormative or cisnormative understandings of human identities. I use *queer* and *LGBTQ* somewhat interchangeably, in part for language variety, but also as a way of highlighting both the range of nonnormative sexual and gender identities and the shared marginalization that unites them.
5 Nick Couldry, *Why Voice Matters: Culture and Politics after Neoliberalism* (London: Sage, 2010), 1.
6 Couldry, 9.
7 Couldry, 101.
8 John Hartley, "Authorship and the Narrative of the Self," in *A Companion to Media Authorship*, ed. Jonathan Gray and Derek Johnson (Malden, Mass.: Wiley-Blackwell, 2013), 29, emphasis in original.
9 John Caughie, *Theories of Authorship* (London: Routledge, 1988), 62.
10 Andrew Sarris, "Notes on the Auteur Theory in 1962," *Film Culture* 27 (Winter 1962–1963): 1–8.
11 Andrew Sarris, *The American Cinema: Directors and Directions, 1929–1968* (New York: E. P. Dutton City, 1968), 24.
12 Pushing beyond the emphasis on aesthetics, Timothy Corrigan has argued that auteurism has a commercial value in its ability to turn directors into stars. See Corrigan, *A Cinema without Walls: Movies and Culture after Vietnam* (New Brunswick, N.J.: Rutgers University Press, 1991), 101–136.

13 See, for example, Pauline Kael, "Circles and Squares," *Film Quarterly* 16, no. 3 (1963): 12–26.

14 James Naremore, "Authorship and the Cultural Politics of Film Criticism," *Film Quarterly* 44, no. 1 (1990): 14–23.

15 Robert Carringer, "Collaboration and Concepts of Authorship," *PMLA* 116, no. 2 (2001): 377. See also Robert Carringer, *The Making of Citizen Kane*, rev. ed. (Berkeley: University of California Press, 1996).

16 Colin Burnett, "Hidden Hands at Work: Authorship, Intentional Flux, and the Dynamics of Collaboration," in *A Companion to Media Authorship*, ed. Gray and Johnson, 112–132.

17 John T. Caldwell, "Authorship below-the-Line," in *A Companion to Media Authorship*, ed. Gray and Johnson, 350.

18 See, for example, Matthew Bernstein, "The Producer as Auteur," in *Auteurs and Authorship: A Film Reader*, ed. Barry Keith Grant (Malden, Mass.: Blackwell, 2008), 180–189; Michael DeAngelis, "Robert Stigwood: Producer, Author, Text," in *Authorship and Film*, ed. David A. Gerstner and Janet Staiger (New York: Routledge, 2003), 247–261; Derek Johnson, "Scoring Authorship: An Interview with Bear McCreary," in *A Companion to Media Authorship*, ed. Gray and Johnson, 391–402; and David Brisbin, "Production Design and the Invisible Arts of Seeing," in *A Companion to Media Authorship*, ed. Gray and Johnson, 370–390.

19 Roland Barthes, "The Death of the Author," in *Image Music Text*, trans. and ed. Stephen Heath (New York: Hill and Wang, 1977), 147.

20 See Michel Foucault, "What Is an Author?," in *Language, Counter-memory, Practice: Selected Essays and Interviews by Michel Foucault*, ed. Donald F. Bouchard, trans. Donald F. Bouchard and Sherry Simon (Ithaca, N.Y.: Cornell University Press, 1977), 113–138.

21 See, for example, Kristina Busse, "The Return of the Author: Ethos and Identity Politics," in *A Companion to Media Authorship*, ed. Gray and Johnson, 48–68; Catherine Grant, "Secret Agents: Feminist Theories of Women's Film Authorship," *Feminist Theory* 2, no. 1 (2001): 113–130; Andy Medhurst, "That Special Thrill: *Brief Encounter*, Homosexuality and Authorship," in *Queer Screen: A Screen Reader*, ed. Jackie Stacey and Sarah Street (London: Routledge, 2007), 41–52; Kaja Silverman, "The Female Authorial Voice," in *Film and Authorship*, ed. Virginia Wright Wexman (New Brunswick, N.J.: Rutgers University Press, 2003), 50–75.

22 Janet Staiger, "Authorship Approaches," in *Authorship and Film*, ed. Gerstner and Staiger, 27.

23 Amy Villarejo, "Movies and the Politics of Authorship," in *American Cinema of the 1990s: Themes and Variations*, ed. Chris Holmlund (New Brunswick, N.J.: Rutgers University Press, 2008), 85.

24 Alexander Doty, *Making Things Perfectly Queer: Interpreting Mass Culture* (Minneapolis: University of Minnesota Press, 1993), 38. See also DeAngelis, "Robert Stigwood," 247–261; and Alexander Dhoest, "How Queer Is *L'Air de Paris*?: Marcel Carné and Queer Authorship," *Scope: An Online Journal of Film Studies* (May 2003), http://www.nottingham.ac.uk/scope/documents/2003/may-2003/dhoest.pdf.

25 Andrea Weiss, "Transgressive Cinema: Lesbian Independent Film," in *Queer Cinema: The Film Reader*, ed. Harry Benshoff and Sean Griffin (New York: Routledge, 2004), 44.

26 Walter Metz, "John Waters Goes to Hollywood: A Poststructural Authorship Study," in *Authorship and Film*, ed. Gerstner and Staiger, 157–174; Michael DeAngelis, "Authorship and New Queer Cinema: The Case of Todd Haynes," in *Auteurs and Authorship*, ed. Grant, 292–303; Marica Landy, "Storytelling and Information in Todd Haynes' Films," in *The Cinema of Todd Haynes*, ed. James Morrison (London: Wallflower Press, 2007), 7–24. See also B. Ruby Rich, "The New Queer Cinema," in *Queer Cinema*, ed. Benshoff and Griffin, 53–59; and Villarejo, "Movies and the Politics of Authorship."

27 Richard Delgado, "Storytelling for Oppositionists and Others: A Plea for Narrative," in *Critical Race Theory: The Cutting Edge*, 2nd ed., ed. Richard Delgado and Jean Stefancic (Philadelphia: Temple University Press, 2000), 61.

28 Delgado, 61.

29 Pearl Bowser, Jane Gaines, and Charles Musser, eds., *Oscar Micheaux and His Circle: African-American Filmmaking and Race Cinema of the Silent Era* (Bloomington: Indiana University Press, 2001).

30 Jun Okada, "'Noble and Uplifting and Boring as Hell': Asian American Film and Video, 1971–1982," *Cinema Journal* 49, no. 1 (2009): 23.

31 Stephen Michael Charbonneau, "Branching Out: Young Appalachian Selves, Autoethnographic Aesthetics, and the Founding of Appalshop," *Journal of Popular Film and Television* 37, no. 3 (2009): 137.

32 Gloria Ladson-Billings, "Just What Is Critical Race Theory, and What's It Doing in a Nice Field like Education?," in *Race Is . . . Race Isn't: Critical Race Theory and Qualitative Studies in Education*, ed. Laurence Parker, Donna Deyhle, and Sofia Villenas (Boulder, Colo.: Westview Press, 1999), 16.

33 Richard Delgado and Jean Stefancic, *Critical Race Theory: An Introduction* (New York: New York University Press, 2012), 49.

34 Joseph E. Davis, "Narrative and Social Movements: The Power of Stories," in *Stories of Change: Narrative and Social Movements*, ed. Joseph E. Davis (Albany, N.Y.: SUNY Press, 2002), 17.

35 Davis, 19.

36 Davis, 21.

37 Robert Benford, "Controlling Narratives and Narratives as Control within Social Movements," in *Stories of Change*, ed. Davis, 54.

38 Christopher Pullen, *Gay Identity, New Storytelling, and the Media* (New York: Palgrave Macmillan, 2009), 13.

39 Christopher Pullen, *Documenting Gay Men: Identity and Performance in Reality Television and Documentary Film* (London: McFarland, 2007), 10.

40 Ken Plummer, *Telling Sexual Stories: Power, Change, and Social Worlds* (New York: Routledge, 1995), 85.

41 Plummer, 35.

42 Plummer, 35.

43 Katie Zezima and David Weigel, "GOP Takes Platform Further to Right on LGBT Issues; Trump Stays Out of It," *Washington Post*, July 14, 2016, A8.

44 Ted G. Jelen, "Catholicism, Homosexuality, and Same-Sex Marriage in the United States," in *Faith, Politics, and Sexual Diversity in Canada and the United States*, ed. David Royside and Clyde Wilcox (Vancouver: University of British Columbia Press, 2011), 209.

45 Dawne Moon, "Religious Views of Homosexuality," in *Handbook of Lesbian and Gay Studies*, ed. Diane Richardson and Steven Seidman (London: Sage, 2002), 313.

46 John Blum, William McFeely, Edmund Morgan, Arthur Schlesinger, Kenneth Stampp, and C. Vann Woodward, *The National Experience: A History of the United States,* 6th ed. (San Diego: Harcourt Brace Jovanovich, 1985), 830.
47 Blum et al., 908.
48 Robert Eberwein, *Sex Ed: Film, Video, and the Framework of Desire* (New Brunswick, N.J.: Rutgers University Press, 1999), 141.
49 Joey L. Mogul, Andrea J. Ritchie, and Kay Whitlock, *Queer (In)Justice: The Criminalization of LGBT People in the United States* (Boston: Beacon Press, 2011), 72.
50 Mogul, Ritchie, and Whitlock, 53–57.
51 104th Congress, 2nd Session, H.R. 3396—Defense of Marriage Act (1996).
52 103rd Congress, 1st Session, H.R. 4201—National Defense Authorization Act for Fiscal Year 1994 (1993). Section 546 of this act established the "Don't Ask, Don't Tell" policy that prevented officials from asking soldiers about their sexual orientation but still allowed them to discharge soldiers who were found to be gay.
53 U.S. Senate Investigations Subcommittee of the Committee on Expenditures, *Employment of Homosexuals and Other Sex Perverts in the U.S. Government* (Washington, D.C.: Government Printing Office, 1950). See also David K. Johnson, *The Lavender Scare: The Cold War Persecution of Gays and Lesbians in the Federal Government* (Chicago: University of Chicago Press, 2004).
54 Michael Bronski, *A Queer History of the United States* (Boston: Beacon Press, 2011), 220.
55 Walter L. Williams and Yolanda Retter, eds., *Gay and Lesbian Rights in the United States: A Documentary History* (Westport, Conn.: Greenwood Press, 2003), 144.
56 James Dobson, *Marriage Under Fire: Why We Must Win the Battle* (Portland, Ore.: Multnomah Press, 2004), 19.
57 Harry M. Benshoff and Sean Griffin, *Queer Images: A History of Gay and Lesbian Film in America* (Lanham, Md.: Rowman & Littlefield, 2006), 26.
58 Laura Horak, *Girls Will Be Boys: Cross-Dressed Women, Lesbians, and American Cinema, 1908–1934* (New Brunswick, N.J.: Rutgers University Press, 2016), 168.
59 Benshoff and Griffin, *Queer Images*, 26.
60 Vito Russo, *The Celluloid Closet: Homosexuality in the Movies,* rev. ed. (New York: Harper and Row, 1987), 59.
61 Larry Gross, *Up from Invisibility: Lesbians, Gay Men, and the Media in America* (New York: Columbia University Press, 2001), 59–61.
62 Steven Seidman, *Beyond the Closet: The Transformation of Gay and Lesbian Life* (New York: Routledge, 2002), 160.
63 For discussions of bisexual and transgender characters on-screen, see Maria San Filippo, *The B Word: Bisexuality in Contemporary Film and Television* (Bloomington: Indiana University Press, 2013); and John Phillips, *Transgender on Screen* (New York: Palgrave Macmillan, 2006).
64 Stephen Tropiano, *The Prime Time Closet: A History of Gays and Lesbians on TV* (New York: Applause, 2002), 3.
65 Edward Alwood, "A Gift of Gab: How Independent Broadcasters Gave Gay Rights Pioneers a Chance to Be Heard," in *Media Queered: Visibility and Its Discontents,* ed. Kevin G. Barnhurst (New York: Peter Lang, 2007), 41.
66 Steven Capsuto, *Alternate Channels: The Uncensored Story of Gay and Lesbian Images on Radio and Television* (New York: Ballantine Books, 2000), 4–5.
67 Gross, *Up from Invisibility*, 46–49; Capsuto, *Alternate Channels*, 5.

68 Gross, *Up from Invisibility*, 143–145.
69 Ron Becker, *Gay TV and Straight America* (New Brunswick, N.J.: Rutgers University Press, 2006), 81.
70 Steven F. Hick and John G. McNutt, "Communities and Advocacy on the Internet: A Conceptual Framework," in *Advocacy, Activism, and the Internet: Community Organization and Social Policy*, ed. Steven F. Hick and John G. McNutt (Chicago: Lyceum Books, 2002), 8.
71 Carrie A. Rentschler, "Expanding the Definition of Media Activism," in *A Companion to Media Studies*, ed. Angharad N. Valdivia (Oxford: Blackwell, 2003), 530.
72 For a more complete discussion of queer communities and film festivals, see chapter 4.
73 Jeffrey Weeks, *Making Sexual History* (Cambridge: Polity Press, 2000), 183.
74 Kath Weston, *Families We Choose: Lesbians, Gays, Kinship*, 2nd ed. (New York: Columbia University Press, 1997), 123.

Chapter 1 Challenging Oppressive Myths

1 Craig A. Rimmerman, *The Lesbian and Gay Movements: Assimilation or Liberation?*, 2nd ed. (Boulder, Colo.: Westview Press, 2014), 5.
2 Steven Seidman, *Beyond the Closet: The Transformation of Gay and Lesbian Life* (New York: Routledge, 2002), 184.
3 John Lauritsen and David Thorstad, *The Early Homosexual Rights Movement (1864–1935)*, rev. ed. (Ojai, Calif.: Times Change Press, 1995), 8, 37.
4 John D'Emilio, *Sexual Politics, Sexual Communities: The Making of a Homosexual Minority in the United States, 1940–1970*, 2nd ed. (Chicago: University of Chicago Press, 1998), 23–24.
5 D'Emilio, 66.
6 Rimmerman, *Lesbian and Gay Movements*, 18.
7 Lillian Faderman, *The Gay Revolution: The Story of a Struggle* (New York: Simon & Schuster, 2015), 91–92.
8 Marcia M. Gallo, *Different Daughters: A History of the Daughters of Bilitis and the Rise of the Lesbian Rights Movement* (New York: Carroll & Graf, 2006), 10.
9 Rimmerman, *Lesbian and Gay Movements*, 19.
10 D'Emilio, *Sexual Politics*, 3.
11 Susan Stryker, *Transgender History* (Berkeley, Calif.: Seal Press, 2008), 59–65.
12 Martin Duberman, *Stonewall* (New York: Dutton Press, 1993), 224.
13 Michael Bronski, *A Queer History of the United States* (Boston: Beacon Press, 2011), 211.
14 Bronski, 213.
15 Steven Capsuto, *Alternate Channels: The Uncensored Story of Gay and Lesbian Images on Radio and Television* (New York: Ballantine Books, 2000), 59–105; Kathryn C. Montgomery, *Target: Prime Time: Advocacy Groups and the Struggle over Entertainment Television* (New York: Oxford University Press, 1989), 75–100.
16 Steven Epstein, "Gay and Lesbian Movements in the United States: Dilemmas of Identity, Diversity, and Political Strategy," in *The Global Emergence of Gay and Lesbian Politics: National Imprints of a Worldwide Movement*, ed. Barry D. Adam, Jan Willem Duyvendak, and Andre Krouwel (Philadelphia: Temple University Press, 1999), 55.

17 Epstein, 64.
18 See, for example, Kevin G. Barnhurst, ed., *Media Queered: Visibility and Its Discontents* (New York: Peter Lang, 2007).
19 Suzanna Danuta Walters, *All the Rage: The Story of Gay Visibility in America* (Chicago: University of Chicago Press, 2001), 15.
20 Grant Lukenbill, *Untold Millions: Positioning Your Business for the Gay and Lesbian Consumer Revolution* (New York: Harper Collins, 1995), 2.
21 Dean Spade, "A Politics beyond Recognition," in *Cruising the Archive: Queer Art and Culture in Los Angeles, 1945–1980*, ed. David Frantz and Mia Locks (Los Angeles: ONE National Gay and Lesbian Archives, 2011), 102–106.
22 John D'Emilio, *In a New Century: Essays on Queer History, Politics, and Community Life* (Madison: University of Wisconsin Press, 2014), 56.
23 D'Emilio, 57.
24 Benedict Anderson, *Imagined Communities* (London: Verso, 1983).
25 Dorothy Noyes, "Group," *Journal of American Folklore* 108, no. 430 (1995), 466.
26 Kath Weston, *Families We Choose: Lesbians, Gays, Kinship*, 2nd ed. (New York: Columbia University Press, 1997), 129.
27 Weston, 134.
28 A. H. Maslow, *Motivation and Personality* (New York: Harper, 1954).
29 Kimberly D. Hudson, "Toward a Conceptual Framework for Understanding Community Belonging and Well-Being: Insights from a Queer-Mixed Perspective," *Journal of Community Practice* 23 (2015): 29.
30 Jeffrey Weeks, *Making Sexual History* (Cambridge: Polity Press, 2000), 182.
31 Patricia Hill Collins, "The New Politics of Community," *American Sociological Review* 75, no. 1 (2010): 16.
32 Martin Meeker, *Contacts Desired: Gay and Lesbian Communications and Community, 1940s–1970s* (Chicago: University of Chicago Press, 2006), 21.
33 Meeker, 23–26.
34 David R. Coon, "Sun, Sand, and Citizenship: The Marketing of Gay Tourism," *Journal of Homosexuality* 59, no. 4 (2012): 517.
35 Larry Gross, *Up from Invisibility: Lesbians, Gay Men, and the Media in America* (New York: Columbia University Press, 2001), 24.
36 Stryker, *Transgender History*, 53.
37 Katherine Sender, *Business Not Politics: The Making of the Gay Market* (New York: Columbia University Press, 2004), 26.
38 Richard Dyer, *Now You See It: Studies on Lesbian and Gay Film* (London: Routledge, 1990), 120.
39 Harry M. Benshoff and Sean Griffin, *Queer Images: A History of Gay and Lesbian Film in America* (Lanham, Md.: Rowman & Littlefield, 2006), 119.
40 Janet Staiger, "Finding Community in the Early 1960s: Underground Cinema and Sexual Politics," in *Queer Cinema: The Film Reader*, ed. Harry Benshoff and Sean Griffin (New York: Routledge, 2004), 182.
41 For a detailed comparison of *Some of Your Best Friends* and *Word Is Out*, see Christopher Pullen, *Documenting Gay Men: Identity and Performance in Reality Television and Documentary Film* (London: McFarland, 2007), 93–98.
42 Benshoff and Griffin, *Queer Images*, 154.
43 Andrea Weiss, "Transgressive Cinema: Lesbian Independent Film," in *Queer Cinema*, ed. Benshoff and Griffin, 44.

44 Dyer, *Now You See It*, 203.

45 Curran Nault, "No Skin off My Ass: Bruce LaBruce and the Curious Case of Queer Punk Love," in *Queer Love in Film and Television: Critical Essays*, ed. Pamela Demory and Christopher Pullen (New York: Palgrave Macmillan, 2013), 170–171.

46 Catherine Saalfield, "On the Make: Activist Video Collectives," in *Queer Looks: Perspectives on Lesbian and Gay Film and Video*, ed. Martha Gever, Pratibha Parmar, and John Greyson (New York: Routledge, 1993), 27.

47 Benshoff and Griffin, *Queer Images*, 212.

48 Saalfield, "On the Make," 26.

49 Alexandra Juhasz, *AIDS TV: Identity, Community, and Alternative Video* (Durham, N.C.: Duke University Press, 1995), 3.

50 Michele Aaron, "New Queer Cinema: An Introduction," in *New Queer Cinema: A Critical Reader*, ed. Michele Aaron (New Brunswick, N.J.: Rutgers University Press, 2004), 3.

51 B. Ruby Rich, *New Queer Cinema: The Director's Cut* (Durham, N.C.: Duke University Press, 2013), 18.

52 Aaron, "New Queer Cinema," 3.

53 Aaron, 5.

54 B. Ruby Rich, "A Queer and Present Danger," *Sight and Sound* 10, no. 3 (2000): 23.

55 Christine Vachon with Austin Bunn, *A Killer Life: How an Independent Film Producer Survives Deals and Disasters in Hollywood and Beyond* (New York: Simon & Schuster, 2006), 30–31.

56 Christine Vachon with David Edelstein, *Shooting to Kill: How an Independent Producer Blasts through the Barriers to Make Movies That Matter* (New York: Avon Books, 1998), 19.

57 Vachon, *Killer Life*, 4.

58 Vachon, 107.

59 Vachon, 153.

60 As Sherry B. Ortner points out, this strategy has become common throughout the independent film world as small companies seek to balance more serious, "message films" with broader crowd pleasers. See Sherry B. Ortner, *Not Hollywood: Independent Film at the Twilight of the American Dream* (Durham, N.C.: Duke University Press, 2013), 267.

61 All comments from Christopher Racster are taken from a phone interview with the author conducted on September 15, 2009. For further discussion of Mythgarden, see David R. Coon, "Mythgarden: Collaborative Authorship and Counter-storytelling in Queer Independent Film," *Journal of Film and Video* 70, no. 3–4 (2018).

62 All comments from Chad Allen are taken from a phone interview with the author conducted on October 21, 2009.

63 All comments from Robert Gant are taken from a phone interview with the author conducted on March 24, 2010.

64 Jonathan Alexander and Elizabeth Losh, "'A YouTube of One's Own?': 'Coming Out' Videos as Rhetorical Action," in *LGBT Identity and Online New Media*, ed. Christopher Pullen and Margaret Cooper (New York: Routledge, 2010), 46.

65 Dan Savage, introduction to *It Gets Better: Coming Out, Overcoming Bullying, and Creating a Life Worth Living*, ed. Dan Savage and Terry Miller (New York: Penguin Books, 2011), 1–8. See also Stephen Tropiano, "'A Safe and Supportive Environment': LGBTQ Youth and Social Media," in *Queer Youth and Media*

Cultures, ed. Christopher Pullen (New York: Palgrave Macmillan, 2014), 46–63.

Chapter 2 Documenting and Preserving Stories from the LGBTQ Movements

1 All comments from Michelle Kristel are taken from a phone interview with the author conducted on May 25, 2011.
2 See the In the Life Media website, accessed March 9, 2012, http://www.itlmedia.org/.
3 "About Us," *In the Life Media*, accessed March 9, 2012, http://www.itlmedia.org/pages/aboutus.
4 John Carmody, "The TV Column," *Washington Post*, June 18, 1992, C6.
5 For more about LGBTQ representation in 1990s television, see Ron Becker, *Gay TV and Straight America* (New Brunswick, N.J.: Rutgers University Press, 2006).
6 All comments from Jacqueline Gares are taken from a phone interview with the author conducted on June 6, 2011.
7 All comments from Erik Satre are taken from a phone interview with the author conducted on August 16, 2011.
8 All comments from Chuy Sanchez are taken from a phone interview with the author conducted on June 17, 2011.
9 All comments from Eleanor Moonier are taken from a phone interview with the author conducted on July 13, 2011.
10 Ben H. Bagdikian, *The New Media Monopoly* (Boston: Beacon Press, 2004), 242.
11 In the Life Media fundraising letter (n.d.), author's personal collection.
12 Bill Nichols, *Introduction to Documentary*, 2nd ed. (Bloomington: Indiana University Press, 2010), 7.
13 Tom Snow and Dean Pitchford, "One More Time," 1992.
14 Nichols, *Introduction to Documentary*, 79.
15 Nichols, 12.
16 Stella Bruzzi, *New Documentary*, 2nd ed. (London: Routledge, 2006), 11.
17 Thomas Waugh, "Walking on Tippy Toes: Lesbian and Gay Liberation Documentary of the Post-Stonewall Period 1969–84," in *Between the Sheets, in the Streets: Queer, Lesbian, Gay Documentary*, ed. Chris Holmlund and Cynthia Fuchs (Minneapolis: University of Minnesota Press, 1997), 110.
18 Bruzzi, *New Documentary*, 186.
19 Marc Stein, "Canonizing Homophile Sexual Respectability: Archives, History, and Memory," *Radical History Review*, no. 120 (2014): 53–73.
20 Christopher Pullen, *Documenting Gay Men: Identity and Performance in Reality Television and Documentary Film* (London: McFarland, 2007), 6.
21 Pullen, 5.
22 Rahat Imran, *Activist Documentary Film in Pakistan: The Emergence of a Cinema of Accountability* (London: Routledge, 2016), 186.
23 Laurie Ouellette, *Viewers like You? How Public TV Failed the People* (New York: Columbia University Press, 2002), 39.
24 Ouellette, 40.
25 William Hoynes, *Public Television for Sale: Media, the Market, and the Public Sphere* (Boulder, Colo.: Westview Press, 1994), 154.

26 Barry Dornfeld, *Producing Public Television, Producing Public Culture* (Princeton, N.J.: Princeton University Press, 1998), 5.
27 Ouellette, *Viewers like You?*, 4.
28 James Ledbetter, *Made Possible By . . . : The Death of Public Broadcasting in the United States* (London: Verso, 1997), 232.
29 Patricia Aufderheide, "Public Television and the Public Sphere," *Critical Studies in Mass Communication* 8 (1991): 169.
30 Glenda R. Balas, *Recovering a Vision for Public Television* (Lanham, Md.: Rowman & Littlefield, 2003), 16.
31 Laurie Ouellette, "TV Viewing as Good Citizenship? Political Rationality, Enlightened Democracy, and PBS," *Cultural Studies* 13, no. 1 (1999): 67.
32 Dorothee Benz, "In the Life: PBS Keeps Its Distance from Gay Programming," *Fair*, June 1993, http://fair.org/extra-online-articles/in-the-life/.
33 B. J. Bullert, *Public Television: Politics and the Battle over Documentary Film* (New Brunswick, N.J.: Rutgers University Press, 1997), 100.
34 For detailed discussions of the controversies surrounding both *Tongues Untied* and *Stop the Church*, see chapters 5 and 6 of Bullert, *Public Television*.
35 In addition to its exchange program, APT provides a syndication service, which collects and distributes comedies, dramas, and feature film packages from domestic and foreign producers. APT also offers a premium service that provides special programs intended for use during stations' fundraising campaigns.
36 "Exchange," *American Public Television*, accessed January 19, 2016, http://www.aptonline.org/aptweb.nsf/vProducers/Producers-Exchange.
37 WNYC served as the presenting organization for the first four seasons of the show, and WNET served in this capacity for the remaining seasons.
38 Jens Jensen, "'Interactivity': Tracking a New Concept in Media and Communication Studies," in *Computer Media and Communication: A Reader*, ed. Paul Mayer (Oxford: Oxford University Press, 1999), 163.
39 Graham Meikle, *Future Active: Media Activism and the Internet* (London: Routledge, 2002), 32.
40 Tim Berners-Lee, *Weaving the Web* (London: Orion Business Books, 1999), 182–183.
41 Meikle, *Future Active*, 26.
42 "Outfest UCLA Legacy Project for LGBT Moving Image Preservation," *UCLA Film and Television Archive*, accessed January 28, 2016, https://www.cinema.ucla.edu/collections/outfest-ucla-legacy-project-lgbt-moving-image-preservation.
43 Kelly Graml, "Groundbreaking Television Coverage of LGBT Milestones Now Online," UCLA Film and Television Archive press release, June 30, 2015, accessed January 28, 2016, https://www.cinema.ucla.edu/sites/default/files/UCLA_IntheLife_2015.pdf.
44 Aaron Devor, "Preserving the Footprints of Transgender Activism: The Transgender Archives at the University of Victoria," *QED: A Journal in GLBTQ Worldmaking* 1, no. 2 (2014): 201.
45 "Universal Declaration on Archives," *International Council on Archives*, accessed January 29, 2016, http://www.ica.org/13343/universal-declaration-on-archives/universal-declaration-on-archives.html.

46 Judith [Jack] Halberstam, "Unfound," in *Cruising the Archive: Queer Art and Culture in Los Angeles, 1945–1980*, ed. David Frantz and Mia Locks (Los Angeles: ONE National Gay and Lesbian Archives, 2011), 158.
47 Daniel Marshall, Kevin P. Murphy, and Zeb Tortorici, "Editors' Introduction—Queering Archives: Historical Unravelings," *Radical History Review*, no. 120 (2014): 2.
48 Sara Edenheim, "Lost and Never Found: The Queer Archive of Feelings and Its Historical Propriety," *Differences: A Journal of Feminist Cultural Studies* 24, no. 3 (2014): 41.
49 Don Romesburg, "Presenting the Queer Past: A Case for the GLBT History Museum," *Radical History Review*, no. 120 (2014): 132.
50 David Frantz and Mia Locks, "Some Introductory Remarks," in *Cruising the Archive*, ed. Frantz and Locks, 13.
51 Stein, "Canonizing Homophile Sexual Respectability," 55.
52 Stein, 62.
53 Ann Cvetkovich, *An Archive of Feelings: Trauma, Sexuality, and Lesbian Public Cultures* (Durham, N.C.: Duke University Press, 2003), 241.
54 Cvetkovich, 269.
55 Alexandra Juhasz, "Video Remains: Nostalgia, Technology, and Queer Archive Activism," *GLQ* 12, no. 2 (2006): 319–328.
56 Ann Cvetkovich, "The Queer Art of the Counterarchive," in *Cruising the Archive*, ed. Frantz and Locks, 32.
57 All comments from Mark Quigley are taken from a phone interview with the author conducted on April 6, 2017.
58 Romesburg, "Presenting the Queer Past," 131.

Chapter 3 Training Filmmakers and Educating Audiences

1 "The Women Are All Right: Power Up Celebrates 10 Years of Chipping Away at Hollywood's Glass Ceiling," *The Advocate*, November 2010, 18.
2 "About POWER UP," *POWER UP*, accessed April 21, 2016, http://www.powerupfilms.org/index.php?option=com_content&view=article&id=11&Itemid=2.
3 Joshua D. Atkinson, *Alternative Media and Politics of Resistance: A Communication Perspective* (New York: Peter Lang, 2010), 22.
4 Atkinson, 16.
5 Nick Couldry and James Curran, "The Paradox of Media Power," in *Contesting Media Power: Alternative Media in a Networked World*, ed. Nick Couldry and James Curran (Lanham, Md.: Rowman & Littlefield, 2003), 7.
6 Ellie Rennie, "Community Media Production: Access, Institutions, and Ethics," in *The International Encyclopedia of Media Studies, Volume II: Media Production*, ed. Vicki Mayer (New York: Blackwell, 2013), 3.
7 For a discussion of Scribe Video Center, see Cindy Hing-Yuk Wong, "Grassroots Authors: Collectivity and Construction in Community Video," in *Authorship and Film*, ed. David A. Gerstner and Janet Staiger (New York: Routledge, 2003), 213–231.
8 Rennie, "Community Media Production," 2–3.
9 DeeDee Halleck, *Hand-Held Visions: The Impossible Possibilities of Community Media* (New York: Fordham University Press, 2002), 386.

10 Laura Mulvey, "Visual Pleasure and Narrative Cinema," *Screen* 16, no. 3 (1975): 6–18.
11 Harry M. Benshoff and Sean Griffin, *Queer Images: A History of Gay and Lesbian Film in America* (Lanham, Md.: Rowman & Littlefield, 2006), 167.
12 All comments from Lisa Thrasher are taken from a phone interview with the author conducted on November 16, 2012.
13 Rachel Shatto, "Pow-Pow-Power Up!," *Curve*, October 2010, 37.
14 All comments from Christopher Racster are taken from a phone interview with the author conducted on September 15, 2009.
15 Seehwa Cho, *Critical Pedagogy and Social Change: Critical Analysis on the Language of Possibility* (New York: Routledge, 2013), 1.
16 Joe L. Kincheloe, *Critical Pedagogy Primer* (New York: Peter Lang, 2004), 46–48.
17 Cho, *Critical Pedagogy*, 16.
18 John Smyth, *Critical Pedagogy for Social Justice* (New York: Continuum, 2011), 111, emphasis in original.
19 Smyth, 114.
20 Kevin Kumashiro, *Troubling Education: Queer Activism and Antioppressive Pedagogy* (New York: RoutledgeFalmer, 2002), 31.
21 Kumashiro, 32.
22 Stacy Codikow, "About the Mentorship Program," *POWER UP*, accessed May 10, 2016, http://www.powerupfilms.org/index.php?option=com_content&view=article&id=201&Itemid=61.
23 Codikow.
24 Codikow.
25 Christine E. Sleeter, *Multicultural Education as Social Activism* (Albany, N.Y.: SUNY Press, 1996), 223.
26 Kumashiro, *Troubling Education*, 39.
27 Kumashiro, 40.
28 Kumashiro, 42.
29 "Power Premiere," *POWER UP*, accessed May 13, 2016, http://www.powerupfilms.org/index.php?option=com_content&view=section&id=11&Itemid=31.
30 "About POWER UP," *POWER UP*, accessed May 14, 2016, http://www.powerupfilms.org/index.php?option=com_content&view=article&id=11&Itemid=2.
31 Robert Eberwein, *Sex Ed: Film, Video, and the Framework of Desire* (New Brunswick, N.J.: Rutgers University Press, 1999), 141.
32 David R. Coon, "Putting Women in Their Place: Gender, Space, and Power in *24* and *Alias*," *Feminist Media Studies* 11, no. 2 (2011): 231–244.
33 Tom Lisanti and Louis Paul, *Film Fatales: Women in Espionage Films and Television, 1962–1973* (London: McFarland, 2002), 15–16.
34 Angela Smith, "Letting Down Rapunzel: Feminism's Effects on Fairy Tales," *Children's Literature in Education* 46, no. 4 (2015): 424–437.
35 See, for example, Jason Cianciotto and Sean Cahill, *LGBT Youth in America's Schools* (Ann Arbor: University of Michigan Press, 2012); and Stuart Biegel, *The Right to Be Out: Sexual Orientation and Gender Identity in America's Public Schools* (Minneapolis: University of Minnesota Press, 2010).
36 B. Ruby Rich, *New Queer Cinema: The Director's Cut* (Durham, N.C.: Duke University Press, 2013), 203.
37 Rich, 205.

38 Andrea Sperling, interviewed in "The Nitty Gritty behind the Itty Bitty Titty Committee," bonus feature, *Itty Bitty Titty Committee* DVD.
39 Christine Harold, "Pranking Rhetoric: 'Culture Jamming' as Media Activism," *Critical Studies in Media Communication* 21, no. 3 (2004): 192.
40 Harold, 192.
41 Jamie Babbit, interviewed in "The Nitty Gritty behind the Itty Bitty Titty Committee," bonus feature, *Itty Bitty Titty Committee* DVD.
42 Patricia Bradley, *Mass Media and the Shaping of American Feminism, 1963–1975* (Jackson: University of Mississippi Press, 2003), 50–51.
43 Sherrie A. Innes, *The Lesbian Menace: Ideology, Identity, and the Representation of Lesbian Life* (Amherst: University of Massachusetts Press, 1997), 116.
44 In contrast to the radical politics of the C(I)A, Sadie's girlfriend, Courtney, runs a nonprofit organization that takes a more liberal, assimilationist approach, seeking slow and steady change through formal meetings, educational outreach, and fundraisers.
45 Kumashiro, *Troubling Education*.
46 Michael Warner, *The Trouble with Normal: Sex, Politics, and the Ethics of Queer Life* (Cambridge, Mass.: Harvard University Press, 2000), 60.
47 John D. H. Downing, with Tamara Villarreal Ford, Geneve Gil, and Laura Stein, *Radical Media: Rebellious Communication and Social Movements* (London: Sage, 2001), xi.
48 Rich, *New Queer Cinema*, 211.

Chapter 4 Connecting Diverse Communities through Film and Media Festivals

1 "General Info," *Three Dollar Bill Cinema*, accessed April 15, 2017, https://www.threedollarbillcinema.org/about/info.
2 All comments from Jason Plourde are taken from an interview with the author conducted on August 8, 2013.
3 Mark Peranson, "First You Get the Power, Then You Get the Money: Two Models of Film Festivals," in *The Film Festival Reader*, ed. Dina Iordanova (St. Andrews, Scotland: St. Andrews Film Studies, 2013), 191–203.
4 Marijke de Valck, *Film Festivals: From European Geopolitics to Global Cinephilia* (Amsterdam: Amsterdam University Press, 2007); Thomas Elsaesser, *European Cinema: Face to Face with Hollywood* (Amsterdam: Amsterdam University Press, 2005); Dina Iordanova, "The Film Festival Circuit," in *Film Festival Reader*, ed. Iordanova, 109–126; Ragan Rhyne, "Film Festival Circuits and Stakeholders," in *Film Festival Reader*, ed. Iordanova, 135–150.
5 Peranson, "First You Get the Power," 194.
6 Julian Stringer, "Regarding Film Festivals: Introduction," in *Film Festival Reader*, ed. Iordanova, 63.
7 Daniel Dayon, "Looking for Sundance: The Social Construction of a Film Festival," in *Film Festival Reader*, ed. Iordanova, 45–58.
8 B. Ruby Rich, "Why Do Film Festivals Matter?," in *Film Festival Reader*, ed. Iordanova, 158.
9 Dina Iordanova, "Film Festivals and Dissent: Can Film Change the World?," in *Film Festival Yearbook 4: Film Festivals and Activism*, ed. Dina Iordanova and Leshu

Torchin (St. Andrews, Scotland: St. Andrews Film Studies, 2012), 13; see also Leshu Torchin, "Networked for Advocacy: Film Festivals and Activism," in *Film Festival Yearbook 4*, ed. Iordanova and Torchin, 1–12.

10 Sonia Tascón, *Human Rights Film Festivals: Activism in Context* (New York: Palgrave Macmillan, 2015).

11 Skadi Loist and Ger Zielinski, "On the Development of Queer Film Festivals and Their Media Activism," in *Film Festival Yearbook 4*, ed. Iordanova and Torchin, 49–62; Ragan Rhyne, "Pink Dollars: Gay and Lesbian Film Festivals and the Economy of Visibility" (PhD diss., New York University, 2007).

12 See, for example, Vito Russo, *The Celluloid Closet*, rev. ed. (New York: Harper and Row, 1987); and Harry Benshoff and Sean Griffin, *Queer Images: A History of Gay and Lesbian Film in America* (Lanham, Md.: Rowman & Littlefield, 2006).

13 "Festival Program Guide Archives," *Frameline*, accessed April 15, 2017, http://www.frameline.org/now-showing/festival-program-guide-archives.

14 Cindy Hing-Yuk Wong, *Film Festivals: Culture, People, and Power on the Global Screen* (New Brunswick, N.J.: Rutgers University Press, 2011), 179.

15 Wong, 181.

16 Loist and Zielinski, "Queer Film Festivals," 52.

17 Tascón, *Human Rights Film Festivals*, 9.

18 Benshoff and Griffin, *Queer Images*, 172–173; Loist and Zielinski, "Queer Film Festivals," 50.

19 Iordanova, "Film Festivals and Dissent," 23.

20 Chris Straayer and Tom Waugh, eds., "Queer Film and Video Festival Forum, Take One," *GLQ* 11, no. 4 (2005): 582.

21 Ger Zielinski, "On the Production of Heterotopia, and Other Spaces, in and around Lesbian and Gay Film Festivals," *Jump Cut* 54 (Fall 2012), https://www.ejumpcut.org/archive/jc54.2012/gerZelinskiFestivals/index.html.

22 "About Us," *Appalachian Queer Film Festival*, accessed October 7, 2014, http://aqff.org/about-us/.

23 Torchin, "Networked for Advocacy," 8.

24 All comments from Keith Bacon are taken from an interview with the author conducted on December 16, 2013.

25 All comments from Kathleen Mullen are taken from an interview with the author conducted on July 29, 2015.

26 "Frequently Asked Questions," *Without a Box*, accessed July 10, 2014, https://www.withoutabox.com/index.php?cmd=faq.festival.

27 Susan Stryker, *Transgender History* (Berkeley, Calif.: Seal Press, 2008), 34.

28 Stryker, 113.

29 Stryker, 123.

30 John Phillips, *Transgender on Screen* (New York: Palgrave Macmillan, 2006), 51.

31 Phillips, 85.

32 All comments from Sam Berliner are taken from an interview with the author conducted on August 27, 2014.

33 Nicole Richter, "Trans Love in New Trans Cinema," in *Queer Love in Film and Television: Critical Essays*, ed. Pamela Demory and Christopher Pullen (New York: Palgrave Macmillan, 2013), 163.

34 Christopher A. Shelley, *Transpeople: Repudiation, Trauma, Healing* (Toronto: University of Toronto Press, 2008), 137.

35 Tascón, *Human Rights Film Festivals*, 11.
36 Richard Fung, "Programming the Public," *GLQ* 5, no. 1 (1999): 90.
37 Roya Rastegar, "The De-fusion of Good Intentions: Outfest's Fusion Film Festival," *GLQ* 15, no. 3 (2009): 489.
38 Skadi Loist, "A Complicated Queerness: LGBT Film Festivals and Queer Programming Strategies," in *Coming Soon to a Festival near You: Programming Film Festivals*, ed. Jeffrey Ruoff (St. Andrews, Scotland: St. Andrews Film Studies, 2012), 159–160.
39 Joshua Gamson, "The Organizational Shaping of Collective Identity: The Case of Lesbian and Gay Film Festivals in New York," *Sociological Forum* 11, no. 2 (1996): 246.
40 Gamson, 246–249.
41 Rastegar, "De-fusion of Good Intentions," 490.
42 Fung, "Programming the Public," 91.
43 Loist, "Complicated Queerness," 165.
44 "Who We Are," *Advocates for Informed Choice*, accessed October 21, 2015, http://aiclegal.org/who-we-are/mission/.
45 Janet Harbord, "Film Festivals—Time-Event," in *Film Festival Reader*, ed. Iordanova, 132.
46 Nicole Brodeur, "SIFF to Reopen the Egyptian Theater," *Seattle Times*, May 16, 2014, http://www.seattletimes.com/seattle-news/siff-to-reopen-the-egyptian-theatre/.
47 "Organizational Overview," *Northwest Film Forum*, accessed August 10, 2015, http://www.nwfilmforum.org/live/page/about.
48 Rich, "Why Do Film Festivals Matter?," 161–162.
49 Rich, 161.
50 Petra Doan, "Why Plan for the LGBTQ Community," in *Planning and LGBTQ Communities: The Need for Inclusive Queer Spaces*, ed. Petra Doan (New York: Routledge, 2015), 8.
51 Petra Doan, "Beyond Queer Space: Planning for Diverse and Dispersed LGBTQ Populations," in *Planning and LGBTQ Communities*, ed. Doan, 251.
52 See, for example, Eric O. Clarke, *Virtuous Vice* (Durham, N.C.: Duke University Press, 2000); David Evans, *Sexual Citizenship: The Material Construction of Sexualities* (New York: Routledge, 1993); Katherine Sender, *Business Not Politics: The Making of the Gay Market* (New York: Columbia University Press, 2004); Suzanna Danuta Walters, *All the Rage: The Story of Gay Visibility in America* (Chicago: University of Chicago Press, 2001).

Chapter 5 Developing the Next Generation of Storytellers

1 "About Us," *Reel Grrls*, accessed July 24, 2015, http://reelgrrls.org/about. For a more detailed discussion of this program, see Mary Celeste Kearney, *Girls Make Media* (New York: Routledge, 2006), 111–113.
2 All comments from Danny Tayara are taken from an interview with the author conducted on August 27, 2014.
3 Kearney, *Girls Make Media*, 99.
4 David Buckingham, *Media Education: Literacy, Learning and Contemporary Culture* (Cambridge: Polity Press, 2003), 10.
5 Buckingham, 11.
6 Kearney, *Girls Make Media*, 120.

7 Buckinghham, *Media Education*, 13, emphasis in original.
8 Brian Goldfarb, *Visual Pedagogy: Media Cultures in and beyond the Classroom* (Durham, N.C.: Duke University Press, 2002), 66.
9 "Mission & History," *Educational Video Center*, accessed October 23, 2016, http://evc.org/mission-history/.
10 Steven Goodman, *Teaching Youth Media: A Critical Guide to Literacy, Video Production, and Social Change* (New York: Teachers College Press, 2003), 3.
11 Kearney, *Girls Make Media*, 121.
12 Goodman, *Teaching Youth Media*, 7.
13 Goldfarb, *Visual Pedagogy*, 80.
14 Lora Taub-Pervizpour, "Youth as Cultural Producers/Cultural Productions of Youth," in *The International Encyclopedia of Media Studies, Volume II: Media Production*, ed. Vicki Mayer (New York: Blackwell, 2013), 2.
15 Kevin Kumashiro, *Troubling Education: Queer Activism and Antioppressive Pedagogy* (New York: RoutledgeFalmer, 2002), 31. Also see the discussion of critical pedagogy and antioppressive education in chapter 3.
16 All comments from Theo are taken from an interview with the author conducted on October 26, 2016. Because they are not public figures and some are under the age of eighteen, Reel Queer Youth participants are identified in this chapter by first name only or a pseudonym.
17 Alexander Doty, *Making Things Perfectly Queer: Interpreting Mass Culture* (Minneapolis: University of Minnesota Press, 1993); Sean Griffin, *Tinker Belles and Evil Queens: The Walt Disney Company from the Inside Out* (New York: New York University Press, 2000); Harry Benshoff, *Monsters in the Closet: Homosexuality and the Horror Film* (Manchester: Manchester University Press, 1997).
18 Ben Gove, "Framing Gay Youth," *Screen* 37, no. 2 (1996): 180.
19 See, for example, Michaela D. E. Meyer and Megan M. Wood, "Sexuality and Teen Television: Emerging Adults Respond to Representations of Queer Identity on *Glee*," *Sexuality & Culture* 17 (2013): 434–448; and Raffi Sarkissian, "Queering TV Conventions: LGBT Teen Narratives on *Glee*," in *Queer Youth and Media Cultures*, ed. Christopher Pullen (New York: Palgrave Macmillan, 2014), 145–157.
20 Glyn Davis, "'Saying It Out Loud': Revealing Television's Queer Teens," in *Teen TV: Genre, Consumption, and Identity*, ed. Glyn Davis and Kay Dickinson (London: BFI, 2004), 131.
21 Bryan Wuest, "Stories like Mine: Coming Out Videos and Queer Identities on YouTube," in *Queer Youth and Media Cultures*, ed. Pullen, 25.
22 Jonathan Alexander and Elizabeth Losh, "'A YouTube of One's Own?': 'Coming Out' Videos as Rhetorical Action," in *LGBT Identity and Online New Media*, ed. Christopher Pullen and Margaret Cooper (New York: Routledge, 2010), 38.
23 Matthew G. O'Neill, "Transgender Youth and YouTube Videos: Self-Representation and Five Identifiable Trans Youth Narratives," in *Queer Youth and Media Cultures*, ed. Pullen, 36.
24 Sarah Banet-Weiser, "Branding the Post-feminist Self: Girls' Video Production and YouTube," in *Mediated Girlhoods: New Explorations of Girls' Media Culture*, ed. Mary Celeste Kearney (New York: Peter Lang, 2011), 284.
25 Harry Benshoff and Sean Griffin, *Queer Images: A History of Gay and Lesbian Film in America* (Lanham, Md.: Rowman & Littlefield, 2006), 11.
26 Maxine Greene, foreword to Goodman, *Teaching Youth Media*, x.

27 Nick Couldry, *Why Voice Matters: Culture and Politics after Neoliberalism* (London: Sage, 2010), 1.

28 Michael Sadowski, *In a Queer Voice: Journeys of Resilience from Adolescence to Adulthood* (Philadelphia: Temple University Press, 2013), 3–5.

29 Laura Kann et al., "Sexual Identity, Sex of Sexual Contacts and Health-Related Behaviors among Students in Grades 9–12—United States and Selected Sites, 2015," *MMWR Surveillance Summaries* 65, no. 9 (2016): 1–202.

30 Sadowski, *In a Queer Voice*, 8.

31 All comments from Finn Cottom are taken from an interview with the author conducted on November 29, 2013.

32 Christopher Pullen, *Gay Identity, New Storytelling, and the Media* (New York: Palgrave Macmillan, 2009), 17.

33 Pullen, 40.

34 Ken Plummer, *Telling Sexual Stories: Power, Change, and Social Worlds* (New York: Routledge, 1995), 35.

35 Jeffrey Weeks, *Making Sexual History* (Cambridge: Polity Press, 2000), 192.

36 All comments from Jason Plourde are taken from an interview with the author conducted on August 8, 2013.

37 Lynne Hillier and Lyn Harrison, "Building Realities Less Limited than Their Own: Young People Practicing Same-Sex Attraction on the Internet," *Sexualities* 10, no. 1 (2007): 82–100. See also Stephen Tropiano, "'A Safe and Supportive Environment': LGBTQ Youth and Social Media," in *Queer Youth and Media Cultures*, ed. Pullen, 46–62.

38 In 2017, organizers launched a second workshop about an hour south of Seattle on the campus of the University of Washington Tacoma.

39 "2013 National School Climate Survey," *Gay, Lesbian, and Straight Education Network*, accessed August 14, 2015, http://www.glsen.org/article/2013-national-school-climate-survey.

40 "About Capitol Hill Housing," *Capitol Hill Housing*, accessed July 30, 2015, http://capitolhillhousing.org/about/.

41 See Sheila L. Cavanagh, *Queering Bathrooms: Gender, Sexuality, and the Hygienic Imagination* (Toronto: University of Toronto Press, 2010).

42 Taub-Pervizpour, "Youth as Cultural Producers," 13.

43 Shawna, Q&A session after Reel Queer Youth screening, October 17, 2015.

44 Tobey, Q&A session after Reel Queer Youth screening, October 17, 2015.

45 Goodman, *Teaching Youth Media*, 57.

46 Suzanna Danuta Walters, *All the Rage: The Story of Gay Visibility in America* (Chicago: University of Chicago Press, 2001), 28.

47 Joseph P. Goodwin, *More Man than You'll Ever Be: Gay Folklore and Acculturation in Middle America* (Bloomington: Indiana University Press, 1989), xiv.

48 Shelley L. Craig, Lauren McInroy, Lance T. McCready, and Ramona Alaggia, "Media: A Catalyst for Resilience in Lesbian, Gay, Bisexual, Transgender, and Queer Youth," *Journal of LGBT Youth* 12, no. 3 (2015): 254–275.

Conclusion Stories of Some of Our Lives

1 "About," *ACT UP Oral History Project*, accessed March 9, 2017, http://www.actuporalhistory.org/index1.html.

2 "About StoryCorps," *StoryCorps*, accessed March 10, 2017, https://storycorps.org/about/.

3 Vincent Doyle, *Making Out in the Mainstream: GLAAD and the Politics of Respectability* (Montreal: McGill-Queen's University Press, 2016), 4–7.

4 Hazel Markus and Paula Nurius, "Possible Selves," *American Psychologist* 41, no. 9 (1986): 954–969.

5 Markus and Nurius, 954.

6 Robert Benford, "Controlling Narratives and Narratives as Control within Social Movements," in *Stories of Change: Narrative and Social Movements*, ed. Joseph E. Davis (Albany, N.Y.: SUNY Press, 2002), 55.

7 Leshu Torchin, "Networked for Advocacy: Film Festivals and Activism," in *Film Festival Yearbook 4: Film Festivals and Activism*, ed. Dina Iordanova and Leshu Torchin (St. Andrews, Scotland: St. Andrews Film Studies, 2012), 1.

8 George Yúdice, "Testimonio and Postmodernism," in *The Real Thing: Testimonial Discourse and Latin America*, ed. Georg M. Gugelberger (Durham, N.C.: Duke University Press, 1996), 44.

9 Torchin, "Networked for Advocacy," 2.

10 Roger Hallas, *Reframing Bodies: AIDS, Bearing Witness, and the Queer Moving Image* (Durham, N.C.: Duke University Press, 2009), 12.

11 Hallas, 12–14.

12 Hallas, 14.

13 Leshu Torchin, "*Ravished Armenia*: Visual Media, Humanitarian Advocacy, and the Formation of Witnessing Publics," *American Anthropologist* 108, no. 1 (2006): 215.

14 Michael Warner, *Publics and Counterpublics* (New York: Zone Books, 2002), 66.

15 Warner, 67.

16 Warner, 75.

17 Nancy Fraser, "Rethinking the Public Sphere: A Contribution to the Critique of Actually Existing Democracy," *Social Text* 25–26 (1990): 67.

18 Fraser, 67.

19 Ken Plummer, *Telling Sexual Stories: Power, Change and Social Worlds* (New York: Routledge, 1995), 30.

Bibliography

Aaron, Michele. "New Queer Cinema: An Introduction." In *New Queer Cinema: A Critical Reader*, edited by Michele Aaron, 3–14. New Brunswick, N.J.: Rutgers University Press, 2004.

Alexander, Jonathan, and Elizabeth Losh. "'A YouTube of One's Own?': 'Coming Out' Videos as Rhetorical Action." In *LGBT Identity and Online New Media*, edited by Christopher Pullen and Margaret Cooper, 37–50. New York: Routledge, 2010.

Allen, Dennis W. "Homosexuality and Narrative." *Modern Fiction Studies* 41, no. 3–4 (1995): 609–634.

Alwood, Edward. "A Gift of Gab: How Independent Broadcasters Gave Gay Rights Pioneers a Chance to Be Heard." In *Media Queered: Visibility and Its Discontents*, edited by Kevin G. Barnhurst, 27–43. New York: Peter Lang, 2007.

Anderson, Benedict. *Imagined Communities*. London: Verso, 1983.

Aslinger, Ben. "Creating a Network for Queer Audiences at Logo TV." *Popular Communication* 7 (2009): 107–121.

Atkinson, Joshua D. *Alternative Media and Politics of Resistance: A Communication Perspective*. New York: Peter Lang, 2010.

Aufderheide, Patricia. "Public Television and the Public Sphere." *Critical Studies in Mass Communication* 8 (1991): 168–183.

Balas, Glenda. *Recovering a Vision for Public Television*. Lanham, Md.: Rowman & Littlefield, 2003.

Banet-Weiser, Sarah. "Branding the Post-Feminist Self: Girls' Video Production and YouTube." In *Mediated Girlhoods: New Explorations of Girls' Media Culture*, edited by Mary Celeste Kearney, 277–294. New York: Peter Lang, 2011.

Barnhurst, Kevin G., ed. *Media Queered: Visibility and Its Discontents*. New York: Peter Lang, 2007.

Barthes, Roland. *Image Music Text*. New York: Hill and Wang, 1977.

Becker, Ron. *Gay TV and Straight America*. New Brunswick, N.J.: Rutgers University Press, 2006.

Benford, Robert D. "Controlling Narratives and Narratives as Control within Social Movements." In *Stories of Change: Narrative and Social Movements*, edited by Joseph E. Davis, 53–75. Albany: SUNY Press, 2002.

Benshoff, Harry. *Monsters in the Closet: Homosexuality and the Horror Film*. Manchester: Manchester University Press, 1997.

Benshoff, Harry M., and Sean Griffin. *Queer Images: A History of Gay and Lesbian Film in America*. Lanham, Md.: Rowman & Littlefield, 2006.

Bernstein, Matthew. "The Producer as Auteur." In *Auteurs and Authorship: A Film Reader*, edited by Barry Keith Grant, 180–189. Malden, Mass.: Blackwell, 2008.

Besen, Wayne R. *Anything but Straight: Unmasking the Scandals and Lies behind the Ex-gay Myth*. New York: Harrington Park Press, 2003.

Biegel, Stuart. *The Right to Be Out: Sexual Orientation and Gender Identity in America's Public Schools*. Minneapolis: University of Minnesota Press, 2010.

Bowser, Pearl, Jane Gaines, and Charles Musser, eds. *Oscar Micheaux and His Circle: African-American Filmmaking and Race Cinema of the Silent Era*. Bloomington: Indiana University Press, 2001.

Bradley, Patricia. *Mass Media and the Shaping of American Feminism, 1963–1975*. Jackson: University of Mississippi Press, 2003.

Brisbin, David. "Production Design and the Invisible Arts of Seeing." In *A Companion to Media Authorship*, edited by Jonathan Gray and Derek Johnson, 370–390. Malden, Mass.: Wiley-Blackwell, 2013.

Bronski, Michael. *A Queer History of the United States*. Boston: Beacon Press, 2011.

Bruzzi, Stella. *New Documentary*. 2nd ed. London: Routledge, 2006.

Buckingham, David. *Media Education: Literacy, Learning and Contemporary Culture*. Cambridge: Polity Press, 2003.

Bullert, B. J. *Public Television: Politics and the Battle over Documentary Film*. New Brunswick, N.J.: Rutgers University Press, 1997.

Burnett, Colin. "Hidden Hands at Work: Authorship, the Intentional Flux, and the Dynamics of Collaboration." In *A Companion to Media Authorship*, edited by Jonathan Gray and Derek Johnson, 112–132. Malden, Mass.: Wiley-Blackwell, 2013.

Busse, Kristina. "The Return of the Author: Ethos and Identity Politics." In *A Companion to Media Authorship*, edited by Jonathan Gray and Derek Johnson, 48–68. Malden, Mass.: Wiley-Blackwell, 2013.

Caldwell, John T. "Authorship below-the-Line." In *A Companion to Media Authorship*, edited by Jonathan Gray and Derek Johnson, 349–369. Malden, Mass.: Wiley-Blackwell, 2013.

Campbell, Jane, and Theresa Carilli, eds. *Queer Media Images: LGBT Perspectives*. Lanham, Md.: Lexington Books, 2013.

Capsuto, Steven. *Alternate Channels: The Uncensored Story of Gay and Lesbian Images on Radio and Television*. New York: Ballantine Books, 2000.

Carringer, Robert. "Collaboration and Concepts of Authorship." *PMLA* 116, no. 2 (2001): 370–379.

———. *The Making of Citizen Kane*. Rev. ed. Berkeley: University of California Press, 1996.

Caughie, John. *Theories of Authorship*. London: Routledge, 1988.

Cavanagh, Sheila L. *Queering Bathrooms: Gender, Sexuality, and the Hygienic Imagination*. Toronto: University of Toronto Press, 2010.

Chambers, Samuel A. *The Queer Politics of Television*. London: I. B. Tauris, 2009.

Charbonneau, Stephen Michael. "Branching Out: Young Appalachian Selves, Autoethnographic Aesthetics, and the Founding of Appalshop." *Journal of Popular Film and Television* 37, no. 3 (2009): 137–145.

Cho, Seehwa. *Critical Pedagogy and Social Change: Critical Analysis on the Language of Possibility*. New York: Routledge, 2013.

Cianciotto, Jason, and Sean Cahill. *LGBT Youth in America's Schools*. Ann Arbor: University of Michigan Press, 2012.

Clarke, Eric O. *Virtuous Vice*. Durham, N.C.: Duke University Press, 2000.

Collins, Patricia Hill. "The New Politics of Community." *American Sociological Review* 75, no. 1 (2010): 7–30.

Coon, David. R. "Mythgarden: Collaborative Authorship and Counter-storytelling in Queer Independent Film." *Journal of Film and Video* 70, no. 3–4 (2018).

Coon, David R. "Putting Women in Their Place: Gender, Space, and Power in *24* and *Alias*." *Feminist Media Studies* 11, no. 2 (2011): 231–244.

———. "Sun, Sand, and Citizenship: The Marketing of Gay Tourism." *Journal of Homosexuality* 59, no. 4 (2012): 511–534.

Corrigan, Timothy. *A Cinema without Walls: Movies and Culture after Vietnam*. New Brunswick, N.J.: Rutgers University Press, 1991.

Couldry, Nick. *Why Voice Matters: Culture and Politics after Neoliberalism*. London: Sage, 2010.

Couldry, Nick, and James Curran. "The Paradox of Media Power." In *Contesting Media Power: Alternative Media in a Networked World*, edited by Nick Couldry and James Curran, 3–15. Lanham, Md.: Rowman & Littlefield, 2003.

Craig, Shelley L., Lauren McInroy, Lance T. McCready, and Ramona Alaggia. "Media: A Catalyst for Resilience in Lesbian, Gay, Bisexual, Transgender, and Queer Youth." *Journal of LGBT Youth* 12, no. 3 (2015): 254–275.

Cvetkovich, Ann. *An Archive of Feelings: Trauma, Sexuality, and Lesbian Public Cultures*. Durham, N.C.: Duke University Press, 2003.

———. "The Queer Art of the Counterarchive." In *Cruising the Archive: Queer Art and Culture in Los Angeles, 1945–1980*, edited by David Frantz and Mia Locks, 32–35. Los Angeles: ONE National Gay and Lesbian Archives, 2011.

Davis, Glyn. "'Saying It Out Loud': Revealing Television's Queer Teens." In *Teen TV: Genre, Consumption, and Identity*, edited by Glyn Davis and Kay Dickinson, 127–140. London: BFI, 2004.

Davis, Joseph E. "Narrative and Social Movements: The Power of Stories." In *Stories of Change: Narrative and Social Movements*, edited by Joseph E. Davis, 3–29. Albany: SUNY Press, 2002.

Dayon, Daniel. "Looking for Sundance: The Social Construction of a Film Festival." In *The Film Festival Reader*, edited by Dina Iordanova, 45–57. St. Andrews, Scotland: St. Andrews Film Studies, 2013.

DeAngelis, Michael. "Authorship and New Queer Cinema: The Case of Todd Haynes." In *Auteurs and Authorship: A Film Reader*, edited by Barry Keith Grant, 292–303. Malden, Mass.: Blackwell, 2008.

———. "Robert Stigwood: Producer, Author, Text." In *Authorship and Film*, edited by David A. Gerstner and Janet Staiger, 247–261. New York: Routledge, 2003.

Delgado, Richard. "Storytelling for Oppositionists and Others: A Plea for Narrative." In *Critical Race Theory: The Cutting Edge*, edited by Richard Delgado and Jean Stefancic, 60–70. Philadelphia: Temple University Press, 2000.

Delgado, Richard, and Jean Stefancic. *Critical Race Theory: An Introduction*. New York: New York University Press, 2012.

D'Emilio, John. *In a New Century: Essays on Queer History, Politics, and Community Life*. Madison: University of Wisconsin Press, 2014.

———. *Sexual Politics, Sexual Communities: The Making of a Homosexual Minority in the United States, 1940–1970*. 2nd ed. Chicago: University of Chicago Press, 1998.

———. *The World Turned: Essays on Gay History, Politics, and Culture*. Durham, N.C.: Duke University Press, 2002.

de Valck, Marijke. *Film Festivals: From European Geopolitics to Global Cinephilia*. Amsterdam: Amsterdam University Press, 2007.

Devor, Aaron H. "Preserving the Footprints of Transgender Activism: The Transgender Archives at the University of Victoria." *QED: A Journal in GLBTQ Worldmaking* 1, no. 2 (2014): 200–204.

Dhoest, Michael. "How Queer Is *L'Air de Paris*?: Marcel Carné and Queer Authorship." *Scope: An Online Journal of Film Studies* (May 2003), http://www.nottingham.ac.uk/scope/documents/2003/may-2003/dhoest.pdf.

Doan, Petra, ed. *Planning and LGBTQ Communities: The Need for Inclusive Queer Spaces*. New York: Routledge, 2015.

Dobson, James. *Marriage under Fire: Why We Must Win the Battle*. Portland, Ore.: Multnomah Press, 2004.

Dornfeld, Barry. *Producing Public Television, Producing Public Culture*. Princeton, N.J.: Princeton University Press, 1998.

Doty, Alexander. *Making Things Perfectly Queer: Interpreting Mass Culture*. Minneapolis: University of Minnesota Press, 1993.

Downing, John D. H., Tamara Villarreal Ford, Geneve Gil, and Laura Stein. *Radical Media: Rebellious Communication and Social Movements*. London: Sage, 2001.

Doyle, Vincent. *Making Out in the Mainstream: GLAAD and the Politics of Respectability*. Montreal: McGill-Queen's University Press, 2016.

Duberman, Martin. *Stonewall*. New York: Dutton Press, 1993.

Dyer, Richard. *Now You See It: Studies on Lesbian and Gay Film*. London: Routledge, 1990.

Eberwein, Robert. *Sex Ed: Film, Video, and the Framework of Desire*. New Brunswick, N.J.: Rutgers University Press, 1999.

Edenheim, Sara. "Lost and Never Found: The Queer Archive of Feelings and Its Historical Propriety." *Differences: A Journal of Feminist Cultural Studies* 24, no. 3 (2014): 36–62.

Elsaesser, Thomas. *European Cinema: Face to Face with Hollywood*. Amsterdam: Amsterdam University Press, 2005.

Epstein, Steven. "Gay and Lesbian Movements in the United States: Dilemmas of Identity, Diversity, and Political Strategy." In *The Global Emergence of Gay and Lesbian Politics: National Imprints of a Worldwide Movement*, edited by Barry D. Adam, Jan Willem Duyvendak, and Andre Krouwel, 30–90. Philadelphia: Temple University Press, 1999.

Evans, David. *Sexual Citizenship: The Material Construction of Sexualities*. New York: Routledge, 1993.

Faderman, Lillian. *The Gay Revolution: The Story of a Struggle*. New York: Simon & Schuster, 2015.

Farmer, Brett. *Spectacular Passions: Cinema, Fantasy, Gay Male Spectatorships*. Durham, N.C.: Duke University Press, 2000.

Foucault, Michel. "What Is an Author?" In *Language, Counter-memory, Practice: Selected Essays and Interviews by Michel Foucault*, edited by Donald F. Bouchard, 113–138. Ithaca, N.Y.: Cornell University Press, 1977.

Frantz, David, and Mia Locks. "Some Introductory Remarks." In *Cruising the Archive: Queer Art and Culture in Los Angeles, 1945–1980*, edited by David Frantz and Mia Locks, 12–17. Los Angeles: ONE National Gay and Lesbian Archives, 2011.

Fung, Richard. "Programming the Public." *GLQ* 5, no. 1 (1999): 73–93.

Gallo, Marcia M. *Different Daughters: A History of the Daughters of Bilitis and the Rise of the Lesbian Rights Movement*. New York: Carroll & Graf, 2006.

Gamson, Joshua. "The Organizational Shaping of Collective Identity: The Case of Lesbian and Gay Film Festivals in New York." *Sociological Forum* 11, no. 2 (1996): 231–261.

Gershenson, Olga, and Barbara Penner, eds. *Ladies and Gents: Public Toilets and Gender*. Philadelphia: Temple University Press, 2009.

Goldfarb, Brian. *Visual Pedagogy: Media Cultures in and Beyond the Classroom*. Durham, N.C.: Duke University Press, 2002.

Goodman, Steven. *Teaching Youth Media: A Critical Guide to Literacy, Video Production, and Social Change*. New York: Teachers College Press, 2003.

Goodwin, Joseph P. *More Man than You'll Ever Be: Gay Folklore and Acculturation in Middle America*. Bloomington: Indiana University Press, 1989.

Gove, Ben. "Framing Gay Youth." *Screen* 37, no. 2 (1996): 174–192.

Grant, Catherine. "Secret Agents: Feminist Theories of Women's Film Authorship." *Feminist Theory* 2, no. 1 (2001): 113–130.

Gray, Jonathan, and Derek Johnson, eds. *A Companion to Media Authorship*. Malden, Mass.: Wiley-Blackwell, 2013.

Griffin, Sean. *Tinker Belles and Evil Queens: The Walt Disney Company from the Inside Out*. New York: New York University Press, 2000.

Gross, Larry. *Up from Invisibility: Lesbians, Gay Men, and the Media in America*. New York: Columbia University Press, 2001.

Halberstam, Judith [Jack]. "Unfound." In *Cruising the Archive: Queer Art and Culture in Los Angeles, 1945–1980*, edited by David Frantz and Mia Locks, 158–161. Los Angeles: ONE National Gay and Lesbian Archives, 2011.

Hallas, Roger. *Reframing Bodies: AIDS, Bearing Witness, and the Queer Moving Image*. Durham, N.C.: Duke University Press, 2009.

Halleck, DeeDee. *Hand-Held Visions: The Impossible Possibilities of Community Media*. New York: Fordham University Press, 2002.

Harbord, Janet. "Film Festivals—Time-Event." In *The Film Festival Reader*, edited by Dina Iordanova, 127–133. St. Andrews, Scotland: St. Andrews Film Studies, 2013.

Harold, Christine. "Pranking Rhetoric: Culture Jamming as Media Activism." *Critical Studies in Media Communication* 21, no. 3 (2004): 189–211.

Hartley, John. "Authorship and the Narrative of the Self." In *A Companion to Media Authorship*, edited by Jonathan Gray and Derek Johnson, 23–47. Malden, Mass.: Wiley-Blackwell, 2013.

Hick, Steven F., and John G. McNutt. "Communities and Advocacy on the Internet: A Conceptual Framework." In *Advocacy, Activism, and the Internet: Community Organization and Social Policy*, edited by Steven F. Hick and John G. McNutt, 3–18. Chicago: Lyceum Books, 2002.

Hillier, Lynne, and Lyn Harrison. "Building Realities Less Limited than Their Own: Young People Practicing Same-Sex Attraction on the Internet." *Sexualities* 10, no. 1 (2007): 82–100.

Himberg, Julia. "Multicasting: Lesbian Programming and the Changing Landscape of Cable TV." *Television & New Media* 15, no. 4 (2014): 289–304.

Horak, Laura. *Girls Will Be Boys: Cross-Dressed Women, Lesbians, and American Cinema, 1908–1934*. New Brunswick, N.J.: Rutgers University Press, 2016.

Hoynes, William. *Public Television for Sale: Media, the Market, and the Public Sphere*. Boulder, Colo.: Westview Press, 1994.

Hudson, Kimberly D. "Toward a Conceptual Framework for Understanding Community Belonging and Well-Being: Insights from a Queer-Mixed Perspective." *Journal of Community Practice* 23 (2015): 27–50.

Imran, Rahat. *Activist Documentary Film in Pakistan: The Emergence of a Cinema of Accountability*. London: Routledge, 2016.
Innes, Sherrie A. *The Lesbian Menace: Ideology, Identity, and the Representation of Lesbian Life*. Amherst: University of Massachusetts Press, 1997.
Iordanova, Dina. "The Film Festival Circuit." In *The Film Festival Reader*, edited by Dina Iordanova, 109–126. St. Andrews, Scotland: St. Andrews Film Studies, 2013.
———. "Film Festivals and Dissent: Can Film Change the World?" In *Film Festival Yearbook 4: Film Festivals and Activism*, edited by Dina Iordanova and Leshu Torchin, 13–30. St. Andrews, Scotland: St. Andrews Film Studies, 2012.
Jelen, Ted. G. "Catholicism, Homosexuality, and Same-Sex Marriage in the United States." In *Faith, Politics, and Sexual Diversity in Canada and the United States*, edited by David Royside and Clyde Wilcox, 207–218. Vancouver: University of British Columbia Press, 2011.
Johnson, David K. *The Lavender Scare: The Cold War Persecution of Gays and Lesbians in the Federal Government*. Chicago: University of Chicago Press, 2004.
Johnson, Derek. "Scoring Authorship: An Interview with Bear McCreary." In *A Companion to Media Authorship*, edited by Jonathan Gray and Derek Johnson, 391–402. Malden, Mass.: Wiley-Blackwell, 2013.
Juhasz, Alexandra. *AIDS TV: Identity, Community, and Alternative Video*. Durham, N.C.: Duke University Press, 1995.
Kael, Pauline. "Circles and Squares." *Film Quarterly* 16, no. 3 (1963): 12–26.
Kann, Laura, Emily O'Malley Olsen, Tim McManus, William A. Harris, Shari Shanklin, Katherine Flint, Barbara Queen, Richard Lowry, David Chyen, List Whittle, Jemekia Thornton, Connie Lim, Yoshimi Yamakawa, Nancy Brener, and Stephanie Zaza. "Sexual Identity, Sex of Sexual Contacts and Health-Related Behaviors among Students in Grades 9–12—United States and Selected Sites, 2015." *MMWR Surveillance Summaries* 65, no. 9 (2016): 1–202.
Kearney, Mary Celeste. *Girls Make Media*. New York: Routledge, 2006.
Kincheloe, Joe L. *Critical Pedagogy Primer*. New York: Peter Lang, 2004.
Kumashiro, Kevin. *Troubling Education: Queer Activism and Antioppressive Pedagogy*. New York: RoutledgeFalmer, 2002.
Ladson-Billings, Gloria. "Just What Is Critical Race Theory, and What's It Doing in a Nice Field like Education?" In *Race Is . . . Race Isn't: Critical Race Theory and Qualitative Studies in Education*, edited by Laurence Parker, Donna Deyhle, and Sofia Villenas, 7–30. Boulder, Colo.: Westview Press, 1999.
Landy, Marcia. "Storytelling and Information in Todd Haynes' Films." In *The Cinema of Todd Haynes*, edited by James Morrison, 7–24. London: Wallflower Press, 2007.
Lauritsen, John, and David Thorstad. *The Early Homosexual Rights Movement (1864–1935)*. Rev. ed. Ojai, Calif.: Times Change Press, 1995.
Ledbetter, James. *Made Possible By . . . : The Death of Public Broadcasting in the United States*. London: Verso, 1997.
Lisanti, Tom, and Louis Paul. *Film Fatales: Women in Espionage Films and Television, 1962–1973*. London: McFarland, 2002.
Loist, Skadi. "A Complicated Queerness: LGBT Film Festivals and Queer Programming Strategies." In *Coming Soon to a Festival near You: Programming Film Festivals*, edited by Jeffrey Ruoff, 157–172. St. Andrews, Scotland: St. Andrews Film Studies, 2012.
Loist, Skadi, and Ger Zielinski. "On the Development of Queer Film Festivals and Their Media Activism." In *Film Festival Yearbook 4: Film Festivals and Activism*, edited by Dina

Iordanova and Leshu Torchin, 49–62. St. Andrews, Scotland: St. Andrews Film Studies, 2012.

Lukenbill, Grant. *Untold Millions: Positioning Your Business for the Gay and Lesbian Consumer Revolution*. New York: Harper Collins, 1995.

Lynch, Frederick R. "Nonghetto Gays: An Ethnography of Suburban Homosexuals." In *Gay Culture in America: Essays from the Field*, edited by Gilbert Herdt, 165–201. Boston: Beacon Press, 1992.

Markus, Hazel, and Paula Nurius. "Possible Selves." *American Psychologist* 41, no. 9 (1986): 954–969.

Marshall, Daniel, Kevin P. Murphy, and Zeb Tortorici. "Editors' Introduction: Queering Archives: Historical Unravelings." *Radical History Review*, no. 120 (2014): 1–11.

Mayer, Vicki, Miranda J. Banks, and John Thornton Caldwell, eds. *Production Studies: Cultural Studies of Media Industries*. New York: Routledge, 2009.

Mayne, Judith. "A Parallax View of Lesbian Authorship." In *Film and Authorship*, edited by Virginia Wright Wexman, 76–86. New Brunswick, N.J.: Rutgers University Press, 2003.

Medhurst, Andy. "That Special Thrill: *Brief Encounter*, Homosexuality, and Authorship." In *Queer Screen: A Screen Reader*, edited by Jackie Stacey and Sarah Street, 41–52. London: Routledge, 2007.

Meeker, Martin. *Contacts Desired: Gay and Lesbian Communications and Community, 1940s–1970s*. Chicago: University of Chicago Press, 2006.

Meikle, Graham. *Future Active: Media Activism and the Internet*. New York: Routledge, 2002.

Metz, Walter. "John Waters Goes to Hollywood: A Poststructural Authorship Study." In *Authorship and Film*, edited by David A. Gerstner and Janet Staiger, 157–174. New York: Routledge, 2003.

Meyer, Michaela D. E., and Megan M. Wood. "Sexuality and Teen Television: Emerging Adults Respond to Representations of Queer Identity on *Glee*." *Sexuality & Culture* 17 (2013): 434–448.

Miller, Diane Helene. *Freedom to Differ: The Shaping of the Gay and Lesbian Struggle for Civil Rights*. New York: New York University Press, 1998.

Mogul, Joey L., Andrea J. Ritchie, and Kay Whitlock. *Queer (In)Justice: The Criminalization of LGBT People in the United States*. Boston: Beacon Press, 2011.

Montgomery, Kathryn C. *Target: Prime Time: Advocacy Groups and the Struggle over Entertainment Television*. New York: Oxford University Press, 1989.

Moon, Dawne. "Religious Views of Homosexuality." In *Handbook of Lesbian and Gay Studies*, edited by Diane Richardson and Steven Seidman, 313–328. London: Sage, 2002.

Mulvey, Laura. "Visual Pleasure and Narrative Cinema." *Screen* 16, no. 3 (1975): 6–18.

Naremore, James. "Authorship and the Cultural Politics of Film Criticism." *Film Quarterly* 44, no. 1 (1990): 14–23.

Nault, Curran. "No Skin off My Ass: Bruce LaBruce and the Curious Case of Queer Punk Love." In *Queer Love in Film and Television: Critical Essays*, edited by Pamela Demory and Christopher Pullen, 169–179. New York: Palgrave Macmillan, 2013.

———. *Queercore: Queer Punk Media Subculture*. New York: Routledge, 2017.

Nichols, Bill. *Introduction to Documentary*. 2nd ed. Bloomington: Indiana University Press, 2010.

Noyes, Dorothy. "Group." *Journal of American Folklore* 108, no. 430 (1995): 449–478.

Okada, Jun. "'Noble and Uplifting and Boring as Hell': Asian American Film and Video, 1971–1982." *Cinema Journal* 49, no. 1 (2009): 20–40.

O'Neill, Matthew G. "Transgender Youth and YouTube Videos: Self-Representation and Five Identifiable Trans Youth Narratives." In *Queer Youth and Media Cultures*, edited by Christopher Pullen, 34–45. New York: Palgrave Macmillan, 2014.

Ortner, Sherry B. *Not Hollywood: Independent Film at the Twilight of the American Dream*. Durham, N.C.: Duke University Press, 2013.

Ouellette, Laurie. *Viewers like You? How Public TV Failed the People*. New York: Columbia University Press, 2002.

Peñaloza, Lisa. "We're Here, We're Queer, and We're Going Shopping! A Critical Perspective on the Accommodation of Gays and Lesbians in the U.S. Marketplace." *Journal of Homosexuality* 31, no. 1–2 (1996): 9–41.

Peranson, Mark. "First You Get the Power, Then You Get the Money: Two Models of Film Festivals." In *The Film Festival Reader*, edited by Dina Iordanova, 191–203. St. Andrews, Scotland: St. Andrews Film Studies, 2013.

Phillips, John. *Transgender on Screen*. New York: Palgrave Macmillan, 2006.

Plummer, Ken. *Telling Sexual Stories: Power, Change and Social Worlds*. New York: Routledge, 1995.

Ponticelli, Christy M. "Crafting Stories of Sexual Identity Reconstruction." *Social Psychology Quarterly* 62, no. 2 (1999): 157–172.

Pullen, Christopher. *Documenting Gay Men: Identity and Performance in Reality Television and Documentary Film*. London: McFarland, 2007.

———. *Gay Identity, New Storytelling, and the Media*. New York: Palgrave Macmillan, 2009.

Rastegar, Roya. "The De-Fusion of Good Intentions: Outfest's Fusion Film Festival." *GLQ* 15, no. 3 (2009): 481–497.

Rennie, Ellie. "Community Media Production: Access, Institutions, and Ethics." In *The International Encyclopedia of Media Studies, Volume II: Media Production*, edited by Vicki Mayer, 1–19. New York: Blackwell, 2013.

Rentschler, Carrie A. "Expanding the Definition of Media Activism." In *A Companion to Media Studies*, edited by Angharad N. Valdivia, 529–547. Oxford: Blackwell, 2003.

Rhyne, Ragan. "Film Festival Circuits and Stakeholders." In *The Film Festival Reader*, edited by Dina Iordanova, 135–150. St. Andrews, Scotland: St. Andrews Film Studies, 2013.

Rich, B. Ruby. *New Queer Cinema: The Director's Cut*. Durham, N.C.: Duke University Press, 2013.

———. "Why Do Film Festivals Matter?" In *The Film Festival Reader*, edited by Dina Iordanova, 157–165. St. Andrews, Scotland: St. Andrews Film Studies, 2013.

Richter, Nicole. "Trans Love in New Trans Cinema." In *Queer Love in Film and Television: Critical Essays*, edited by Pamela Demory and Christopher Pullen, 161–167. New York: Palgrave Macmillan, 2013.

Rimmerman, Craig A. *The Lesbian and Gay Movements: Assimilation or Liberation?* 2nd ed. Boulder, Colo.: Westview Press, 2014.

Romesburg, Don. "Presenting the Queer Past: A Case for the GLBT History Museum." *Radical History Review*, no. 120 (2014): 131–144.

Russo, Vito. *The Celluloid Closet: Homosexuality in the Movies*. Rev. ed. New York: Harper and Row, 1987.

Saalfield, Catherine. "On the Make: Activist Video Collectives." In *Queer Looks: Perspectives on Lesbian and Gay Film and Video*, edited by Martha Gever, Pratibha Parmar, and John Greyson, 21–37. New York: Routledge, 1993.

Sadowski, Michael. *In a Queer Voice: Journeys of Resilience from Adolescence to Adulthood*. Philadelphia: Temple University Press, 2013.

Samar, Vincent J., ed. *The Gay Rights Movement*. Chicago: Fitzroy Dearborn, 2001.

San Filippo, Maria. *The B Word: Bisexuality in Contemporary Film and Television*. Bloomington: Indiana University Press, 2013.

Sarkissian, Raffi. "Queering TV Conventions: LGBT Teen Narratives on *Glee*." In *Queer Youth and Media Cultures*, edited by Christopher Pullen, 145–157. New York: Palgrave Macmillan, 2014.

Sarris, Andrew. *The American Cinema: Directors and Directions, 1929–1968*. New York: Dutton, 1968.

———. "Notes on the Auteur Theory in 1962." *Film Culture* 27 (Winter 1962–1963): 1–8.

Savage, Dan, and Terry Miller, eds. *It Gets Better: Coming Out, Overcoming Bullying, and Creating a Life Worth Living*. New York: Penguin Books, 2011.

Seidman, Steven. *Beyond the Closet: The Transformation of Gay and Lesbian Life*. New York: Routledge, 2002.

Sender, Katherine. *Business Not Politics: The Making of the Gay Market*. New York: Columbia University Press, 2004.

Shelley, Christopher A. *Transpeople: Repudiation, Trauma, Healing*. Toronto: University of Toronto Press, 2008.

Silverman, Kaja. "The Female Authorial Voice." In *Film and Authorship*, edited by Virginia Wright Wexman, 50–75. New Brunswick, N.J.: Rutgers University Press, 2003.

Sleeter, Christine E. *Multicultural Education as Social Activism*. Albany: SUNY Press, 1996.

Smith, Angela. "Letting Down Rapunzel: Feminism's Effects on Fairy Tales." *Children's Literature in Education* 46, no. 4 (2015): 424–437.

Smyth, John. *Critical Pedagogy for Social Justice*. New York: Continuum, 2011.

Spade, Dean. "A Politics beyond Recognition." In *Cruising the Archive: Queer Art and Culture in Los Angeles, 1945–1980*, edited by David Frantz and Mia Locks, 102–106. Los Angeles: ONE National Gay and Lesbian Archives, 2011.

Staiger, Janet. "Authorship Approaches." In *Authorship and Film*, edited by David A. Gerstner and Janet Staiger, 27–57. New York: Routledge, 2003.

———. "Finding Community in the Early 1960s: Underground Cinema and Sexual Politics." In *Queer Cinema: The Film Reader*, edited by Harry Benshoff and Sean Griffin, 167–188. New York: Routledge, 2004.

Stein, Marc. "Canonizing Homophile Sexual Respectability: Archives, History, and Memory." *Radical History Review*, no. 120 (2014): 53–73.

Streitmatter, Rodger. *Unspeakable: The Rise of the Gay and Lesbian Press in America*. Boston: Faber and Faber, 1995.

Stringer, Julian. "Regarding Film Festivals: Introduction." In *The Film Festival Reader*, edited by Dina Iordanova, 59–68. St. Andrews, Scotland: St. Andrews Film Studies, 2013.

Stryker, Susan. *Transgender History*. Berkeley, Calif.: Seal Press, 2008.

Tascon, Sonia M. *Human Rights Film Festivals: Activism in Context*. New York: Palgrave Macmillan, 2015.

Taub-Pervizpour, Lora. "Youth as Cultural Producers/Cultural Productions of Youth." In *The International Encyclopedia of Media Studies, Volume II: Media Production*, edited by Vicki Mayer, 1–23. New York: Blackwell, 2013.

Torchin, Leshu. "Networked for Advocacy: Film Festivals and Activism." In *Film Festival Yearbook 4: Film Festivals and Activism*, edited by Dina Iordanova and Leshu Torchin, 1–11. St. Andrews, Scotland: St. Andrews Film Studies, 2012.

———. "*Ravished Armenia*: Visual Media, Humanitarian Advocacy, and the Formation of Witnessing Publics." *American Anthropologist* 108, no. 1 (2006): 214–220.

Tropiano, Stephen. *The Prime Time Closet: A History of Gays and Lesbians on TV*. New York: Applause, 2002.

———. "'A Safe and Supportive Environment': LGBTQ Youth and Social Media." In *Queer Youth and Media Cultures*, edited by Christopher Pullen, 46–63. New York: Palgrave Macmillan, 2014.

Vachon, Christine, and Austin Bunn. *A Killer Life: How an Independent Film Producer Survives Deals and Disasters in Hollywood and Beyond*. New York: Simon & Schuster, 2006.

Vachon, Christine, and David Edelstein. *Shooting to Kill: How an Independent Producer Blasts through the Barriers to Make Movies That Matter*. New York: Avon Books, 1998.

Villarejo, Amy. "Movies and the Politics of Authorship." In *American Cinema of the 1990s: Themes and Variations*, edited by Chris Holmlund, 70–90. New Brunswick, N.J.: Rutgers University Press, 2008.

Walters, Suzanna Danuta. *All the Rage: The Story of Gay Visibility in America*. Chicago: University of Chicago Press, 2001.

Walton, Gerald, ed. *The Gay Agenda: Claiming Space, Identity, and Justice*. New York: Peter Lang, 2014.

Warner, Michael. *Publics and Counterpublics*. New York: Zone Books, 2002.

———. *The Trouble with Normal: Sex, Politics, and the Ethics of Queer Life*. Cambridge, Mass.: Harvard University Press, 2000.

Waugh, Thomas. "Walking on Tippy Toes: Lesbian and Gay Liberation Documentary of the Post-Stonewall Period 1969–84." In *Between the Sheets, in the Streets: Queer, Lesbian, Gay Documentary*, edited by Chris Holmlund and Cynthia Fuchs, 107–124. Minneapolis: University of Minnesota Press, 1997.

Weeks, Jeffrey. *Making Sexual History*. Malden, Mass.: Blackwell, 2000.

———. "Necessary Fictions: Sexual Identities and the Politics of Diversity." In *Sexualities and Society: A Reader*, edited by Jeffrey Weeks, Janet Holland, and Matthew Waites, 122–131. Cambridge: Polity Press, 2003.

Weiss, Andrea. "Transgressive Cinema: Lesbian Independent Film." In *Queer Cinema: The Film Reader*, edited by Harry Benshoff and Sean Griffin, 43–52. New York: Routledge, 2004.

Weston, Kath. *Families We Choose: Lesbians, Gays, Kinship*. 2nd ed. New York: Columbia University Press, 1997.

Williams, Walter L., and Yolanda Retter, eds. *Gay and Lesbian Rights in the United States: A Documentary History*. Westport, Conn.: Greenwood Press, 2003.

Wolkomir, Michelle. *Be Not Deceived: The Sacred and Sexual Struggles of Gay and Ex-gay Christian Men*. New Brunswick, N.J.: Rutgers University Press, 2006.

Wong, Cindy Hing-Yuk. *Film Festivals: Culture, People, and Power on the Global Screen*. New Brunswick, N.J.: Rutgers University Press, 2011.

———. "Grassroots Authors: Collectivity and Construction in Community Video." In *Authorship and Film*, edited by David A. Gerstner and Janet Staiger, 213–231. New York: Routledge, 2003.

Wuest, Bryan. "Stories like Mine: Coming Out Videos and Queer Identities on YouTube." In *Queer Youth and Media Cultures*, edited by Christopher Pullen, 19–33. New York: Palgrave Macmillan, 2014.

Yudice, George. "Testimonio and Postmodernism." In *The Real Thing: Testimonial Discourse and Latin America*, edited by Georg M. Gugelberger, 42–57. Durham, N.C.: Duke University Press, 1996.

Zielinski, Ger. "On the Production of Heterotopia and Other Spaces in and around Lesbian and Gay Film Festivals." *Jump Cut* 54 (2012), https://www.ejumpcut.org/archive/jc54.2012/gerZelinskiFestivals/index.html.

Index

Page numbers in *italics* refer to figures.

About the Author

DAVID R. COON is an associate professor of media studies at the University of Washington Tacoma. He teaches courses about film, television, advertising, video production, and improvisational theater. His first book, *Look Closer: Suburban Narratives and American Values in Film and Television* (2014), investigates recent challenges to the dominant ideologies embedded in the suburban American Dream. He has published essays examining film, television, advertising, gender, sexuality, and space in the *Journal of Popular Film and Television*, *Feminist Media Studies*, the *Journal of Homosexuality*, and *Polymath: A Journal of Interdisciplinary Arts and Sciences*.